# TRANSFORMATIONS
## A HISTORY OF
## UBC CONTINUING STUDIES

SCOTT MᶜLEAN AND ERIC DAMER

THE UNIVERSITY OF BRITISH COLUMBIA

UBC Continuing Studies
The University of British Columbia
410-5950 University Boulevard
Vancouver, British Columbia, Canada
V6T 1Z3


Library and Archives Canada Cataloguing in Publication

McLean, Scott, 1965-
      Transformations : a history of UBC Continuing Studies / Scott McLean and Eric Damer.

Includes index.
ISBN 978-0-88865-008-5


      1. University of British Columbia.  Continuing Studies--History.
2. University of British Columbia.  Dept. of University Extension.
3. University of British Columbia.  Centre for Continuing Education.
4. Continuing education--British Columbia--Vancouver--History.
5. University extension--British Columbia--Vancouver--History.
I. Damer, Eric, 1964- II. University of British Columbia.  Continuing Studies III. Title.

LC5254.3.V36M35 2012      378.1'750971133      C2012-902980-7


With gratitude for financial support from the Social Sciences and Humanities Research Council (SSHRC) and the Wilson Fund (UBC Continuing Studies endowment).

Special thanks to the UBC Continuing Studies marketing team and all current UBC Continuing Studies program areas.

Design and production by Lisa Evans

Historical photographs (marked *UBCA*) courtesy of UBC Archives; other photos from UBC Continuing Studies collections. Additional photos courtesy Francis Andrew; Martin Dee; David Gordon Duke; Don Erhardt; Brian Houle; Jo Ledingham; Yolande Morin; Judith Plessis; and UBC Continuing Studies program participants.

Index prepared by Eric Damer

Printed in Canada by Rhino Print Solutions

FSC
www.fsc.org

MIX
Paper from
responsible sources
FSC® C014515

*Transformations: A History of UBC Continuing Studies* is dedicated to all instructors, staff and students who have contributed to the success of UBC Continuing Studies and its historical predecessors: the Centre for Continuing Education; the Department of University Extension; and the University Extension Committee.

Countless adult students have used their UBC lifelong learning experiences to transform educational, cultural, and economic life in British Columbia and beyond.

# Table of Contents

# Leadership and Organizational Change

UBC officially
established in 1908

University Extension
Committee established
in 1918

Leonard Klinck,
UBC President,
1918-1942

Robert England,
Director, Department of
University Extension,
1936-1937

Norman MacKenzie,
UBC President,
1944-1962

John Friesen, Director,
Department of
University Extension,
1953-1967

| | 1915 | | 1925 | | 1935 | | 1945 | | 1955 | |

| 1910 | | 1920 | | 1930 | | 1940 | | 1950 | | 1960 |

Frank Wesbrook,
UBC President,
1913-1918

Department of
University Extension
established in 1936

Major post-war
expansion drove UBC
enrolment from 2,500
in 1943 to 10,000 in
1959

Degree-credit
enrolment at UBC
remained under 2,000
in the 1920s

Gordon Shrum, Director,
Department of
University Extension,
1937-1953

*Continuing Studies*

Centre for Continuing Education established in 1970

Jindra Kulich, Director, Centre for Continuing Education, 1975-1989

Walter Uegama, Associate Vice President, Continuing Studies, 1991-2000

Jane Hutton, Associate Vice President, Continuing Studies, 2000-2007

Judith Plessis, Executive Director, UBC Continuing Studies, 2007-present

**1965**  **1975**  **1985**  **1995**  **2005**  **2015**

**1970**  **1980**  **1990**  **2000**  **2010**

Gordon Selman, Director of University Extension, 1967 1970, and Director of the Centre for Continuing Education, 1970-1975

Centre for Continuing Education's Women's Resources Centre initiated by Pat Thom established in 1973

Anne Ironside, Acting Director, Centre for Continuing Education, 1989-1991

UBC Continuing Studies established in 1991, and Continuing Studies Building opened in 1997

UBC Robson Square opened in 2001

UBC degree credit enrolment reached over 50,000 students from across Canada and 140 other countries

# Provost's Message

*Dr. David Farrar, Provost and Vice President Academic,*
*The University of British Columbia*

## A PROUD HISTORY OF CONTINUING EDUCATION

Over the past 100 years, the University of British Columbia has played a vital role in the economic, social, and cultural life of our province. For 75 of those years, leading edge continuing education programs at UBC have helped transform the lives of adult learners and provided members of our communities access to the rich educational resources of the university.

This book highlights the significant impact of continuing education programs within the historical development of UBC. From extension lectures in 1936 to the expansive breadth of offerings available through UBC Continuing Studies and UBC's faculty-based continuing education units in 2012, adult learning has played an important role throughout the history of our university and our province.

Beginning as University Extension under President Klinck in the 1930s, continuing education programs at UBC went through a great shift in the 1970s. The professional continuing education programs moved directly under the jurisdiction of the faculties while an innovative lifelong learning unit, the Centre for Continuing Education, was established. Dedicated to local, national, and international programs in disciplines ranging from additional language learning to liberal arts and computer technology, "the Centre" provided the vision for the central continuing education unit we know today. In the 1990s, the Centre for Continuing Education was renamed UBC Continuing Studies and developed into a leader among interdisciplinary continuing education units in Canada. UBC Continuing Studies now offers over 1200 non-credit courses a year in face-to-face, online and mixed-mode formats.

You will enjoy reading about the outstanding people who helped develop continuing education to its present stature, from UBC faculty committed to community engagement to the remarkable adult students who transform society through lifelong learning.

Over a million people have participated in UBC continuing education programs over the last seven decades – the university is proud to share their history in this engaging book!

# Foreword

*Dr. Judith Plessis, Executive Director, UBC Continuing Studies*

The University of British Columbia's commitment to adult education is rooted in the earliest days of the university's more than 100 year history, but began more formally in 1936 when the Department of University Extension was formed to recognize that, in the words of UBC President Klinck, "in a complex society such as ours, learning must be a continuous process throughout life."

UBC has shown a strong commitment to the adult learner and continuing education for over seven decades. On the occasion of this 75th anniversary, we are pleased to honour the myriad of contributions by committed visionaries, leaders, administrators, staff, instructors, and – most importantly – students. The individual stories within this volume demonstrate how the curiosity and dedication of adult learners have made our work as continuing educators incredibly rewarding.

Continuing education at UBC began with public lectures and programs for adults in agriculture, forestry, mining and botany. The book's first chapters trace how university extension programs reflected the economic and social needs of the day in British Columbia. The history of continuing education at UBC is entwined with both our province's and our university's history, and the mission to "provide a program of continuing education in all academic and cultural fields throughout British Columbia" is enshrined in the *University Act*.

From the vision of pioneering leaders such as Robert England, Gordon Shrum, and John Friesen to the more recent leadership of Jane Hutton, I am humbled by the legacies of inspired directors and program leaders who developed enduring programs with limited resources. As an instructor and administrator with UBC Continuing Studies for over three decades, I am proud to be associated with the outstanding men and women who laid the foundations for UBC Continuing Studies and UBC's faculty-based continuing professional education units that originated in the Department of University Extension. With this commemorative publication, the university pays homage to the hundreds of continuing education professionals who are not mentioned by name in this book, but whom we applaud for their roles in the success of promoting lifelong learning at UBC.

Educational programs for adults at UBC have played a significant social role from the early days of Extension Lectures to Living Room Learning in the 1950s. Instructors and staff within the Centre for Continuing Education in the 1970s became activists for social change under the tutelage of dynamic leaders. Innovative program directors like Ruth Sigal helped build unique community and continuing education enterprises such as the UBC Women's Resources Centre, which served as a model for service and outreach in the community for decades. In the 1980s and 1990s, under the leadership of Jindra Kulich, Anne Ironside, and Walter Uegama, the Centre for Continuing Education shifted to become UBC Continuing Studies, consolidating its role as an interdisciplinary unit of program development and part-time credit study across the university as well as a leader in community outreach learning programs for adults. It is noteworthy that several well-established academic departments and professional continuing education units within UBC faculties originated from earlier extension programs. For example, the Department of Adult Education within the Faculty of Education benefited from the leadership of adult educators John Friesen and Gordon Selman, former Directors of University Extension.

Over the past 75 years, over a million adult learners have participated in UBC continuing education programs. Continuing education programs continue to transform individual lives and communities as thousands of adults complete courses and certificate programs, from Project Management to Aboriginal Health and Community Administration. Our continuing education students today have a deep impact on their professional and personal networks both locally and around the globe.

I welcome you to step back into this rich history of continuing education at UBC.

# Preface

*Dr. Scott M<sup>c</sup>Lean and Dr. Eric Damer*

SCOTT M<sup>c</sup>LEAN is the Director of Continuing Education at the University of Calgary. From 1994 to 2005, he was on faculty with the University of Saskatchewan Extension Division. Scott has taught adult basic education in Nunavut, developed university extension programs in leadership and health promotion, published widely, consulted internationally, and taught graduate seminars in the field of adult and continuing education.

Our interest in the history of UBC Continuing Studies goes back many years. As the Director of Community Development Programs at the University of Saskatchewan in the latter 1990s, Scott became curious about how and why universities had become active in adult and continuing education. He started doing research in the area, and from 2004 to 2007 received funding from the Social Sciences and Humanities Research Council (SSHRC) to examine the history of extension at the University of Saskatchewan and the University of Alberta. Scott found this research to be enjoyable and interesting, and in applying for a 2008–2011 SSHRC grant, chose to focus on UBC, McGill University, and the University of Montreal because they were large and prestigious institutions, and because they were set in large urban centres – in contrast to the historically rural contexts of the University of Saskatchewan and the University of Alberta.

After starting his research on these three universities, Scott realized that UBC had a particularly rich and interesting history in extension and continuing education work. He was impressed by the diversity and scope of the programming that UBC had developed and delivered, and noted the consistent commitment of those involved to include liberal arts and civic engagement work in that programming. Scott met with Judith Plessis, and they agreed to explore how this research could develop into a book.

Scott and Judith consulted with Dr. Herbert Rosengarten – a long serving instructor with UBC Continuing Studies, former Executive Director of the UBC President's office, and former Head of the Department of English – regarding how best to proceed with the project. Herbert recommended engaging Eric, given Eric's excellent writing skills and wealth of knowledge regarding the history of UBC and its communities. As a graduate student at UBC in the 1990s, Eric had written a thesis on the history of the Vancouver Institute, a venerable lecture series that has linked "town and gown" since 1916. With a new interest in the history of UBC and its relationship with the wider community, Eric continued with a dissertation on the history of the university's adult education program and further studies on the institution's past. The current history of UBC Continuing Studies and its predecessors fits perfectly with Eric's research interests.

Research for this book was based primarily upon written materials available through UBC Archives and through an informal document storage system housed at UBC Continuing Studies. We comprehensively reviewed the historical records available from these two sources, and used those records to organize our narrative. We consulted existing historical works on the Department of University Extension, notably those written by Gordon Selman, to ensure the comprehensiveness of our manuscript. We have footnoted all places in which our history or analysis is derived from the scholarly work of others.

In addition to archival research, we interviewed a number of current and former members of staff with UBC Continuing Studies and the Centre for Continuing Education. These interviews were useful in explaining events from relatively recent years, where coverage in the archives is not as robust as it is for earlier decades. While we do not identify the names of those interviewed for this project, we do express sincere appreciation to all those who agreed to speak with us as part of our research for this book.

Readers will note that we have not organized the book along simple chronological lines. We have separated the text into three major eras, divided by the years 1936 and 1970, because it was in each of these periods that UBC made fundamental changes to its organizational structures relating to extension and continuing education. Within the second and third eras, we have further structured our narrative according to the major, substantive goals pursued through extension and continuing education programming at UBC: assisting people to earn a better living; enabling people to understand and appreciate their world in an increasingly complete manner; and encouraging citizens to participate actively in public affairs.

We would like to acknowledge several people who have assisted the research, writing, and editing of this book. Judith Plessis and Mary Holmes provided excellent editorial contributions. Graphic design and production services were provided by Lisa Evans, with support from the UBC Continuing Studies marketing team. As Executive Director of UBC Continuing Studies, Judith Plessis sponsored the publication of the book, and provided both inspiration and guidance for its completion.

We received helpful comments on earlier drafts of the book from Herbert Rosengarten, Francis Andrew, Don Black, Deena Boeck, Mackie Chase, Beth Hawkes, Jane Hutton, William Koty, Ramona Montagnes, Peter Moroney, Tanya Reid, Karen Rolston, Andrew Scales, Walter Uegama, Mike Weiss, and Vince Wong.

We express our appreciation to Candice Bjur and Chris Hives at the University of British Columbia Archives, and to Sarah Munro who provided valuable proofreading services.

Research for the book was supported by a Standard Research Grant from the Social Sciences and Humanities Research Council of Canada. University of Calgary PhD students Heather Rollwagen and Prabhjote (Jyoti) Gondek provided research assistance, thanks to SSHRC support.

ERIC DAMER holds graduate degrees from the University of British Columbia, where he studied the history of adult and higher education in the province. He has taught the history of education as a sessional instructor, and has published three previous books on UBC, including *UBC: The First 100 Years*, co-authored with Herbert Rosengarten in 2009.

# In 2001, Ruth Sigal won a Women of Distinction, Life Achievement Award for her quarter-century of work with the Women's Resources Centre,

*an important unit within UBC Continuing Studies, as well as for her roles as a founding member of the Vancouver Crisis Centre and of a suicide research program at Vancouver General Hospital. Under her guidance, from 1978-2001, the Women's Resources Centre grew from a volunteer staff of seven, helping two hundred people a year, to a team of sixty dedicated volunteers, helping some 25,000 people a year with personal growth and career development. "I believe that each one of us has a seed inside us and all you have to do is water it," Ruth said of her philosophy. As a Holocaust survivor, Ruth had a particular empathy and a need to make a contribution in the world. "I feel that I need to help people, especially people who are underprivileged," she said. Ruth was the co-founder, with Lillian Boraks-Nemetz, of a local organization to support people who were hidden as children during the Holocaust. She also worked extensively in schools and at UBC to educate people about the Holocaust and about discrimination and racism more broadly.*

# UBC and the people of British Columbia

As a public institution, the University of British Columbia undertakes research, teaching, and service work of importance to the people of the province, and receives support from those people in the form of government grants, private donations, and the payment of tuition and fees. Given this relationship, UBC presidents have consistently worked to build strong connections between the university and the communities it serves. In 1916, Frank Wesbrook, UBC's founding president, articulated a vision of "the people's university":

> *We, the present student body, Staff, Senate, Board of Governors and members of Convocation of this infant University, may well be envied by those who have gone before and by those who will come after. To us has come the opportunity of making our Province, our Dominion, our Empire and our world, a better place in which to live... To meet in full our obligation, may ours be a Provincial University without provincialism. May our sympathies be so broadened and our service so extended to all the people of the Province that we may indeed be the people's University, whose motto is "tuum est" ("It is yours").*[1]

Subsequent presidents of the university have promoted the idea that UBC belongs to the people of the province, and exists to serve those people in their quest for a better life. Following the Second World War, during a time of unprecedented growth for the university, President Norman MacKenzie reiterated UBC's commitment to serving British Columbians:

> *It is my wish – a wish shared by all members of the University – that every person in this province should be fully aware of the University's capacity to serve them. Our outlook is entirely practical: we are a part of the communities to which we look for support and we feel that such support should be forthcoming in return for services rendered... We would like to see all citizens of the province convinced of our willingness to assist actively, whenever and wherever possible, in any plan to further the welfare of communities and individuals in British Columbia.*[2]

Although UBC and the communities it serves changed dramatically over the course of the twentieth century, the institution's commitment to service remained strong. In 2002, President Martha Piper wrote of the importance of university-community engagement:

> *Never has it been more important for a university to key its work to the problems of the community it serves. Never has it been more important for universities to collaborate with communities, addressing their concerns and working with them to identify and meet their needs.*[3]

The development of
the human potential,
individual fulfilment,
and the development of
society as a whole, are
of prime importance
to our society and to
this province. Lifelong,
continuous learning is
one of the main forces
in this development.

Jindra Kulich
Director of Continuing
Education
1978

Throughout its history, UBC has lived up to such commitments in numerous ways: by providing higher and professional education to students who live and work in British Columbia; by conducting and disseminating the results of research on questions of importance to the province; by giving faculty members and students the opportunity to engage in public service and outreach work; and by encouraging members of the public to participate in scholarly, cultural, and recreational activities sponsored by the university. Of the various ways that UBC has engaged with communities outside the boundaries of the campus, this book tells the story of one: the delivery of continuing education and extension programs and services.

Over the years, several UBC units have taken major responsibility for the provision of educational programs and services to people other than those pursuing degrees through on-campus study during daytime hours. In 1918, UBC established a University Extension Committee to promote, facilitate, and monitor off-campus lectures by members of the university. In 1936, UBC formed a Department of University Extension, which, for the next thirty-four years, organized educational activities such as extension lectures, evening courses, conferences, workshops, summer schools, residential training programs, travel seminars, study-discussion groups, degree-credit courses (offered via correspondence or in the evenings), radio broadcasts, and the circulation of library books, slide shows, movies, and phonograph records.

In 1970, the Department of University Extension became known as the Centre for Continuing Education; in 1992, this unit was transformed into UBC Continuing Studies. With each administrative re-incarnation came shifts in programming emphasis. Since 1970, these units have delivered a blend of degree-credit and non-degree-credit courses and programs oriented increasingly toward learners already possessing some level of higher education. Degree-credit programs have focussed primarily on part-time students, with courses delivered via distance education, or at times or in places outside the conventional academic session. Non-degree-credit programs have included stand-alone lectures, workshops, and conferences, as well as courses leading to certificates and diplomas.

This book narrates the history of those units at UBC whose primary mandate has been the provision of extension and continuing education: the University Extension Committee, the Department of University Extension, the Centre for Continuing Education, and UBC Continuing Studies. Of course, this is not the whole story of adult education at UBC. Over the years, members of a broad spectrum of faculties, schools, and departments have undertaken a tremendous amount of extension work and developed ambitious continuing education programs. In recent decades, many professional faculties have established continuing professional education units (see p. 213). While such decentralized activities have been of great significance to the university and the province, they are not described in this book.

The focus of this book is on the programs and services offered by central extension and continuing education units at UBC. Chapter One narrates the early history of extension at UBC, and explains how the Department of University Extension was formed. Chapter Two summarizes the social, institutional, and administrative changes that characterized the period from 1936 through 1970. Chapters Three through Five describe the major programs and services offered by the Department of University Extension during that time. Each chapter is dedicated to one of the three pillars of extension programming at UBC: professional education; cultural development and personal growth; and civic engagement and citizenship education. Chapters Six through Nine use a comparable approach to describe the programs and services offered by the Centre for Continuing Education and UBC Continuing Studies from 1970 to 2012. Chapter Ten reviews the major patterns in extension and continuing education programming at UBC over the years, and connects those patterns with important social changes in British Columbia.

The significance of extension and continuing education work at UBC can be highlighted by illustrating the scope of its reach among the people of British Columbia. In the 1940s, over 45,000 people each year listened to extension lectures delivered by UBC faculty members, and nearly 500,000 people each year watched movies or slide shows that the Department of University Extension circulated to community-based organizations

**Top left:** The UBC campus at Point Grey, 1925. **Top right:** Frank Wesbrook, UBC's first President (1913-1918), and an early supporter of university extension. **Bottom:** Leonard Klinck, UBC's first Dean of Agriculture and its second President (1918-1944). Klinck provided strong support for extension initiatives at UBC. *UBCA 1.1/174, 3.1/1464, 1.1/1328*

**Top:** The Buchanan Building, site of many continuing education courses after 1958. **Bottom:** Participants in an early UBC short course in agriculture, 1919.
*UBCA 1.1/242-5, 13.1/20*

around British Columbia. In the 1950s, about twenty thousand books were borrowed each year from the Extension Library Service. Between 1940 and 1965, over forty thousand people attended evening classes organized by the Department of University Extension in Vancouver. In the 1960s, about 2,500 students each year enrolled in degree-credit courses delivered through correspondence methods, off-campus, or in the evenings. In the 1970s, an average of nearly thirty thousand people each year participated in lectures, courses, and workshops organized by the Centre for Continuing Education. In the 1980s and 1990s, over ten thousand women each year took part in career and personal counselling sessions organized by the Women's Resources Centre. Between 2000 and 2010, UBC Continuing Studies taught over twenty different languages, and developed about thirty distinct programs of study leading to certificates. Clearly, thousands of British Columbians have benefitted from the opportunities for professional, cultural, and civic development provided by UBC through extension and continuing education work.

## STAYING THE COURSE

Extension and continuing education work at UBC has been guided by an enduring com-mitment to provide programs and services that address the professional, cultural, and civic aspirations of adult learners - to help people earn a better living, understand themselves and their world more fully, and participate actively in the public affairs that influence their lives. This commitment was first expressed in 1935, when President Klinck unveiled a "Plan for Adult Education in British Columbia" in a speech to the Vancouver Institute.[4] In that speech, Klinck stated:

> Adult education aims to give education to the citizens of today no less than to the citizens of tomorrow. One of its functions is to educate a thoughtful citizenship; to make us civil persons as well as persons who are trained to make a good living or skilled in the use of things of the mind. (p. 5)

Klinck suggested that adults desired further education in part so that "they may be able to discharge more intelligently their responsibilities as citizens" (p. 5). Further, he indi-cated that "cultural" and "vocational" forms of education were actually closely linked and that "in the great majority of individuals these two motives or interests are indis-solubly mixed" (p. 8).

*Ours is the task of helping to adjust the rights of the individual to the needs of all, of the obligations of each to the other and to the world.*

*Frank Wesbrook*
*UBC President*
*1916*

The UBC approach to extension and continuing education was a long-standing commit-ment, expressed in comparable terms by John Friesen some thirty years later in his 1965 annual report as Director of Extension.[5] In that report, Friesen posed the question: "What are the concerns of adults for further education?" His response was: "We submit that they are threefold: to make a living, to enrich experience and purpose in life, and to par-ticipate actively in citizen affairs" (p. 5).

At times, the balance between professional, liberal, and civic education has been strained. In his 1968 annual report, Director Gordon Selman gave a five-year overview of changes to university extension, and wrote:

> We take considerable satisfaction in the overall growth of the program and in the rapid expansion of continuing education in the professions. The need for general or liberal education in our society, however, is greater than ever, not less, and it is to be regretted that financial pressures on the Department's program have forced us to decrease the staff time we can devote to these broad and basic fields. (p. 5)

An increasing focus on continuing professional education was one of the reasons given by UBC for changing the name of the Department of University Extension to the Centre for Continuing Education. In 1970, President Walter Gage explained that "the new name means that UBC as an institution will place greater emphasis on the continuing educa-tion of graduates and education at an advanced level."[6] The same year, the Acting Director of Continuing Education, Jack Blaney, explained: "the term continuing educa-tion" reflected "the greater emphasis which is being given to programs which build upon undergraduate and professional education."[7]

Although professional education gained greater prominence in the 1960s and 1970s, a commitment to liberal and civic education endured. In 1978, Director of Continuing Education Jindra Kulich described the scope of university continuing education as follows:

> In the modern diverse society, continuing education must provide a mosaic of opportunities for adults to better cope with the major roles they play. Among these roles are those of the professional or employee, the family member and citizen, and the individual.[8]

In a similar manner, Associate Vice President (Continuing Studies) Walter Uegama asserted in 1994 that "demands of modern life have made personal development and enrichment more critical; the need for an informed and participating citizenry is greater than ever; employment currently requires more frequent, more sophisticated re-fitting of skills and knowledge."[9] A commitment to professional, liberal, and civic goals remains central to UBC Continuing Studies today. In its Five-Year Plan for 2009-2014, UBC Continuing Studies echoed earlier visions by asserting: "We anticipate and respond to emerging learner needs and broaden access to UBC by offering innovative educational programs that advance our students' careers, enrich their lives, and inform their role in a civil and sustainable society" (p. 1). Although the balance between goals has varied, UBC extension and continuing education units have preserved a strong tradition of assisting adult learners to earn a living, to understand themselves and their world, and to participate actively in public affairs.

## TRANSFORMATIONS

While UBC extension and continuing education units have maintained this tradition, the nature of their work has evolved substantially over the past seventy-five years, reflecting profound social and institutional changes. Most fundamentally, the people of British Columbia have changed. The population of the province has grown substantially, and its composition has evolved. Between 1911 and 2001, the population of British Columbia grew tenfold, from just over 390,000 to just over 3,900,000.[10] In the last half of the twentieth century, the population of the province grew by an average of nearly 55,000 people each year, and fewer than half of British Columbians were born in the province. Changing patterns of immigration created a population that is culturally and linguistically diverse, particularly in metropolitan areas. In the first half of the twentieth century, migration from central and eastern Canada and immigration from the United Kingdom and the United States gave British Columbia a population with predominantly British heritage. In the latter decades of the 1900s, immigration from Asia created a more diverse population. In 2001, one-quarter of British Columbians spoke a first language other than English, and four-fifths of those people spoke an Asian language.[11]

As well as becoming larger and more diverse, the population of British Columbia became substantially more urban over the course of the 1900s. In 1911, just over half of British Columbians lived in cities; by 2001, this figure had risen to 85 percent. The growth in the number and size of cities reflected a profound transformation of the provincial economy. In 1921, 30 percent of employed British Columbians worked in the primary industries of agriculture, mining, forestry, and fishing; by 2001, this figure had fallen to 5 percent. By 2001, about two-thirds of British Columbians worked in the service sector, in fields such as retail trade, health and social services, accommodation and food services, education, professional and technical services, and public administration. Other than these fields, the only sectors employing more than 4 percent of British Columbians in 2001 were manufacturing (9 percent), construction (6 percent), and transportation and warehousing (6 percent).

The rise of women's participation in the labour force over the course of the twentieth century was even more dramatic than the process of urbanization and the rise of the service sector. In 1911, women constituted just 8 percent of employed British Columbians; by 2001 this figure had climbed to over 47 percent. Between 1951 and 2001, the proportion of adult women participating in the labour market increased from 23 percent to 60 percent in British Columbia. Trends in labour market participation, urbanization, and occupations were linked. Over the course of the twentieth century, British Columbians increasingly depended upon working for wages to make a living. The traditional, rural economy where men produced primary commodities and women worked at home and in the community was replaced by a postmodern, urban economy

## NUMBER OF CREDIT STUDENTS

| | |
|---|---|
| 1920-21 | 962 |
| 1930-31 | 1,973 |
| 1940-41 | 2,650 |
| 1950-51 | 6,432 |
| 1960-61 | 11,621 |
| 1970-71 | 22,509 |
| 1980-81 | 24,951 |
| 1990-91 | 28,352 |
| 2000-01 | 35,382 |
| 2010-11 | 50,485 |

## % FEMALE

| | |
|---|---|
| 1920-21 | 40% |
| 1930-31 | 39% |
| 1940-41 | 32% |
| 1950-51 | 23% |
| 1960-61 | 29% |
| 1970-71 | 40% |
| 1980-81 | 48% |
| 1990-91 | 51% |
| 2000-01 | 57% |
| 2010-11 | 55% |

in which both men and women participated in the paid workforce. The evolution of extension and continuing education at UBC reflected the transformation of economic and social life in the province.

Over the past century, British Columbia has also witnessed substantial political and cultural change. In 1915, when UBC was established, most of the adult population of the province, including women and people of Asian and Aboriginal heritage, were excluded from voting. Radio and television broadcasts had not yet appeared, and neither computers nor the Internet had been invented. Although some people had automobiles, long-distance travel was time-consuming, expensive, and unpredictable. Governments provided few social programs, such as welfare assistance, unemployment insurance, or universal access to medical care, which are now taken for granted. Issues such as environmental sustainability and global citizenship were not prominent concerns. In short, the world in 1915 was dramatically different from ours.

Given these great societal changes, it is not surprising that participation in university education grew dramatically over the course of the twentieth century, in Canada and British Columbia. In 1901, Canadian universities granted 1,214 undergraduate degrees.[12] In 2001, they granted 129,240.[13] While some of this remarkable expansion was due to population growth, age-specific rates of participation and educational attainment also

| FACULTIES | SCHOOLS AND COLLEGES |
|---|---|
| Applied Science | Architecture and Landscape Architecture |
| Arts | Audiology and Speech Sciences |
| Business | Community and Regional Planning |
| Dentistry | Environmental Health |
| Education | Health Disciplines |
| Forestry | Human Kinetics |
| Graduate Studies | Interdisciplinary Studies |
| Land and Food Systems | Journalism |
| Law | Library, Archival and Information Studies |
| Medicine | Music |
| Pharmaceutical Sciences | Nursing |
| Science | Population and Public Health |
| | Social Work |

increased substantially. The proportion of Canadian youth aged eighteen to twenty-four enrolled full-time in university increased from 3 percent in 1920 to more than 20 percent in 1996.[14] Further, between 1950 and 1996, the proportion of the adult Canadian population holding a university degree increased from 2 percent to 12 percent. In recent years, participation in university education has continued to grow: between 2000 and 2006, full-time university enrolment increased by 31 percent in Canada, to a high of 815,000 students.[15]

Within British Columbia, the trend toward higher levels of educational attainment has been dramatic. Table 0.1 summarizes the growth of undergraduate and graduate enrolment at UBC from 1920 to 2010, vividly indicating the tremendous growth at UBC over the course of the 1900s, while Table 0.2 illustrates a major evolution in the gender composition of the student population. Women comprised a decreasing proportion of students in the first half of the century, and then grew to comprise a strong majority of students by the end of the century. By 2009, UBC had over 240,000 alumni, residing in more than 120 countries.[16]

The post-secondary system in British Columbia has also expanded dramatically in recent decades. Until 1960, UBC had a virtual monopoly on university education in the province, with Victoria College and the Vancouver School of Art serving other post-secondary needs. In the 1960s and 1970s, two new universities and a dozen colleges were established in the province. In 2009, the Association of Universities and Colleges of Canada recognized eleven degree-granting post-secondary institutions in British Columbia, while the Association of Canadian Community Colleges had a further sixteen members in the province. The rapid expansion of post-secondary education in the second half of the twentieth century reflected the social and economic changes outlined above, and helped shape extension and continuing education work at UBC.

This work also changed due to the evolving nature of UBC. When it opened its doors in 1915, UBC had just three poorly-staffed faculties, no graduate programs, no permanent facilities, and little emphasis on research by faculty members. As Table 0.3 indicates, by 2011, UBC had twelve faculties and thirteen schools and colleges.

Many of these academic units engaged extensively in graduate and professional education. Some of them were active both on the Point Grey campus and at UBC Okanagan, which opened in Kelowna in 2005. In addition to these campuses, UBC had facilities at Robson Square in downtown Vancouver, and at the Great Northern Way campus near False Creek, and utilized, through the Faculty of Medicine, substantial space in hospitals around the province. In 2009, UBC researchers undertook nearly $470 million in externally-funded work. Overall, UBC evolved into a major research and teaching institution, employing almost 14,000 people and operating with annual revenues of over $1.5 billion. From a small university engaged primarily in undergraduate teaching in the

Totem pole by artists Bill Reid and Doug Cranmer, at the UBC Museum of Anthropology. In recent decades, UBC Continuing Studies has collaborated with First Nations to provide high-quality, relevant programs in health, education, management, and other fields.

liberal arts and sciences, UBC grew to become a major institution, extensively involved in scholarly research and graduate and professional education. Without question, the institutional context for extension and continuing education work changed dramatically over the course of the twentieth century.

Tradition and change have both characterized extension and continuing education at UBC. At all times, UBC has supported adult learners in their quest to make a better living, understand their world, and influence public affairs. Many of the programs and services outlined in the following chapters crossed the boundaries of these categories, preparing people for various forms of career success, personal development, and civic engagement. At all times, too, the nature of extension and continuing education – both content and format – remained dynamic, reflecting a changing social and institutional context. Vocational programs in agriculture, home economics, and fisheries education were superseded by programs in business management and continuing professional education, which in turn were superseded by those in information technology and intercultural communication. Cultural programs that were once focussed on the classical heritage of Western civilization were replaced by programs focussed on "New Age" spirituality and the learning of languages from around the world. Public affairs programs dealing with the Great Depression and Second World War were superseded by those dealing with the Cold War and decolonization, and then by those dealing with nuclear weapons and environmental sustainability. Communications media used in presenting programs have also evolved, from public lectures and books to radio broadcasts, phonographic records, films, television, teleconferences, computer-mediated instruction, and the Internet.

At once rooted in tradition and constantly changing, the work of extension and continuing education at UBC has both anticipated and responded to the changing needs of the university and the communities served by the university. As the following chapters show, thousands of British Columbians have pursued professional, personal, and community development through the programs and services of UBC extension and continuing education units. Through supporting the educational aspirations of these people, UBC has both strengthened the communities in which those people live, and nurtured positive relationships between those communities and the university.

While diverse, the stories narrated in this book consistently relate to the theme of "Transformations." The society within which UBC exists has changed massively between 1915 and 2011. The organizational units tasked with major responsibility for extension and continuing education work have been fundamentally restructured on several occasions. The programs organized by these units have evolved dramatically over time. The students participating in such programs have, in many cases, experienced substantial personal growth and professional development as a result of their involvement with UBC. Transformations – of lives, programs, institutions, and society – are at the core of this book, and a significant part of the heritage of UBC Continuing Studies.

Vancouver School of Theology overlooking Carr and Duke Halls (visible on the right), which were for many years the site of UBC Continuing Studies administrative offices and classrooms.

# In 1934, Professor A.F. Barss proposed the establishment of an extension service and defined the following characteristics of an ideally qualified Director of Extension at UBC.

- *"Personality", as being of greater value than actual previous training.*

- *A relatively young man.*

- *A University graduate (possibly from this University) acquainted with all phases of University work.*

- *A man with experience in newspaper work, or some phases of journalism, including writing, advertising, making up copy, illustrating, publicity work.*

- *A man with "platform" ability who can not only think and write, but who can talk interestingly and convincingly, as well.*

- *A man who meets people easily, and works with others harmoniously, has tact and diplomacy.*

- *A man with organizing ability, who can work out plans and then get others to assist in carrying out those plans; this presupposes that the technical work, where and when called for, would be done by the men best informed in the separate technical fields.*

- *A man with previous experience in University Extension work, or somewhat similar type of publicity work.*

*Chapter One*

# Building the foundations of extension, 1915-1935

The University of British Columbia was officially established on March 7, 1908, when the Provincial Legislature passed "An Act to Establish and Incorporate a University for the Province of British Columbia." Nearly forty years of discussion, debate, and outright feuding had delayed the creation of a provincial university, but finally the time was right. British Columbia was growing quickly: population, especially in the urban centres of Vancouver, Victoria, and New Westminster, was soaring, reaching over 390,000 by 1911 from a mere 98,000 twenty years earlier.[1] Heralded by the arrival of the Canadian Pacific Railway in 1886, industrial production in the province was escalating, with great profits being made in the forest, mining, fishing, and shipping industries. In politics, the provincial Conservatives under Premier Richard McBride enjoyed a parliamentary majority with which to settle such controversial questions as the establishment and location of a provincial university, and gave strong support to the university movement.

UBC opened its doors in September 1915, with a total of 379 students and three faculties: Arts and Science, Applied Science, and Agriculture. Despite the formalities that marked the occasion, the opening was considerably less impressive than organizers had hoped. Two and a half years earlier, when Frank Fairchild Wesbrook was appointed president, the Conservatives had in mind a monumental stone university located on Point Grey to signify British Columbia's aspirations of leadership in the British Empire. Wesbrook, drawing fondly on his experiences as a medical student in England, added the ambition to create a "Cambridge on the Pacific." Alas, recession and then the First World War put an end to these plans. Despite Wesbrook's considerable skill and charisma, government support dwindled. Instead of opening in a neo-Tudor monument to higher education, UBC opened in a collection of dilapidated wooden buildings in the Fairview district of Vancouver, next to the Vancouver General Hospital. Formerly used as a college of McGill University, the university campus was dubbed the "Fairview Shacks" by students and faculty, until the campus finally moved to Point Grey in 1925.

For many years after UBC opened, its existence was precarious. The early political supporters had moved on, replaced by politicians who were openly critical of the institution. UBC had no alumni, no endowments, no physical plant to speak of, and no wealthy benefactors, although it did have

general support from a range of people within government, various industries, and students themselves. UBC faculty, administrators, and students were optimistic that they were pioneers in creating a university that would provide educational leadership for a progressive and prosperous society. UBC's first priority was to attract students, partly to make good on its claims for educational leadership, and partly to build popular support. From the beginning, providing education to people other than degree-seeking students was a significant priority for the university. The *UBC Calendar* for 1915-16 explained the university's three goals:

> *The Province, through the University, undertakes to furnish instruction in the various branches requisite for a liberal education, and in the technical branches that have a bearing upon the life and industries of the Province. It will aim to encourage research work in all departments, to produce creative scholars, and so do its share in enlarging the domain of knowledge. It is the intention to organize an extension division, upon a broad basis, to assist the people of the Province to assimilate the useful knowledge so rapidly advancing, and to carry it to those whose circumstances deprive them of the opportunity of attendance within its walls. (p. 22)*

From the outset, teaching, research, and extension work were considered to be the primary functions of UBC. However, in the early years, extension activities were largely deferred in light of other significant challenges.

Extension work at UBC was inspired by university extension movements in England and the United States. The earliest, sustained university extension initiatives began in the 1870s through Cambridge, Oxford, and the London Society for the Extension of University Teaching.[2] Those movements were intended to expand access to university lectures beyond the privileged few admitted to places such as Oxford and Cambridge, and to maintain the relevance of these universities in a changing social and political context. In practical terms, most early extension work involved public evening lectures by university professors. Having been a student at Cambridge, President Wesbrook would have been familiar with this tradition.

The English model of university extension came to North America in the 1880s and 1890s. In Canada, Queen's University established an Extra-mural Programme in 1889, and its leaders joined colleagues from the University of Toronto and McGill University in establishing a Canadian Association for the Extension of University Teaching in 1891. In the United States, educators established an American Society for the Extension of University Teaching in 1890, and universities including those of Chicago, Wisconsin, and Kansas developed successful extension programs in the subsequent decade. UBC's first extension services were public lectures. During the winter and spring of 1916, for example, UBC administrators and faculty joined with local proponents in the community to form the Vancouver Institute as Vancouver's premier lecture series.[3]

UBC was also strongly influenced by ideas from south of the border. In the United States, university extension took on a rather different character after 1900. The notion of

democratizing higher education remained important, but rather than expanding access to university lectures, the new, American model of extension provided a range of educational services to communities and industries. In this model, extension meant applying research, delivering seminars and non-credit courses, and providing diverse community services for social, economic, and cultural development. At land-grant and state universities across the United States, extension work became a third pillar of scholarly activity, along with teaching and research. By 1914, at least thirty American universities had established general extension divisions, and a further twenty-five agricultural colleges undertook extension work. [4]

President Wesbrook seated centre and campus planners at work, 1913. *UBCA 1.1/816*

By the time UBC opened its doors to students in 1915, both the University of Alberta and the University of Saskatchewan had Extension Departments.[5] In his inaugural address in 1908, the founding president of the University of Alberta, Henry Marshall Tory, expounded upon the importance of university extension:

> *The modern state university has sprung from a demand on the part of the people themselves for intellectual recognition, a recognition which only a century ago was denied them... The people demand that knowledge shall not be the concern of scholars alone. The uplifting of the whole people shall be its final goal. Mr. Chancellor, I consider that the extension of the activities of the university on such lines as will make its benefits reach directly or indirectly the mass of the people, carrying its ideals of refinement and culture into their homes and its latent spiritual and moral power into their minds and hearts, is a work second to none.[6]*

At UBC, as at other western Canadian universities, early extension programming was often directed to rural people with modest formal education. From 1915 to 1935, UBC provided a variety of extension services, the most significant of which are outlined here.

## AGRICULTURAL EXTENSION

UBC was founded, in part, to provide agricultural research and education. After President Wesbrook, the second person hired was the Dean of Agriculture, Leonard Klinck. In 1918, Klinck accepted the duties of president following Wesbrook's unexpected death from a chronic infection. Although agriculture was not foremost in the minds of many university supporters in the early years, the site selection committee of 1910 that chose Point Grey as the future UBC campus included several prominent educators who saw the value of turning British Columbia's limited agricultural lands into prosperous family farms. For these men, education was key to producing dedicated and capable farmers during the settlement of the Canadian west. The Dominion government supported agricultural education when it passed the *Agricultural Instruction Act* in 1913, providing money for schools in British Columbia and for UBC.

Two Weeks' Short Course
IN
POULTRY HUSBANDRY

*January 5th to 17th inclusive, 1931*

Rhode Island Red Hen No. 12862 has laid 1016 eggs in five years.

The University of British Columbia

THE FACULTY OF AGRICULTURE
POULTRY DEPARTMENT

1931
UNIVERSITY
SHORT COURSE
IN
HORTICULTURE

*January 19th to January 30th*

*The New Greenhouses*

Members of the Faculty of Agriculture were among the first to undertake extension work at UBC, although the Faculty itself was not fully staffed until 1917. In 1916 and 1917, faculty members reported giving public lectures, contributing to short courses sponsored by the provincial Department of Agriculture, and instructing in a Summer School for teachers of agriculture organized by the provincial Department of Education. From January 8 to 26, 1917, the Faculty of Agriculture sponsored a "Short Course in Horticulture" with forty-four full-time participants who attended lectures on soils, crops, fertilizers, pesticides, fruits, and vegetables.[7] The five-dollar registration fee was waived for three First World War veterans.

Returning veterans were the students in the first UBC extension program that went beyond the lecture or short course format. From 1918 to 1920, the Faculty of Agriculture delivered six, three-month vocational training courses for a total of 466 veterans, who studied agronomy, animal husbandry, dairying, horticulture, and poultry production.[8] For several years during and following the war, UBC also offered returning soldiers a series of popular vocational courses in motor mechanics, gas engines, steam engineering, and basic electrical engineering. Veterans could also learn skills as machinists and chauffeurs. These programs were coordinated by the Department of Mechanical Engineering, which negotiated with Ottawa for equipment, personnel, and buildings. Like other courses, these vocational programs combined theory with hands-on practical work. Undergraduate students noted the mechanics workshop and joked that faculty were getting repairs in the "garage for profs."[9]

By the end of 1917, the UBC Faculty of Agriculture and the provincial Department of Agriculture had agreed to several principles of co-operation in providing agricultural extension services in British Columbia. The university took responsibility for all agricultural research and for instruction of all courses exceeding three days in duration and having a scientific emphasis. The Department of Agriculture retained responsibility for distributing information bulletins, conducting demonstrations and other field work, and providing information and instruction directly focussed on increasing agricultural production. Federal funds were transferred to UBC through the province, which sometimes lagged in this duty by up to a year.[10] Between 1918 and 1923, the Faculty of Agriculture held thirty-three extension courses at various locations in the province, with a total of 2,255 students in attendance. As a precursor of the future engagement of UBC with community-based and professional organizations, some were co-hosted by the BC Dairymen, the Horticulture Association, Farmers' Institutes, and the Fruit Growers' Association. Most courses lasted for four or five days, and included lectures and demonstrations on topics such as animal husbandry, horticulture, dairying, and poultry production.

Members of the Faculty of Agriculture also conducted surveys, tested soils and crops, and attended agricultural shows where they judged livestock, seeds and crops, and brought attention to their research on poultry breeding, egg laying productivity, cereal

EXTENSION SHORT COURSE

IN

AGRICULTURE

Under the Auspices of the Appledale
Local United Farmers of British Columbia

LECTURES
AND DEMONSTRATIONS

APPLEDALE, B. C.
JANUARY 6, 8, 9, 10, 11, 1923

Offered by the
FACULTY OF AGRICULTURE
of the University of British Columbia

THE MEETINGS WILL BE HELD IN
THE APPLEDALE HALL

Ladies are especially invited

husbandry, dairying, and even flower cultivation. In 1920, UBC hosted the BC Dairymen's Convention and showcased faculty research on dairy bacteriology. By the mid-1920s, UBC researchers had contributed to new milk production regulations, developed several local cheeses, and introduced the "UBC Banner Oat" and the "UBC Spud" to farmers and agricultural educators.[11]

In 1923, rural short courses were discontinued due to the loss of federal government funding, despite the value of agricultural courses, both to participating farmers and to UBC's educational reputation. Critics of UBC still questioned the high per-student cost of the Faculty of Agriculture, and whether faculty research replicated work done by Dominion and Provincial Departments of Agriculture.[12] The support of influential farmers was important to UBC, so Dean Clement trimmed the departmental budgets in 1923 to enable the continuation of extension courses.[13] The following winter, the Faculty of Agriculture began offering annual short courses at the University Farm on Point Grey. Course brochures explained that "lectures and demonstrations are largely practical and are designed for those men and women who wish to extend their knowledge of farming." Each year, the Faculty offered three or four different courses, from one to three weeks duration, on such topics as Agronomy and Animal Husbandry, Dairying, Farm Economics, Horticulture, Poultry Husbandry, and Seed Growing. The courses were open to all interested participants, involved no examinations, and until at least 1931 had a registration fee of only one dollar. Between 1924 and 1930, the annual number of participants at these courses grew from about sixty to about 130.[14]

## MINING

Mining has been an influential industry in British Columbia. The early history of the province was shaped in many ways by large scale mining events: the Fraser River and Cariboo gold rushes populated the region and helped create the province; the Vancouver Island coal mines created the Dunsmuir political dynasty; the Kootenay hard-rock mines and "silver rush" of the 1890s opened the south-east corner of the province; and the Britannia copper mine north of Vancouver was by the 1920s one of the largest in the British Empire. Given the value of mining to the province, many advocates for a provincial university in the early 1900s felt that a mining school should be the province's first priority. Although mining was overshadowed by agriculture when UBC finally opened, the university had a strong Department of Geology, a chemist with industrial experience in smelting, and a program of mining engineering.[15]

Short courses in mining were approved in 1916, and twenty-seven students enrolled in January 1917 for the first six-week session. Covering mining, smelting, geology, chemistry, assaying, and several practical skills essential to the industry, the courses were directed to "prospectors, miners, brokers, businessmen, newspaper men, and others."

*Agricultural conditions are changing not only with the years, but with the seasons and months, and it is only through an extension service that the changing pulse of the agricultural people is immediately detectable...it is through the extension service that the findings and teachings of the faculty are carried to the people in general. The inspiration from students adds something to the vitality of the extension teaching.*

*F.M. Clement*
*UBC Dean of Agriculture*
*1924*

The appeal to the business community was deliberate, as UBC faculty members played important roles in the Chamber of Mines, itself an early ally of the University.[16] Businessmen were trying to "Make Vancouver a Great Mining Centre," and UBC was assisting through its extension work as well as its undergraduate teaching.[17] For the first few years, veterans were invited into the mining courses without charge, and the courses continued until 1930 when responsibility was transferred to the Vancouver School Board.[18] In these years, the main *UBC Calendar* described the mining short courses as:

> *thoroughly practical in nature. They are not primarily intended for those who have had a technical training, but rather for those who have had practical experience in mining and prospecting, or are connected with the business of mining in any way. The courses are designed to give practical and technical knowledge, helpful in practical mining work and mining business. While they are short they are complete in themselves, and require no other preparation than a common-school education or ability to read and write.*

After 1925, UBC established a geological museum in the Applied Science building with mineral specimens provided by faculty and other donors; the museum, located in the Geological Sciences building and known as the "Pacific Museum of the Earth," still operates to the present day.

Participants in a UBC short course in mining, 1917. *UBCA 1.1/138*

## BOTANY

In 1919, UBC began an ongoing, general-interest course in botany held every Tuesday evening during the university session. The impetus for this course was faculty member John Davidson, a passionate and conservation-minded field botanist and teacher known to many as "Botany John." Under Davidson's guidance, UBC's short course in botany, which included lectures, lab work, and field trips, continued for thirty years. By the mid-1920s, one could write an exam following the course and obtain university credit.

Davidson's efforts to popularize botany went far beyond classroom activities. An immigrant from Scotland and formerly the Provincial Botanist, Davidson established western Canada's first botanical garden in Essondale (Coquitlam), which he subsequently moved to Point Grey, on the western side of the UBC campus. By 1928 it had over one thousand specimens, and although the botanical garden has since been relocated further to the south, some of the trees from the original arboretum can still be found in the vicinity of UBC's Longhouse. Davidson's social origins and egalitarian attitude led him to cooperate with myriad community groups interested in botany; he frequently gave lectures and led field trips across the province. He established the Natural History Section of the British Columbia Mountaineering Club, which in 1918 joined with Arbor Day enthusiasts to

Students in a UBC short course in geology, 1919. *UBCA 1.1/16020-2*

form the Vancouver Natural History Society (currently Nature Vancouver). As well, Davidson began UBC's herbarium (over fifteen thousand specimen sheets by 1928) and seed collection, which have since been used by countless professional and amateur botanists. Through his courses, lectures, and field trips, Davidson had an enormous influence on a generation of young botanists, foresters, and naturalists.[19]

## EXTENSION LECTURES

Although faculty members provided public lectures as early as 1916, the establishment of the University Extension Committee in 1918 marked a concerted effort to coordinate extension activity at UBC. It began when the local YMCA asked UBC to provide lectures for soldiers in a local camp.[20] In a 1919 report to the Chancellor and the Board of Governors, the chair of the committee, Chemistry Professor Robert Clark, stated that the purpose of the committee was to "keep before the public, especially in the outlying parts of the Province, the work of the University." This was to be done through occasional publications and public lectures.[21] In 1919, the committee published two illustrated pamphlets (*The University of British Columbia, General Statement of its Scope and Activities*; and *The University of British Columbia, Descriptive Outline of Courses Offered*)[22] but thereafter focussed mostly on the organization and delivery of public lectures. The number of lectures reported by UBC faculty members increased from 24 in 1919 to 135 in 1923.[23] Between 1928 and 1934, UBC faculty members delivered an average of over 260 extension lectures to an average of over 27,500 people, per year.[24] The University Extension Committee also facilitated the delivery of lectures over the radio, via Vancouver-area stations. Radio lectures were first conducted by members of the UBC Faculty of Agriculture in 1925. Between 1926 and 1932, the University Extension Committee organized a fifteen-minute radio lecture each Friday evening during the university term.

Extension lectures were a significant form of contact between faculty members and people external to the university. A majority of lectures were given in the Lower Mainland, but they were also given in such cities as Victoria, Kelowna, Kamloops, and Seattle, and in smaller towns on Vancouver Island and in the Fraser and Okanagan valleys.[25] Lecturers came from all academic departments, and spoke on many different topics (see Table 1.1 on p. 37).

In the delivery of lectures, the University Extension Committee worked with a wide range of community-based organizations. Every year, the Committee informed the organizations of the available lectures, and invited them to arrange for a venue and to advertise the event. The University Extension Committee paid the lecturers' travel expenses, and the lecturers provided their services without charge as part of their UBC duties. Lectures were sometimes stand-alone events, and sometimes provided as part of a thematic series or as part of a tour by a particular speaker (typically arranged in December and April, during campus examinations). Most sponsoring groups charged no admission fee.

*November, 1920*

*Dear Sir:*

*As intimated in the University Calendar, the University Extension Committee is prepared to continue last year's policy, and to send out Lecturers to those parts of the Province where sufficient public interest exists, or can be aroused, to warrant this expenditure of time, effort, and money...*

*Yours truly,*

*R.H. Clark, Chairman*
*H.F. Angus, Secretary*
*University Extension Committee*

Extension lectures were often directed toward members of volunteer organizations, including church groups, the Vancouver Natural History Society, Rotary Clubs, the Vancouver Board of Trade, Canadian Clubs, the University Women's Club, Red Cross groups, the YMCA, and the Art, Historical, and Scientific Association. Lectures were occasionally directed toward members of the prestigious Vancouver Club or Terminal City Club, while lectures to labour organizations were at times met with class-based scepticism.[26] At least once, however, faculty speakers won the respect of an audience of sceptical working people. Economists Theodore Boggs and Henry Angus agreed to a series of weekly lectures at the Central City Mission in the fall of 1920. At first, members in the large audience scorned the speakers as apologists for established interests, but after several lectures the audience responded with respectful disagreement and discussion, recognizing the independent views presented by the speakers.[27]

The University Extension Committee consistently reported a high level of demand for, and satisfaction with, its extension lectures. In his 1919 report, Robert Clark noted:

> *Numerous letters and newspaper clippings have been received in appreciation of these lectures, letters have recently been received from several towns lamenting the fact that they were not included in these lecture tours and asking to be in future years. The attendance and interest manifested has been reported by the lecturers for the most part as excellent. (p. 2)*

Demand continued into the 1930s. W.L. MacDonald, the Secretary of the committee, reported in 1925 that "a very gratifying feature of this year's lectures has been the number of letters from various centres expressing appreciation of the Extension Lectures" (p. 1). Finally, in his report for 1936, O.J. Todd, the Secretary of the Committee, wrote: "the articles appearing in nearly a score of newspapers and the comments (unsolicited) made both to the Committee and to individual lecturers through personal statements and numerous letters have been highly favourable" (pp. 5-6).

Although extension lectures appeared to have been a popular service in the 1920s and 1930s, two constraints were consistently cited: limited funds and the scarce time of faculty members. With reference to the "difficulty of securing lecturers," W.L. MacDonald wrote in 1925 that many faculty members volunteered at the beginning of the session, but refused to follow through when called upon. Consequently, he concluded, "Extension work is falling more and more upon a few willing victims" (pp. 7-8). Financial constraints became pressing in the early 1930s, when economic depression led to significant reductions in the budget of UBC. In his *President's Report* for 1934, Klinck lamented the reduction of extension work due to heavy teaching loads in the undergraduate program, and a reduced professorial staff. Klinck particularly regretted that UBC had lost close, personal contact with residents outside the Vancouver and Victoria areas, and concluded that this "condition is regrettable alike from the standpoint of the University and of the public, and should be rectified as promptly as possible" (p. 5). Despite resource constraints, for nearly two decades the University Extension Committee ensured that the public was connected

*Especially notable is the response of the people of Texada Island and Powell River. From a desire to show their appreciation of Professor Spencer's Lectures and to show their interest in the University, these places donated a sum totalling $51.95 to be used for any purpose the Committee sees fit.*

*W.L. MacDonald, Secretary Extension Lecture Committee 1925*

to UBC through lectures by faculty members at off-campus events hosted by a range of local organizations. Each year, hundreds of lectures were given to thousands of people.

Perhaps the most significant venue for public lectures was the Vancouver Institute, a co-operative project established in 1916 that mixed leadership from UBC and several local societies to sponsor lectures every Saturday evening in the winter months, initially

| DEAN / DEPARTMENT | TITLES OF SELECTED LECTURES |
|---|---|
| UBC President | UBC and its Relation to the Province |
| Dean of Applied Science | Mineral Resources of British Columbia |
| Dean of Agriculture | Rural Migration |
| Dean of Arts and Science | National Ideals in Education |
| Classics | The Spirit of Greek Comedy |
| English | Rudyard Kipling |
| Library | The Place of the Library in the Community |
| Modern Languages | Balzac: The Man |
| History | Clemenceau and the France of his Time |
| Philosophy | Philosophy and Life |
| Economics | The Tariff in Canadian History |
| Biology | Forest Trees of British Columbia |
| Zoology | Food from the Sea |
| Mathematics | The Myths of the Constellations |
| Physics | Modern Problems in Fuel Utilization |
| Chemistry | Gases of the Atmosphere |
| Public Health | Spread and Control of Infectious Diseases |
| Civil Engineering | Road Building |
| Mechanical Engineering | Popular Mechanics |
| Mining and Metallurgy | Petroleum: Its Origin and Products |
| Geology | Gems and Precious Stones |
| Animal Husbandry | Farm Survey |
| Horticulture | Small Fruits for Small Gardens |
| Poultry Husbandry | Factors Influencing Egg Production |
| Dairying | Milk and the Public |

# The Vancouver Institute

### SESSION 1920-1921

#### Officers:

HONORARY PRESIDENT
S. D. SCOTT, LL.D.

PRESIDENT
LEMUEL ROBERTSON, M.A.

FIRST VICE-PRESIDENT
MRS. D. MCINTOSH, M.A.

SECOND VICE-PRESIDENT
C. MCLEAN FRASER, B.A., PH.D., F.R.S.C.

HON. SECRETARY-TREASURER
R. R. EARLE, K.C.

#### OBJECTS

The objects of THE INSTITUTE shall be the study and cultivation of the Arts, Sciences, Literature, Music and kindred subjects, by means of Lectures, Exhibitions, Publications and such other means as may from time to time be deemed advisable.

#### AFFILIATIONS

Organizations having similar objects to those of THE INSTITUTE may affiliate with THE INSTITUTE, provided, however, that such affiliation shall in no wise lessen the identity or interfere in any way with the autonomy or the particular objects or work of the organization so affiliating.

in the small auditorium of the Fairview campus. The Vancouver Institute provided an important vehicle to publicize the university and present UBC faculty members before Vancouver audiences. Lecture topics ranged widely, and included local speakers who were part of an earlier "mutual enlightenment" movement to bring culture and sophistication to a rough, pioneer Vancouver. Through the 1920s, however, professional organizations became more significant in the life of the Vancouver Institute, reflecting the practical orientation of the university and higher learning more generally. Despite some question about its future when UBC moved to the Point Grey campus in 1925, the lecture series eventually moved to the university. The successful lectures series continues to the present, providing lectures of exceptional quality on Saturday evenings during the winter and spring sessions, under joint sponsorship of UBC and community organizations.[28]

## SUMMER SESSION AND PROFESSIONAL EDUCATION

In 1920, UBC opened its doors for six weeks during the summer to certified school teachers. Although most high school teachers at that time held a university degree, elementary teachers typically possessed some high school and a "normal school" training of less than a year. Teachers were organizing themselves as well-educated professionals, in part to improve wages and working conditions, but the summer sessions for teachers introduced by the provincial Department of Education in 1914 did not prove to be popular. In 1919, the new British Columbia Teachers' Federation asked the UBC Senate to provide summer courses, in order to advance a more professionalized teaching service.[29]

Summer courses reinforced specialized high-school subject material (including commerce) and provided additional courses in educational psychology, theory, and methods. Despite its location in the "Fairview Shacks," UBC's Summer School was an instant success, and beginning in 1922, students with full matriculation could earn credit toward a degree in the renamed University Summer Session; by the end of the decade, students could earn a complete BA degree by taking courses during the summer months.[30] Summer Session enjoyed a long life, evolving into a more general university summer term. Credit for extra-mural or "night school" courses, however, remained controversial within the university (President Klinck was not in favour of it) but by 1929 several credit courses administered directly by participating departments could be completed on an extra-mural basis; eighty-three students enrolled in extra-sessional classes in 1935.[31]

Teachers were not the only new professionals looking to UBC. UBC launched a nursing degree program in 1919, the first such program in the British Empire, as the status of, and demand for, nurses was on the rise. The Vancouver General Hospital, adjacent to UBC's Fairview campus, sought a differentiated nursing staff and offered to pay the salary of an educator who could provide the hospital with an elite corps of nurses. UBC accepted the undertaking, and with additional funds from the Red Cross, established in 1920 a four-month course in Public Health Nursing, which expanded to a full-year course two years later. This course, and another in nursing teaching and administration introduced a few years later, was open to UBC graduates and practicing nurses with acceptable credentials, who received a certificate upon successful completion. In 1923, UBC provided a short course in the Summer Session for graduate nurses. Although the course was well received by participants, the poorly funded and unstable Department of Nursing was unable to repeat it in subsequent years.[32]

## ESTABLISHING THE DEPARTMENT OF UNIVERSITY EXTENSION

By the late 1920s, UBC was much more secure than it had been ten years earlier. The university's move to Point Grey in 1925 had followed a successful province-wide campaign organized by students, which included a massive petition and the "Great Trek," a high profile parade through the streets of Vancouver to the promised new campus. UBC's regular student enrolment stood at nearly two thousand by 1929, and the provincial grant, on which the university depended, remained lean but had increased a little each year in the late 1920s thanks in part to a prospering provincial economy. Although crowded, UBC had a reputation for producing competent graduates, conducting worthwhile (if limited) research, and providing community leadership through its various extension activities. The optimism of the 1920s would soon be dashed, however.

The first hint that the university was in for trouble came in the summer of 1929, when the newly elected Conservatives under Premier Simon Fraser Tolmie and his Minister of Education, Joshua Hinchliffe, ordered an inquiry into UBC's financial management. The investigation revealed nothing of consequence, but its implementation and reception said much about the government's regard for the university. In the view of many cabinet members, UBC was too expensive and overly vocational; Minister Hinchliffe, an Anglican cleric, had earlier clashed with UBC faculty members over appropriate teaching materials, and held a dim view of the struggling university.[33]

When the stock market crashed in the autumn of 1929 and tax revenues began to shrink, the government reduced UBC's annual grant from $587,700 in 1930 to $487,000 in 1931, and to a devastating $250,000 in 1932. Classes were cut, staff laid off, and research put on hold. Faculties competed for shrinking funding, provoking hostility among the Deans and the President, who endured a vote of non-confidence by the University Senate in 1932. Later that spring, a committee of prominent businessmen reviewed the government's situation and recommended drastic cuts to social services, particularly education. They suggested closing the university and providing scholarships for students to study elsewhere.

*Limiting the opportunities of "Contacting" its public lessens the University's powers of leadership and service. Again, spasmodic, desultory or insufficient information about the University tends to result variously in suspicion, disinterestedness or lack of support, if not in actual opposition.*

*A.F. Barss*
*Professor of Horticulture*
*1934*

Fortunately for UBC, public mood was against the "Kidd Report." The government quickly sought to distance itself from its reactionary recommendations, but when British Columbians went to the polls in 1933, the Conservative party was decimated by Duff Patullo's Liberals who promised to pull the province from the Depression with a program of "socialized capitalism." The new government included UBC faculty member George Weir, who soon became Provincial Secretary and Minister of Education. Although the Liberals had no quick solution to the economic crisis, UBC escaped closure and very slowly regained the funding crucial to its operation.

Although the Great Depression initially hampered extension work at UBC, it quickly became the catalyst for a much broader engagement of the university with the educational needs of its communities. As the Depression deepened, UBC turned to the people of British Columbia for popular support: members of the University Extension Committee created a Public Relations Committee and enhanced the Alumni Association; faculty participants in the Vancouver Institute asserted greater influence in the popular lecture series; and UBC organized several successful Open House events. Some friends of the university even contributed money, time, expertise, or other gifts, all valuable contributions during the crisis. One of the biggest monetary gifts came in the fall of 1933, when the Carnegie Corporation of New York granted $50,000 to each of the four provincial universities in western Canada for the development of "projects designed to improve the morale of the professorial staff and to extend the usefulness of the institution." [34]

In January 1934, in response to the opportunity presented by the Carnegie Corporation grant, A.F. Barss submitted "A Proposal to Improve the Relation of the University to the Province."[35] Barss, a Professor of Horticulture, suggested that the university had lost contact with the people of British Columbia:

> *This University is suffering severely from lack of contact with its constituency – the people of this Province. The present condition of relative isolation is having a serious effect on the University as a whole, as well as upon its faculties and the individual staff members. The blame for the shrinkage in the number of students, for the criticisms of the public, for the indifference or hostility of the Press, cannot all be placed on the present depression, but rather may in large measure be credited to the enforced lack of touch with the 'outside.' (p. 1)*

Barss proposed "the establishment of a definite organization under capable leadership which would have the responsibility of developing and maintaining an active public relations (or University extension) service." Following a brief description of the potential activities of this new service, Barss concluded by noting that his proposal fit the terms of the Carnegie grant, could easily adjust to varying demand, and promised long-lasting benefit to university-community relations.

Barss' initial proposal was favourably received by UBC administrators; there were a number of other proposals to consider (including oceanography, campus lighting, a Chair in music, and a study of the economic crisis),[36] but the Vancouver Council of Social

Agencies had written to President Klinck late in 1933 to remind him of UBC's responsibilities to assist residents of British Columbia during the dark days of the Depression. As Klinck discussed the merit of an adult education service with other university presidents, UBC's Senate endorsed in principle the letter from the Council of Social Agencies.[37] Encouraged, Barss wrote a more detailed document in March, 1934: "A Proposal to Improve the Relation of the University to the Province by the establishment of A University Extension Service."[38] He reiterated his view that such a service was both beneficial to the university and to residents of the province, while consistent with the terms of the Carnegie grant.

In this second proposal, Barss provided a list of potential activities "whereby the University might be taken to the people of the Province, or the people of the Province brought to the University": a regular news service; bulletins, circulars, and pamphlets; a university radio program; public lectures; conferences; annual meetings of various organizations; University Open House and inspection tours; field work with service clubs, high schools, and parent-teacher organizations; a library loan service; and adult education programs "as finances and conditions might warrant." Barss' list of educational activities included evening classes, reading courses, short courses, off-campus "extension schools," refresher courses for teachers and technical workers, liberal arts classes, and "unemployed camp schools." Barss concluded his proposal by acknowledging the political benefit of an extension service that would bring "the University actively before the people of the Province, as well as enlarging the influence and usefulness of the University throughout the Province" (p. 5).

Barss' proposals were highly persuasive: $30,000 of the Carnegie Corporation's grant was dedicated to the establishment of a Department of University Extension, with a director, support staff, and a small budget to offset direct costs. President Klinck and other members of the Faculty of Agriculture were supportive, recalling an earlier time when extension tours across the province were regular activities; the winter short courses in agriculture had also been discontinued in 1933. Farming groups valued the extension services, and they still had considerable influence in provincial politics. MLA George Weir, Minister of Education, was in support of adult education; under his leadership, the province established an Extension and Adult Education division in 1934. UBC conducted a survey in March 1935 which revealed that people across the province were interested in what UBC could provide, particularly extension lectures that were already familiar. The dedication of a significant portion of the Carnegie grant to extension work reflected both an interest in the provision of adult education services to the people of British Columbia, and a concern with the position of the university in the province.

On November 16, 1935, UBC President Klinck revealed his vision for the university's new service when he described a "Plan for Adult Education in British Columbia" before a Vancouver Institute audience.[39] Klinck began his speech by observing that adult

education had recently become very significant in North America. He then explored what was meant by "adult education," who would be involved, and what they might wish to learn. Adults, as Klinck defined them, were over 16 years of age and perfectly capable of learning, but not universally interested in education. To Klinck, adult education was a voluntary and co-operative activity in which adults built upon what they already knew through an intentional and ongoing process of learning.

Klinck argued that adult education strove to support vocational preparation, personal growth, and the development of active and responsible citizens. He suggested that the ability to learn and to think creatively and critically were as important as the acquisition of knowledge and skills. He identified "new reasons for adult education" that originated in a "widening gap between scientific progress and social progress" and the "steady rise in the average age of the population" (p. 12). Further, Klinck argued that it was "incontrovertible" that "in a complex society such as ours learning must be a continuous process throughout life." He asserted: "What is needed...is to evolve an educational system for the whole Province – for the whole of life – age as well as youth" (p. 17).

SHORT COURSE CLASS POULTRY HUSBANDRY JAN. 7. 1931.

Klinck described the development of adult education in England, the United States, and Canada, and he summarized the debate regarding the suitability of adult education functions to the mission of universities. He concluded by noting that practically all universities across Canada had embraced extension work, and in fact were increasing their participation in it. To exemplify his claims regarding the growing importance and acceptability of adult education, Klinck described the extension work of St. Francis Xavier University and the University of Alberta, and the establishment of the Canadian Association for Adult Education.

Following this description of the field, Klinck outlined his plans for developing adult education at UBC. He acknowledged that adult education had previously constituted "a very minor part" of UBC policy, and outlined the work of the University Extension Committee. For the future, Klinck indicated that UBC would establish a Department of University Extension whose staff would "meet the majority of requests for extra-mural instruction" so that additional teaching loads would not be imposed upon the professorial staff whose first duty was "to the students who are registered in the regular courses" (p. 16). Klinck outlined the "Purpose of the New Organization" as one of supporting existing educational activities and cooperating with other agencies engaged in adult education, not replacing or subsuming them.

Klinck's "Plan for Adult Education in British Columbia" set an ambitious agenda for UBC, and broadened the scope of the university's extension mandate far beyond the provision of off-campus lectures. To pursue this mandate, UBC drew on the Carnegie Corporation grant to form a Department of University Extension, which was officially established by the Board of Governors on April 27, 1936.

**Top:** Alden Barss, who proposed a Department of University Extension, 1943.
**Bottom:** Students in a short course in poultry husbandry, 1931. *UBCA 51.1/684 (photo from The Totem, courtesy UBC AMS), 24.1/4*

# In the matter of Extension, the University is faced with a very difficult problem owing to the distances to the outlying centres of population.

*To carry on extension work involves a great deal of organization if the internal work of the University is not to be disrupted by the absence of members of the staff for long periods. Yet there is great value in bringing members of the staff into contact with the people in outlying communities. Sometimes the word "education" scares a great many people, but it is gradually becoming clear that unless our interests are vital and significant, our lives are cramped. Education is a form of emancipation from prejudice, narrow views and hasty generalization. The University can do little more than provide avenues of opportunity along which people can march more confidently to a better future.*

Robert England, Director
Department of University Extension
1937

*Chapter Two*

# The Extension era, 1936-1970

The years between the establishment of the Department of University Extension in 1936 and the transformation of that department into the Centre for Continuing Education in 1970 were characterized by major social and institutional developments. At the international level, the Great Depression, Second World War, Cold War, and social movements of the 1960s provided a constantly shifting political-economic landscape for university extension. Within Canada and British Columbia, these years were marked by economic stagnation followed by substantial economic growth, a "baby boom," significant immigration and urbanization, rising levels of formal education, and the substantial cultural changes associated with developments such as television and mass long-distance travel. During these years, UBC expanded dramatically, enrolling unprecedented numbers of students, receiving higher levels of public funding, and undertaking increased amounts of research and graduate teaching.

## THE EARLY YEARS

Launched during the Great Depression, the Department of University Extension ("Extension") served as a means for UBC to assist British Columbians in a time of crisis. From 1938 to 1945, the *UBC Calendar* stated "Through the activities of the Department of University Extension, the University is contributing enduring benefits to the educational and social welfare of the Province." President Klinck gave Extension office space in the Agriculture Building, and hired the first Director of University Extension, Robert England. England, who had spent some fifteen years working in ethnic settlement and community development for schools and for the Canadian National Railway, was President of the Manitoba Adult Education Association and known to several UBC faculty members at the time he joined the university. During the first year, England boosted faculty lectures or presentations, which included fine arts performances, panel discussions, films, and radio broadcasts with the new Canadian Broadcasting Corporation. England also made important contacts with the recently established Canadian Association for Adult Education and with various local groups, including members of the labour movement, school boards, churches, the press, and the Vancouver Symphony. A little over a year after coming to UBC, he returned to Manitoba to be an economic advisor to the Winnipeg Electric Company.[1]

With little money for salaries or programs (despite an additional grant of $30,000 from the provincial government),[2] Klinck looked within the university for England's successor, and decided on Professor of Physics, Gordon Shrum. Although a part-time director, Shrum was a powerful force. A distinguished graduate of the University of Toronto, Shrum had joined the fledgling UBC in 1925 where he proved to be an engaging physics teacher, a supporter of American football and the Officer Training Program (having fought in the First World War), and an influential figure in institutional politics. As Director of University Extension, Shrum immediately launched several new, bold, and highly successful programs. He tapped into federal and provincial funding and hired a staff of dedicated teachers and administrators who provided a range of services at UBC, in the Vancouver region, and across the province.

In his 1938 annual report, Shrum emphasized the importance of extension work in addressing social change: "The speed with which human knowledge is accumulating makes it a matter of paramount importance that the University – in addition to its concern with valuable teaching and scholarly research – should devote a portion of its energy to the dissemination of this knowledge" (p. 15). He added that through the work of his new department, "the University has opened its doors to a large group of earnest men and women who feel the need for more training, more background, and more knowledge of the physical world in which they live" (p. 12). A decade later, in his 1949 annual report, Shrum reiterated his belief that UBC, "through its programme of adult education, is making and should continue to make a unique and indispensable contribution to the cultural development of the Province" (p. 1).

Extension work was made more difficult by the lack of infrastructure for travel and communication. The province had few paved roads between cities, poor radio reception in mountain valleys, and prohibitively expensive telephone/telegraph communications. Even rail travel was subject to interruptions due to weather.[3] In spite of such obstacles, the teachers and program leaders whom Shrum hired provided lectures to large audiences, instructed non-credit courses, and facilitated discussion groups around the province. Shrum also found opportunities to provide innovative extension services during the Second World War, when UBC stood firmly behind the war effort.[4]

The Department of University Extension directly provided training for hundreds of members of the armed forces, including short courses for radio mechanics and members of flight crews. In addition to training armed forces' personnel, the department delivered war-related courses for the general public, and distributed films dealing with the war to communities across British Columbia.

During the Second World War, the Department of University Extension undertook a number of initiatives in support of the Canadian war effort. Shrum described the following initiatives in his annual report for 1940-41:

> Close cooperation has been maintained with the Canadian Legion War Services and other auxiliary services, particularly in providing visual instruction materials for use in educational work and recreational programmes for the armed forces. In the Youth Training Programme, increased emphasis has been placed on first aid, citizenship, physical training and war-time nutrition. In providing new material for the use of study groups and individual readers, emphasis has been placed on literature dealing with the war and with problems of post-war reconstruction. (p. 1)

Gordon Shrum, UBC's second Director of Extension (1937-1953). *UBCA 1.1/3058*

## POST-WAR GROWTH

Crucial to the post-war growth of the Extension was the arrival of Norman MacKenzie as UBC President, chosen by the Board of Governors to replace Klinck in 1944. MacKenzie was perhaps an even greater proponent of extension than his predecessor, and had the right combination of determination, charm, diplomacy, and personal connections to ensure success. A legal scholar and formerly the President of the University of New Brunswick and chairman of the Wartime Information Board, MacKenzie came to UBC with lofty ambitions to expand the university. He soon won the confidence of the university community, and set out to welcome the people of British Columbia to their university. Because extension programming would play an important role in MacKenzie's plans, Extension always had a small claim on the university's operating budget during his tenure.[5]

MacKenzie's view of university extension, as illustrated in his 1953 *President's Report*, fit the UBC tradition well. He described the conventional university functions of research and teaching, and then argued that there was "another primary function of universities in our kind of society" (p. 1). He was referring to university extension, and he indicated that there were people who had "reservations" about the involvement of the university in this function. In the face of these expressed doubts regarding the value of extension work at universities, MacKenzie argued:

> To me the issue is perfectly clear. If we are to have and maintain a society in which every adult citizen is called upon to have opinions and vote on matters not only of local – but of national and international – importance...some agencies must exist or be created to try to develop and obtain as great an understanding of the problems and nature of citizenship - in its broadest sense - as is possible. Also if we are to continue to live in a complex technological world that is changing and developing rapidly, we must have agencies to help keep the adult population informed about the changing world and the implications of those changes both for their lives and livelihood. And finally, if we are to enjoy the real benefits of technological development, we must help multiply the opportunities for self development and individual satisfaction in the leisure time technology has made possible. (p. 3)

MacKenzie continued his report with an explanation of the importance of adult education for purposes of nurturing active and responsible citizens, developing workers' vocational and professional capacities, and providing the opportunity for cultural enrichment. As a member of the Royal Commission on Arts, Sciences, and Letters (1949-1951), MacKenzie was a strong supporter of the cultural as well as the economic development of Canada.

President MacKenzie linked the growing importance of university extension to contemporary social changes. In his foreword to the 1954 annual report of the Department of University Extension, MacKenzie wrote:

> *In an age of technological change it is a vocational necessity to keep abreast of changes that affect our job. In an age of social change and political and social ferment, it is necessary to try and keep ourselves informed about our relationship with other people and other societies. In an age of increasing opportunities for recreation and leisure, when technology has made tremendous strides in the field of communication, it is desirable that we attempt to use them for the enrichment of life. It is for these reasons that the University maintains and supports a Department of University Extension. Through it we attempt to assist people who want to continue their education in technology, in public affairs, and for the cultivation of their own interests. (p. 3)*

In short, changes in the world were making learning increasingly important, and UBC was committed to continuing to respond to this situation by providing an ambitious extension program.

As British Columbia's post-war economy grew, so too did UBC. MacKenzie welcomed a large number of veterans into undergraduate programs, supported by federal funds. Many veterans were housed, fed, and taught in old army huts moved onto campus. In fact, the university's first residence, Acadia Camp, was a former military camp located in the bush east of the campus itself. Teaching appointments increased significantly during these years, particularly in the professional faculties. By the 1950s, the veterans had graduated, student numbers dropped, and growth followed a rate of increase proportional to the numbers of young people intent on attending university. But this too was on the rise as men and women in British Columbia were looking for greater educational opportunity; in fact, the provincial Liberals campaigned for the 1945 election on a platform that promised to increase educational opportunity. Extension (relocated from the Agriculture building to a re-purposed army hut on East Mall) was ready to serve those who were unable to attend degree programs at UBC in person.

Many of those who looked to UBC for education had an economic motive: leaders of business, industry, and the civil service were beginning to look more favourably on schools and universities to select and train managers and professional workers. At the same time, British Columbia was entering an era of increased leisure time, the enjoyment of which could be enhanced by education. Finally, public affairs seemed to demand a more educated perspective. Locally, one might consider British Columbia's prosperity and the rising

**Top:** John Friesen, UBC's third Director of Extension (1953-1967).
**Bottom:** Norman MacKenzie, UBC's third President (1944-1962) and a generous supporter of Extension.
*UBCA 5.1/1014, 23.1/301-37*

number of social democrats elected to public office. Internationally, new political regimes and diplomatic alignments following the war raised serious issues, particularly the role of communism in the early years of the Cold War. Immigration to British Columbia from continental Europe was up for the first time in several decades, and while Anglo-Canadians still dominated most political and economic institutions, members of ethnic minority groups were gaining status and influence. Although Canada had gained legislative independence from Britain with the Statute of Westminster in 1931, the Canadian government had only begun to assert its own foreign policy since the war. These were complex, confusing times that prompted many to seek informed, reliable education.

By the end of the 1940s, the UBC Department of University Extension delivered one of the largest and most wide-ranging programs of university-based adult education in Canada. In 1953, Shrum stepped down to put his energies into new areas, particularly the BC Research Council and the Faculty of Graduate Studies. Through the Canadian Association of Adult Education, Shrum had come to know and respect John Friesen, then Director of Field Services for the Manitoba Wheat Pool, a grain growers' co-operative with a strong educational mandate. Shrum invited Friesen, an old colleague of President MacKenzie, to become Director of UBC's Department of University Extension. Friesen accepted, and within weeks he was hired.[6] As the new full-time director, with a doctorate in adult education from Columbia University, Friesen brought to Extension a very different personality from that of his predecessor. Born and raised in the Mennonite tradition of self-help and mutual aid, Friesen was diplomatic, democratic, humanitarian, and inspirational, with a clear vision for Extension. He subscribed to the views of Cyril Houle, a prominent University of Chicago professor, that universities ought to emphasize adult education in esoteric fields, provide innovative and experimental programming, and address the educational interests of professionals and community leaders. Friesen increased extension programming considerably, particularly in cultural areas and in professional fields, and brought more people to the UBC campus for courses, conventions, and institutes. The number of full-time staff members with Extension increased from ten in 1951 to seventeen in 1957.[7]

John Friesen agreed with President MacKenzie's views about the importance of "lifelong learning." In his 1957 annual report Friesen wrote:

> No longer, on any basis whatsoever, can adult education be seen as confined to remedying deficiencies in the education of the young. It now exists in its own right with its own task of serving a population that feels more and more the need for lifelong learning. What a few Canadians of vision and courage have repeatedly stressed, recent world events are proving with impelling urgency; namely, that our future will be determined in very large measure by the emphasis we choose to place on public education for children, youth and adults. (p. 28)

In the same year, President MacKenzie's annual report reiterated similar views, indicating that UBC was committed to providing ambitious opportunities for lifelong learning.

*The growing number of British Columbians reached through various study programs provided by the Department of University Extension is proof that the goal of the people's university is being realized. The university, more than ever before, brings the maximum of its rich resources into the shops, the farms, the schools, the fishing villages where people live, work, and play.*

*John Friesen, Director
Department of University
Extension
1956*

Friesen and MacKenzie also brought a more international perspective to UBC. Ethnically, the province was more Anglo-Canadian than expatriate British by the end of the 1950s, and immigration from continental Europe had introduced a slightly different social and cultural perspective to the province and particularly to Vancouver.[8] Between 1951 and 1961, British Columbia's British-born population decreased from about 17 percent to 12 percent of the total population, while European-born rose from just under 8 percent to 10 percent. Those born in the province rose from 38 to 45 percent of the population. By 1961, Vancouver had a "Little Italy" (the Italian-born population rose from 1,800 in 1951 to 7,400 in 1961) while Robson Street downtown became known locally as "Robson Strasse" in recognition of the large number of German immigrants (whose numbers rose from 1,400 to 8,600 during the same ten-year period). People of Aboriginal or Asian descent – formerly disenfranchised – won the provincial vote in the late 1940s. The formal opening of UBC's International House in 1959 by Eleanor Roosevelt signified the university's commitment to internationalism, while the educational programs offered by the Faculty of Commerce in Singapore and Malaya in the late 1950s and the creation of a Department of Asian Studies in 1961 signalled a powerful new interest in Asia. Friesen, with the full support of President MacKenzie, embraced and promoted these developments, moving Extension in this new, cosmopolitan direction with language and study-travel courses.

## CHALLENGES IN THE 1960s

By the early 1960s, it was clear that the role of UBC's Department of University Extension was shifting to match significant changes in the nature of the province: population growth, urbanization, the shift in employment away from primary industries, and rising levels of formal education. Extension increasingly catered to the educational interests of urban professionals and community leaders. Nonetheless, Friesen and MacKenzie continued their support for a broad range of programs they believed would contribute to the quality of life across the province.

Political winds also changed in the 1960s in ways that forced changes upon Extension. The Social Credit government, in power since 1952, had worked to hasten the industrialization of rural British Columbia, first with roads, highways, bridges, railroads, and ferries, and then with hydroelectric power in the 1960s. The government supported education, but in some areas more than others: vocational education useful in the province's industries gained the most support, while arts and humanities were considered less important. At the same time, UBC and the various laboratories nearby had raised scientific expertise to levels of national and sometimes international significance. As scholarly and industrial ambition grew, President MacKenzie found himself out of step with a new Board of Governors, and retired in 1962. In his place, the Board of Governors hired John Macdonald, a young Harvard-trained dental microbiologist, who reflected a new set of ambitions.

John Friesen showing students a model of the proposed new International House at UBC, 1957. *UBCA 62.1/6*

President Macdonald investigated the state of post-secondary education in the province and recommended that the government expand the system to accommodate the expected deluge of university-age baby boomers by creating new colleges and universities that would specialize in different aspects of education. As a result of the "Macdonald Report" (1963), the province created the University of Victoria (formerly Victoria College, an adjunct of UBC), Simon Fraser University, and eight new community colleges between 1965 and 1970. UBC, for many years the only university in the province, was to become the premier scholarly university specializing in research and graduate studies to help introduce sophisticated technologies to industry, and help manage accompanying social and cultural changes. The President, Deans, and Department Heads began to review university programs, removing "lower level" courses, encouraging program specialization, setting new enrolment standards, and creating new administrative units to facilitate scholarship. In particular, all departments enhanced their graduate programs; graduate and post-graduate degrees had been available in several departments during the 1950s, but by 1970 all departments offered at least a master's degree.

Extension did not escape these sweeping changes. The historical mission of UBC in the provision of adult education was notably absent from Macdonald's focus on graduate and professional education. In his 1964 *President's Report,* Macdonald explicitly argued that universities should not engage in too broad a range of activities. He asked: "is there any predictable limit to the interests and functions of the University of British Columbia?" (p. 9). He replied that universities ought to confine themselves to functions supporting their central purposes – which he understood as the "fostering of a permanent spirit of inquiry and creativity, the engendering of powers of sound judgement, and the developing of the cultural resources of society" (p. 9). He distinguished between professions and vocations, and argued that vocational instruction was not appropriate to universities. Macdonald clearly believed that UBC should not engage in general forms of adult education and community service, and urged extension work at UBC to take a

**Left and right:** Using the university's new computers for data processing courses in the 1960s.

very different trajectory from that which had been established by Presidents Klinck and MacKenzie.

The Department of University Extension became subject to the critique of the President and his supporters. Extension was directed to cut many of its general arts and humanities programs while retaining the professional and business courses that paid their own way and were more in line with the new scholarly ambitions of the university. Extension complied to some extent, expanding its continuing professional education offerings. At the same time, the portion of the UBC budget that had hitherto helped subsidize extension activities was severely cut, from approximately $200,000 in 1964 to $100,000 in 1966. It was a "Mournful decision" according to a March 1964 headline in the *Vancouver Sun*. Troubled by the new directions, John Friesen made the necessary cuts while attempting to maintain a commitment to general programs by subsidizing the less lucrative, and seeking external grants. Nonetheless, morale dropped, and a number of staff members resigned.[9] In 1966, Freisen was invited to join the Population Council in Turkey, and left his UBC position.[10]

The last Director of the Department of University Extension at UBC was Gordon Selman, a local Vancouverite, who for many years had worked with John Friesen and shared many of his values. Selman's term as director (1967-1975) was marked by the transition of the Department of University Extension to a Centre for Continuing Education. Credit courses, continuing professional education, and non-credit courses aligned with academic subjects came to dominate, mostly provided on the UBC campus.[11] Friesen had attempted earlier to create a separate faculty to oversee all UBC extension and continuing education programs; this had been opposed by several established faculties, which were taking control of their own continuing education programs. Selman, frustrated with a continuing lack of cooperation, called upon Senate to draft a new policy outlining the relationship between Extension and the faculties – a policy that eventually led to the creation of a Centre for Continuing Education to take the place of the Department of University Extension. At the same time, he encouraged the university to expand its degree completion options for part-time students, an area where UBC lagged behind other institutions. Selman expanded the continuing professional education provision of Extension, raised fees where possible, and still managed to maintain a healthy array of general interest, non-credit courses. As will be discussed in Chapter Six, the transition from extension work to continuing education at UBC was part of a broad trend shared by most universities in western Canada. First, however, the next three chapters narrate the history of the programs and services provided by the Department of University Extension between 1936 and 1970.

*With every passing year, the need increases in the community of Greater Vancouver for a program through which adults may earn a university degree through part-time study. The demands of the labour market – and of living in a complex society – are creating a growing need for the possession of degrees and a growing demand on the part of persons who cannot attend university on a full-time basis.*

*Gordon Selman, Director
Department of University Extension
1968*

# The Rural Leadership School of 1947 was hewn out of the forest surrounding the University. Bulldozers tore away trees, rocks, and rubble.

*Army huts and supplies rolled in via tractor and truck. In six weeks it was ready for the sixty-nine young people selected from rural communities all over the province, from Dawson Creek to the American border... All of the classes were designed to aid the student to become better fitted for community life. Practical work was stressed in all subjects, agriculture, home economics, the hobbies and handicrafts. It has cost the Dominion-Provincial governments - and incidentally, the taxpayer, between thirty-five and forty thousand dollars to build and equip this camp... In return, we are expected to take back to our communities, not only all that we have learned in classes and practical work, but a heritage of close knit fellowship, of common interests and social usefulness; a deep respect for the rights and opinions of others, regardless of race, color, or creed.*

Pearl Lindsay,
From an essay entitled "Impressions of Camp"
written in 1947

## Chapter Three

# Supporting rural livelihoods and urban careers

Helping people make a living has been a consistent goal of extension and continuing education at UBC. In the 1930s and 1940s, Extension offered numerous programs in agriculture, home economics, and fisheries. The Great Depression and the Second World War influenced the nature of career-related programming during the early years of Extension. In the 1950s and 1960s, in the context of major changes to how people made their living in British Columbia, Extension's focus shifted to include business management programs and continuing professional education in fields such as education, engineering, law, communications, and social work. In addition to delivering its own programs, Extension facilitated the delivery of education by UBC faculties and external agencies, by administering extra-mural degree-credit programs and providing conference services. Whether oriented toward small-scale farmers or professionals working for large corporations, the programs described in this chapter shared the objective of helping people become more effective in their working lives.

## AGRICULTURAL EXTENSION

As described in Chapter One, agricultural extension at UBC began with extension lectures, short courses, and radio broadcasts given by members of the Faculty of Agriculture. With the establishment of the Department of University Extension, such work continued and expanded. In 1937, the Provincial Department of Agriculture collaborated with UBC to bring professors of agriculture into contact with local Farmers' Institutes in seven rural areas across the province.[1] Radio talks on agricultural topics were broadcast on Monday evenings during the winter months, in conjunction with the BC Electric Railway which was introducing electrical lines to the Fraser Valley. In 1938, UBC broadcast daily farm market reports, and regular farm-related talks by faculty members and other experts. Extension also sponsored a field day for livestock breeders and veterinarians. Part of the demand for agricultural education came from new farmers in the Fraser Valley who had left the harsher conditions of the prairies but were unfamiliar with local conditions; "Need Adult Education" declared an article in *The Daily Province* in 1934.[2] From 1937 to the early 1950s, poultry husbandry and gardening were among the evening courses offered on an annual basis by Extension at the

THE UNIVERSITY OF BRITISH COLUMBIA

## Agriculture

### AMATEUR GARDENING AND HORTICULTURE
#### FRUITS, VEGETABLES AND FLOWERS

Instructors: PROFESSORS A. F. BARSS, G. H. HARRIS, C. A. HORNBY, J. W. NEILL, and others.

In this course practical programmes for the propagation, planting and care of vegetables and fruits are stressed and consideration is given to methods of improving the appearance of the home grounds. The discussions are illustrated by the use of moving pictures, slides and charts. Mimeographed notes are distributed to supplement many of the talks.

Time:          Tuesdays, 8:00-9:30 p.m.
First Lecture:     Tuesday, October 16th
Place:           Vancouver Normal School
Fee:             Full course, 16 weeks—$6.00

### PROFESSIONAL GARDENING

Instructors: MEMBERS OF THE UNIVERSITY FACULTY OF AGRICULTURE AND THE B.C. PROFESSIONAL GARDENERS' ASSOCIATION

In co-operation with the B.C. Professional Gardeners' Association, two evening classes will be given. Attendance will be limited to those engaged in professional gardening, e.g. parks employment, or some commercial branch of horticulture, e.g. nursery or greenhouse work. Each course will be given one evening a week at the Normal School, eight evenings in the fall term and eight in the winter term.

1. Elementary course for the inexperienced gardeners.

2. Advanced course for the experienced gardeners.

Both courses should lead toward the Diploma in Horticulture which is granted by the B.C. Professional Gardeners' Association with the co-operation of the University Extension Department. Considerable practical experience is required for the Diploma.

Advanced Course
Time:          Mondays, 8:00-9:30 p.m.
First Lecture:     Monday, October 15th
Place:           Vancouver Normal School
Fee:             Full Course, 16 weeks—$10.00

Elementary Course
Time:          Wednesdays, 8:00-9:30 p.m.
First Lecture:     Wednesday, October 17th
Place:           Vancouver Normal School
Fee:             Full Course, 16 weeks—$10.00

Vancouver Normal School. These courses responded to an interest in urban agriculture and the need for increased food production during the Depression and then Second World War, which saw relief gardens and victory gardens introduced to the Vancouver area.[3]

After a lull caused by the Second World War, Extension expanded its agricultural programming in 1944, within a rapidly changing environment. The era of small family farms in British Columbia was coming to an end, with such farms replaced by a smaller number of larger, specialized, and increasingly mechanized agri-businesses. Although most remained family-owned, many of these businesses prospered as transportation and distribution networks across the province improved, while others faced more competition from imported agricultural products, particularly from the United States.[4] In this context, there was significant demand for education regarding new techniques, technologies, and business practices. Extension responded to this challenge by working with the Faculty of Agriculture and agricultural associations to provide a wide range of programs and services.

In 1945, evening courses in "Poultry Husbandry" and "Soils and Pastures" were delivered at Cloverdale and Langley in the Fraser Valley. Between January and April 1945, Extension organized short courses for seed growers, fruit and vegetable canners, and provincial dairy inspectors and veterinarians. In 1946, Extension appointed a full-time Assistant in Agriculture, Arthur Renney, who set to work "finding out what services were already being provided to the various areas of Province, and determining the ways in which the Extension Department could make the most effective contribution."[5] In that year, a total of eight evening courses were delivered in horticulture, livestock, poultry, and bee-keeping. Three courses were offered in Vancouver, while five were held in Langley, Cloverdale, and Haney. In addition, a "Poultry School of the Air" was broadcast in collaboration with the CBC and the federal and provincial departments of agriculture.

In the latter 1940s and 1950s, agricultural programming through the Department of University Extension continued to include evening courses delivered in the lower Fraser Valley. During the decade following the Second World War, Extension delivered an average of nine agricultural evening courses per year, to an average of nearly forty students per course. Courses included those in animal husbandry, pasture management, horticulture, soils and crops, farm management, bee-keeping, and farm mechanics.

In addition to evening courses, Extension held short courses and field days at various locations on topics such as poultry production, dairying, and pasture management. An annual five-week, intensive short course in dairying was delivered at UBC from 1948 through the 1960s. Beginning in 1947, numerous "farm machinery field days" were held at rural centres to which farmers brought their machinery for instruction on its operation, adjustment, and maintenance. Beginning in 1952, Extension expanded its on-campus program of agricultural short courses by holding such events at the Acadia Camp residential training facility used by the Youth Training School (described later in this chapter). In addition to the annual short course in dairying, courses in the 1950s

1962
BEEMASTERS'
SHORT COURSE

included those relating to flower production, bee-keeping, mink breeding, poultry production, and fruit growing.

In the 1950s, Extension's programming in agriculture included education and leadership development for children and youth. From 1953 to 1955, Extension hosted a 4-H Club Field Day, bringing as many as five hundred rural boys and girls to the UBC campus for demonstrations, lectures, and an introduction to the excitement of learning. From 1955 to 1957, Extension reported hosting between three and four thousand pre-school and elementary school children on tours of the University Farm each year.

**Top left:** Students in dairy short course, ca. 1949. **Top right:** Brochure for apiary course, 1962. **Bottom:** Poultry Husbandry course, ca. 1949. *UBCA 3.1/962-1*

The Department of University Extension relied heavily on the UBC Faculty of Agriculture for lecturers, instructors, advisors, and authors of articles on agricultural topics. Extension also worked closely with provincial and federal departments of agriculture to provide information to farmers across British Columbia. Extension distributed pamphlets and other publications, replied to written inquiries, and even, as of 1955, distributed tape-recorded lectures by professors of agriculture.

In the early 1960s, Extension added annual conferences in cattle production, seed growing, sheep production, and turf grass maintenance to those in dairying and poultry production. Reflecting the trend toward continuing professional education, Extension increased its delivery of programs for professional agrologists, a qualification introduced under provincial legislation in 1947 establishing the BC Institute of Agrologists.[6] For example, in 1963, Extension organized events for staff with the British Columbia Department of Agriculture, the Vancouver Branch of the Agricultural Institute of Canada, the British Columbia Institute of Agrologists, and the British Columbia Federation of Agriculture. For another example, from 1963 to 1970, Extension collaborated with the British Columbia Society of Landscape Architects to deliver an annual conference called "Roadside Development."

## RESIDENTIAL YOUTH TRAINING

Between 1938 and 1959, Extension organized and delivered innovative vocational training programs for rural people as part of a "Dominion-Provincial Youth Training Program" funded by the federal and provincial governments. In the spring of 1938 Extension Director Gordon Shrum discovered that the Technical Branch of the Department of Education in Victoria had funding available from the federal Labour Department (made possible by the 1937 *Unemployment and Agricultural Assistance Act*). Shrum obtained some of these

**Top:** Sewing and dressmaking class at the Youth Training Camp, 1940s. **Bottom:** The original Youth Training "roadshow," 1939. *UBCA 3.1/1253-1, 1.1/12090-2*

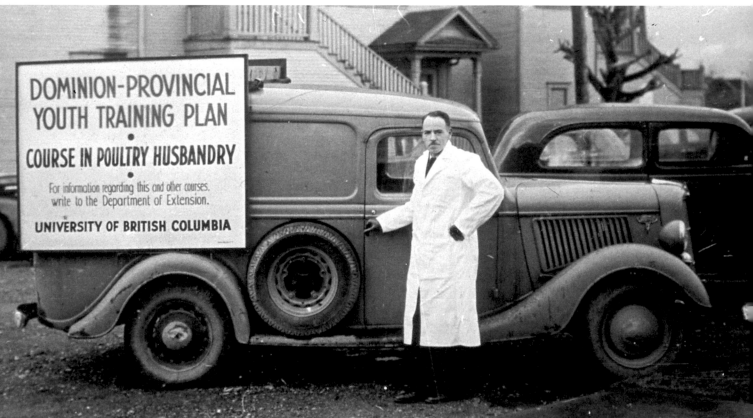

funds for an educational "roadshow" across the Fraser Valley. With equipment loaded into the back of a rented truck, two instructors – experts in poultry husbandry and bee-keeping – visited a new community every day for six weeks, giving talks and demonstrations in whatever vacant hall could be found. The initial program was unorthodox, but so successful that Shrum applied for and received additional funds to continue. Before long, demand was great enough to support two teams of five instructors travelling across the province, and lecturing on a broad range of topics in agriculture and home economics.[7]

In 1939, the program involved sixteen, two-week residential courses held at widely dispersed centres across British Columbia, from the Peace River area to Vancouver Island and the Kootenay region. In that year, 1,059 people between the ages of sixteen and thirty-five attended "Youth Training Schools" for the full two-week period, while over two thousand more participated in associated evening programming. The curriculum included weaving, cooking, dress-making, animal husbandry, dairying, soils, field crops, carpentry, blacksmithing, music appreciation, and practical psychology. Each "school" was organized in collaboration with local community organizations, typically Farmers' Institutes and Women's Institutes. In 1940, Extension delivered two forms of Youth Training Schools: twenty-seven "Rural Occupational Schools" of two to three weeks' duration held in communities across British Columbia (1,023 participants); and one, eight-week "Rural Leadership School" held at Point Grey near the UBC campus, for students having demonstrated leadership potential at the occupational schools (ninety-one participants).

According to Shrum's 1940 annual report, the Youth Training Schools embraced vocational, civic, and liberal goals:

> The schools have sought to present an enlightened educational programme designed with the two-fold purpose of building citizenship and morale, and providing a practical training which will make farm life more worthwhile and attractive. They have tried to reveal the wider possibilities of citizenship both to the young people who take part in the democratic life of the schools and, indirectly, to the communities which request and support the schools as a cooperative venture. They have sought to enhance the value of rural life in the eyes of young people who are not gainfully employed and who as a result may be in the process of becoming discouraged with farm life. Throughout they have endeavoured to encourage individual development and expression by means of an activity programme. (p. 17)

Shrum reported that the program was well received by participants and local observers, quoting the Member of the Legislative Assembly in the Peace River region who stated that the program "is the greatest benefit our young people of the Peace River have received since the formation of this constituency."[8] The combination of "occupational" schools across the province and a "leadership" school at UBC continued until 1942, when declining enrolment attributed to the war effort led to the discontinuation of the program.

The Youth Training Schools resumed in 1947, with an eight-week Rural Leadership School held at UBC's Acadia Camp, and three-week training schools held at Williams Lake and two communities in the Peace River district. The curriculum was again focussed on

*As the rate of change in our society increases – and as our people have more and more leisure, the facilities for adult education become more and more important... The University must provide the facilities whereby men and women can continue their education after they leave school and after they leave university.*

*Dr. Norman MacKenzie*
*UBC President*
*1957*

*Qualifications for Extension Home Economist (ca. 1953)*

*Pleasant personality.*

*Willing to travel and live out of a suitcase for weeks at a time.*

*High academic standing in clothing, good working knowledge of tailoring.*

*Academic course to have included work in interior decoration and home planning.*

*Good foundation in foods and nutrition.*

*Knowledge of and practical work in the following would be a decided asset: making of slip covers and drapes; upholstery; refinishing of furniture; and rug making.*

practical agricultural skills and home economics, with both men and women receiving instruction relating to citizenship, first aid, and recreational leadership. Students could also participate in evening activities such as public speaking, dramatics, physical education, photography, and journalism.

Following 1947, Youth Training Schools were no longer held in rural communities, likely due to both the complexities of organizing itinerant educational events, and the reality that many young adults were leaving rural areas for life in towns and cities. However, an eight-week Youth Training School continued at UBC's residential training centre every year until 1959, providing a total of 768 young adults (an average of sixty-four participants each year) from across the province with an intensive and unique educational experience. Although vocational instruction in agriculture and home economics remained the core activity, students practised leadership and citizenship skills by operating a co-operative food store, publishing a student newspaper and yearbook, and electing a student council to manage the affairs of the School. Students also regularly organized banquets, plays, and dances, and they shared janitorial and food preparation tasks at the School.

The Youth Training School added commercial fishing courses in 1955, providing instruction in navigation, boat care, fish conservation, and oceanography. In forestry courses added in 1958, participants studied mapping, lumber grading, surveying, scaling, and other topics. Agricultural students in the 1950s continued to study animal husbandry, soils and crops, poultry, and horticulture, while those in home economics focussed on child development, inter-personal relations, cooking, sewing, and hygiene. All participants could follow optional courses in subjects such as motor mechanics, carpentry, first aid, public speaking, and photography. As the provincial university, UBC responded to training needs across a broad spectrum of topics and levels as the economy evolved in the twentieth century. Despite the success of this program, in 1959, as part of broader changes to the funding and delivery of vocational education across Canada, the provincial and federal governments stopped funding the Youth Training School, and Extension discontinued the program.

## HOME ECONOMICS AND HANDICRAFTS

In 1938, Extension began providing short courses in collaboration with Women's Institutes in British Columbia. Women's Institutes had become popular across the province since 1909, providing women with opportunities to interact, acquire new skills and knowledge, and engage in charitable and community-based work. With support from the province they became a common feature in small towns and suburbs alike. During the Depression, as many women faced acute pressure to care for their families on severely limited budgets, Women's Institutes were particularly active, sometimes

providing food relief for the hungry across the province and beyond.[9] UBC had little involvement with home economics, refusing to provide a degree program despite the advocacy of women's groups and their offer of funding.[10] Extension, however, responded to the demand for knowledge and skills in home economics.

Initially, home economics courses were part of Extension's Youth Training Program.[11] The new "Homemaking Courses" included instruction in home economics, handicrafts, nutrition, psychology, sewing, cooking, and co-operatives. The Depression prompted great concern for food conservation and the use of alternative technologies for food storage, like dehydration, because of a lack of sugar for canning. Handicrafts were promoted by the provincial advisory board for Women's Institutes not only as a way to make do at home during austere times, but also as a possible way to earn a little additional income.[12] As well, home economics was closely identified with "character education" by provincial school authorities at the time, and was consistent with the ethos of the Youth Training Program to extol the virtues of rural life.[13] In 1938-39, UBC gave ten short home economics courses in various communities, with modest financial support from the provincial Ministry of Agriculture. In 1940, the number of short courses expanded to twenty-nine, attracting 684 participants. Extension also provided an instructor in home economics to participate in six "field days" sponsored by federal and provincial departments of agriculture. Further, two-week summer courses in hand-weaving were delivered at UBC in 1939, 1940, and 1941.

Between 1941 and 1945, Extension reduced its home economics service due to wartime constraints. In May 1946, Extension appointed Eileen Cross, a qualified teacher and dietician with a degree from the University of Manitoba and some training at the University of California, as a full-time Home Economist. With the appointment in October of Jessie

**Left:** Home economics summer course in food preparation, 1955. *UBCA 3.1/1095*
**Right:** Description of "Short Course in Home-making," Victoria, June 13–16, 1939.

Stewart, whom Shrum called "one of the most outstanding and versatile handicrafts instructors in all of Canada," Extension created an independent "Home Economics and Handicrafts Division."[14] Several other women were hired as instructors or home economists over the next ten years as the Division expanded, providing instruction in home economics and handicrafts that was consistent with mainstream expectations regarding gender roles at the time.

Extension staff members delivered short courses, demonstrations, and workshops in numerous rural communities across British Columbia on such topics as sewing, handicrafts, and home decoration. Extension also provided judges for fall fairs in rural communities, and distributed information via pamphlets and letters. Between 1948 and 1953, Extension attracted over six hundred participants to thirty-seven rural short courses each year, on average. Topics included sewing, home rejuvenation, leatherwork, frozen foods (encouraged by the growing popularity of domestic refrigeration), tailoring, weaving, and home furnishings.[15] Rural short courses were typically provided by two home economists who travelled extensively across the rough back roads of British Columbia. In their travels, the home economists frequently made "home visits" to provide advice and to assist with diverse problems. Shrum noted in his 1951 annual report that:

> Home visits were numerous, resulting in more efficient kitchens, the redecorating of rooms, and the addition of simple "built-ins" to improve and lessen the work of homemakers. Frequently the home economists assisted with such widely diverse problems as the repair of sewing machines and the planning of budgets. (p. 2)

Home economists had to be versatile, to say the least. Extension's home economics service was extensive, but it did not last for many years. In 1952, the home economists reported visiting more than fifty communities and serving more than 1,400 women; in 1954, they reported replying to more than one thousand written inquiries dealing with issues such as school lunches, nutrition, and food preparation. However, when Eileen Cross resigned in 1955, she was not replaced.

In the early 1960s, in recognition of the increasing number of women who worked outside the home, Extension began exploring continuing education programming for women engaged in business and professional life. Between 1941 and 1961, the number of women in the British Columbia labour force had nearly tripled, accounting for nearly one third of workers in 1961. Proportional to men, women had increased their numbers only in clerical roles, but their total involvement in the professions had nearly tripled during this time period and their participation in business and managerial roles more than tripled.[16] In his 1963 report, Friesen noted that his department held a one-day seminar on "The Role of Women in Business" and that it "also undertook a major study of special programs for the continuing education of women conducted by leading universities throughout the world" (p. 11). In 1965, Extension hosted 210 participants at a conference on "The Role of the University in Continuing Education for Women." This event was "designed to draw attention to the changing life-patterns of women, to inform

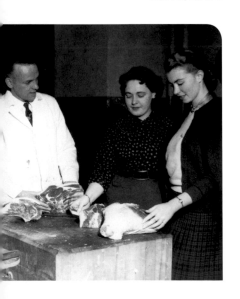

*Meat cutting class, 1956.*
*UBCA 1.1/8545-2*

the community about continuing education services which are already available, and to find out what further services are needed" (pp. 16-17). The following year, Extension opened a counselling service in downtown Vancouver to help women take advantage of educational and occupational opportunities. This service would grow into the Women's Resources Centre, as discussed in Chapter Nine.

## FISHERIES EDUCATION

Beginning in the late 1930s, programming in the theory and practice of co-operatives in the fisheries sector was both an important form of vocational education provided by UBC, and a groundbreaking initiative that helped launch an enduring social movement in the province. Although the Depression had hit bottom in 1933, the legacy of unemployment, desperation, and militancy persisted. One of Canada's best-known educational responses to rural poverty was the "Antigonish Movement" of Nova Scotia organized by the Extension Department of St. Francis Xavier University. Since the early 1920s, activist priests from the university had organized co-operatives and credit unions among rural fishers and their families. When delegates from British Columbia's three largest fishing co-ops asked Shrum late in 1937 to start extension work on their behalf, he contacted St. Francis Xavier University to inquire about their methods and funding. At the same time, the local co-operative movement in greater Vancouver was growing quickly, mixing jobless workers with Christian reformers, utopian visionaries, and political activists who sought legislation to establish credit unions. The province responded in 1938 with legislation to permit these co-operative financial institutions.[17]

In 1938, Extension obtained a grant of $5,000 from the federal Department of Fisheries to bring J.D. Nelson MacDonald from St. Francis Xavier University to conduct a three-day course on co-operatives for fishermen. This initial course was the springboard for a more ambitious program in subsequent years. In 1940, two staff members from St. Francis Xavier University were brought to British Columbia for several months to establish the foundations of an "Educational Programme for British Columbia Fishermen" that lasted for more than twenty years with financial support from the federal Department of Fisheries.

The basic objective of the Programme was "to provide a sound educational basis for fishermen anxious to raise their standard of living by means of cooperative endeavour."[18] It included visits by field workers to fishing communities, the organization of public meetings, technical support for the establishment and operation of credit unions, the distribution of a "Co-op News Letter," and the preparation of courses to be studied by small groups of fishermen. By 1942, UBC had developed several study-group courses, including: "An Introduction to Cooperation," "Credit Unions," "The Cooperative Buying Club," and "A Course for Credit Union Treasurers," some of which used films or radio broadcasts to provide additional resources for group meetings. Also that year, Extension

*Fisheries Short Course (1956)*

*The primary purpose of this course is to extend the knowledge of the fishing industry to practising fishermen beyond their specialized branch. Applicants should be willing and able to convey some of the information gained from the course to other fishermen in their areas.*

organized forty-three "study clubs" in participating fishing communities, and delivered evening classes and conferences of interest to those involved in the fishing industry in Vancouver and surrounding areas. Beginning in 1942, regional two- or three-day conferences were held in a small number of coastal centres.

In his 1941 annual report, Gordon Shrum argued that the Educational Programme for British Columbia Fishermen was having an impact beyond its direct work with the fishermen, by raising morale and generating a "new community spirit" (pp. 70-71). Field workers with Extension not only helped to establish and operate co-operatives and credit unions, but also had a role in the establishment of provincial organizations such as the Fishermen's Co-operative Federation and the Fishermen's Mutual Marine Insurance Society in 1945.

Extension's success in this endeavour depended on the efforts of the field workers, often young UBC graduates, who had considerable obstacles to overcome. Not only did they travel regularly through rough seas along British Columbia's expansive, rugged coast to Prince Rupert, Haida Gwaii (Queen Charlotte Islands), and the west coast of Vancouver Island, but they also encountered widely diverse people, some of whom were migratory and seasonal fishers. Unionized fishers were suspicious of field workers' intentions, and militant or depressed individuals were fairly common.[19] Circumstances for field workers were, to say the least, challenging.

The Educational Programme for British Columbia Fishermen initially focussed on educating people about the aims, principles, and practices of co-operative organization, and on the promotion of co-operatives and credit unions. In the post-war years, as the economy improved and credit unions increased in number, the Department of Fisheries raised its financial support to expand education in co-operative production and marketing of fish, with additional courses and consultation on more technical aspects of the fisheries industry. For example, in 1946, six lectures were delivered weekly to about two hundred fishermen on the subjects of fish handling and preservation. In his 1948 annual report, Shrum noted that "co-operative associations and credit unions, having established themselves, seek to improve their business and educational methods in order to increase their efficiency and financial sustainability" (p. 10). Extension shifted its focus to provide "practical courses designed to contribute to the efficiency or safety of the fishermen in their work." In subsequent years, such courses included instruction in navigation and conservation. Extension increased its distribution of publications, and, from 1951 through 1958, it published and distributed a monthly newsletter, the "Fisheries Forum," to share information about conservation and related issues. In the mid-1950s, over one thousand fishermen received this monthly publication.

Although some aspects of field work declined following the war, Extension continued to employ at least one field worker who travelled extensively along the coast, meeting with fishermen, attending meetings of the co-operatives, discussing problems, and offering

advice. UBC field workers helped the Prince Rupert credit union absorb the collapsed Fisherman's Co-operative Federation following strikes in 1952.[20] In 1956, Extension reported that its field workers had visited "almost every coastal fishing community" and had direct contact with over 1,400 people. Field work continued to be an important component of the fisheries program until the early 1960s.

In 1955, the fisheries program expanded to include a two-week technical course, taught on the UBC campus. The face of commercial fisheries was changing rapidly: new technologies in nets, navigation aids, and on-ship refrigeration were now available; industry concentration had increased, focussing on the mouths of the Fraser and Skeena Rivers; and foreign competition had escalated as ships ranged further in search of fish.[21] Unions, industry, and government cooperated to bring thirty-five active fishermen to UBC in 1955 for the two-week technical course.

In his 1955 annual report, John Friesen noted that "Besides bringing the fishermen up to date in the latest fishing techniques, the course, which was the first of its kind in Canada, aimed at giving them a fuller understanding of the problems of their industry" (p. 15). Extension subsequently delivered its "Technical Fisheries Short Course" on an annual basis until 1968, attracting a total of over five hundred people (an average of thirty-six participants per year). In 1960, the technical fisheries course expanded to three weeks in duration, to allow more in-depth study and to accommodate a field trip to the Pacific Biological Research Station in Nanaimo.

In the 1960s, Extension organized an annual Fisheries Lecture Series. From 1960 through 1963, the twelve-week series was limited to members of staff of companies involved with the British Columbia Fisheries Association. In 1964, the lecture series was opened

**Left:** Fisherman learn about navigational equipment aboard the *Blyth Spirit*, 1961.
**Right:** Fisheries short course, 1960.
*UBCA 3.1/953.2, 1.1/8221.2*

up to members of the public, and a total of sixty-three people attended. This lecture series continued until 1969. In addition to the annual short course and lecture series in the 1960s, Extension offered various workshops on topics of importance to commercial fishing in British Columbia.

## FORESTRY PROGRAMS

In comparison to its substantial involvement with agriculture and fisheries, Extension provided relatively modest educational services relating to the forestry industry. Although one might expect considerable education in one of British Columbia's domin-ant industries, UBC had little history of involvement. Until the introduction of silviculture into the curriculum in the late 1930s, UBC had graduated only a few students in "forest engineering," and they were not in great demand. This changed following the war with the passage of legislation that favoured larger timber holdings and longer-term harvesting rights, intended to encourage better forest management. The subsequent *Foresters' Act* of 1947 created the role of "professional forester," who could be educated in UBC's new Faculty of Forestry. Still, UBC had difficulty in providing extension services to this industry perhaps, as Gordon Shrum noted in his 1953 annual report, because of the "isolated conditions of lumber camps along the coast and in interior regions" (p. 29). The earliest examples of extension work in the forestry sector were a customized training program

Forestry night school class, 1959.
*UBCA 3.1/600-2*

for lumber supervisors delivered for MacMillan and Bloedel in 1953, and short courses in "Fibre Technology" and "Fire Prevention" delivered in 1956.

In 1957, Extension hired a Supervisor of Forestry Services, Alan Campbell, who set to work "establishing close liaison with industry and other organizations providing educational services," as well as conducting "a broad survey of existing services which are available in British Columbia and elsewhere on the continent" (p. 10). In the late 1950s, Extension offered evening courses on subjects such as "Hardwood Timbers" and "Economic Factors Influencing British Columbia's Forest Industry." The Supervisor of Forestry Services served, in these years, as the secretary of a Speakers' Bureau established in collaboration with the Canadian Institute of Forestry. By 1960, Extension no longer maintained a specialized Forestry Service; however, it did continue to provide business and professional education for those working in the forestry sector. For example, in 1963, it offered a "Logging Management" seminar to forty-five managers in the forestry sector, and in 1965 it organized a seminar with over one hundred participants on "British Columbia's Future in Forest Products Trade in Asia and the Pacific."

## CONTINUING PROFESSIONAL EDUCATION

The initiatives described so far in this chapter were focussed on the vocational preparation of people engaged either in the primary industries of farming, fishing, and forestry, or in the management of rural households whose functioning was an essential component of the production of commodities in these industries. However, Extension also provided continuing education for people in a range of urban professions. Over time, as the provincial economy shifted from one based on primary industries to one based on the provision of services, and as the population of British Columbia became increasingly urban, Extension focussed less on agriculture, home economics, and fisheries, and more on a range of new professions.

From its early days, Extension delivered conferences and short courses in collaboration with government agencies, businesses, professional associations, and community-based organizations. Such events typically had professional objectives: a course in electronics was offered in 1937, taught by E.G. Cullwick of the Department of Mechanical and Electrical Engineering, while geology faculty continued to advise mining engineers.[22] In 1938, Extension provided courses on "Leadership Training" (for the Parent-Teacher Federation) and "A Short Course on Social and Cultural Problems" (for practicing social workers), followed in subsequent years by courses on "Public Administration" (for civil servants in Victoria) and popular short courses in Business English, Commercial Law, and Industrial Psychology. In 1942, Extension and the federal Department of Labour co-sponsored a four-week course in "Personnel Administration" to forty human resources managers. This short course was repeated in 1944 and 1947. Business courses like

*Course in Personnel Administration (1944)*

*The course is designed to meet the requirements of executives who, under the stress of present conditions, find it increasingly necessary to delegate the responsibility for the selection, placing, training and direction of employees.*

these were partly prompted by wartime conditions requiring industrial efficiency and high employment.

Short courses and conferences, often held in collaboration with external sponsors, became increasingly important to Extension in the post-war years. In 1947, for example, Extension co-hosted a program in personnel administration, a refresher course for Veteran's Land Act supervisors, a short course for food canners, a training course for vehicle fleet supervisors, and conferences on school building maintenance, playgrounds, and community centres. These were soon followed by similar, co-hosted programs in social work, community recreation, and driver training, to support the trucking and farming industry.

In several cases, collaboration between Extension and off-campus agencies led to regular professional development events or annual conferences. The Institute in Group Work, for example, was organized in 1944 to "meet the very acute shortage of qualified social workers" by providing two weeks of professional training to people working with provincial institutions and community organizations such as the YMCA and church groups. The Welfare Council of Greater Vancouver provided financial assistance, while social work instructors from UBC helped with academic planning at a time when the university was busy preparing professionals for British Columbia's rapidly expanding public welfare services. [23]

The trend toward short courses and conferences relating to professional employment continued in the 1950s. In 1955, Extension delivered short courses in commercial fishing, community planning, engineering, fleet management, and statistical analysis. The following year, Extension offered several new short courses to people in the forestry sector, and with the British Columbia Safety Council delivered one-day short courses in human resource management to over 1,500 participants in nine different cities. The number of short courses and conferences offered continued to rise: from 49 to 100 between 1958 and 1960, with total participation increasing from 4,687 to 7,600.

It was in the 1960s that continuing professional education truly emerged as a major field. In his 1960 annual report, John Friesen noted that continuing education in the professions was:

> becoming, and will continue to be a major concern of higher Adult Education. The Department, in cooperation with the faculties and with professional organizations, has organized a rapidly increasing number of seminars and conferences for a great variety of groups – teachers, police officers, lawyers, agriculturalists, directors of defence, broadcasters, businessmen, physiotherapists, workers with the aging, and many others. (p. 1)

The following year, Friesen reported that Extension collaborated with UBC faculties to provide evening courses, short courses, and conferences in agriculture, architecture, commerce, community planning, education, engineering, fisheries, forestry, law, librarianship, medicine, nursing, pharmacy, public administration, and social work. Such

*Law Refresher Course (1961)*

*The Canadian Bar Association, British Columbia Branch, and the Vancouver Bar Association in conjunction with the Faculty of Law and in collaboration with the Extension Department of the University of British Columbia have arranged the third annual Law Refresher Course to be held at the University of British Columbia on Thursday, May 4th, 1961 and on Friday, May 5th, 1961.*

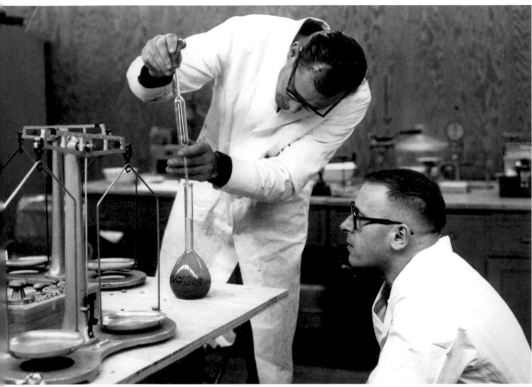

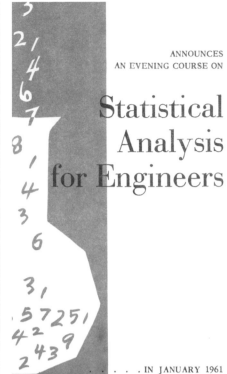

ANNOUNCES
AN EVENING COURSE ON

# Statistical Analysis for Engineers

. . . . IN JANUARY 1961

**Top:** Continuing professional education in the 1960s. **Bottom:** Fleet supervisors' course, 1950. *UBCA 3.1/S48-1*

activity mirrored the increased number of urban professionals in British Columbia's workforce, particularly in the Greater Vancouver area.

In the latter 1960s, over ten thousand people per year enrolled in Extension's short courses and conferences. In health sciences and commerce, Extension remained active until the mid-1960s when the faculties involved assumed complete responsibility. By 1967, Extension employed specialists in education, law, and engineering to work with faculties to develop and deliver continuing professional education programs. In 1969, more than seven thousand participants enrolled in over 160 continuing professional education events in several fields: education (50 percent of enrolments); engineering (19 percent); law (16 percent); agriculture, fisheries and forestry (10 percent); and social work (5 percent). In each field, Extension collaborated with UBC faculties and professional associations, such as the British Columbia Teachers' Federation, the British Columbia Association of Social Workers, and the British Columbia Section of the Canadian Bar Association.

## TEACHER TRAINING AND EARLY CHILDHOOD EDUCATION

Of the various professionals for whom Extension provided continuing education programs, teachers and early childhood educators were among the first and most prominent. In June 1937, Extension organized a short course entitled "Education – Modern Men, Methods and Curricula." The following summer, Extension organized a "Summer School of Athletics" to assist teachers involved in track and field and basketball. In subsequent years, many practicing teachers participated in the "Summer School of the Theatre" described in Chapter Four. Teachers frequently heard UBC lecturers, particularly during President MacKenzie's term as he was particularly keen that teachers (and students) become aware of the university.[24]

In 1956, the establishment of the UBC Faculty of Education created significant demand for additional Extension courses. Extension began offering degree-credit courses on a part-time basis in the evenings and off-campus, as well as refresher courses in mathematics directed toward high school teachers. In 1963, Extension and the Faculty of Education created a formal "Education–Extension Program" to provide non-credit courses for

**Left:** Brochure for preschool Extension program, 1961.
**Right:** Alice Borden (L), early childhood education teacher, 1955.
*UBCA 14.1/4.3*

PLAY EQUIPMENT
FOR THE
PRE-SCHOOL PROGRAM

EXTENSION DEPARTMENT
THE UNIVERSITY OF BRITISH COLUMBIA

teachers, school trustees, educational administrators, and interested members of the general public. In that year, Extension offered over thirty education courses. By the late 1960s, the educational sector was UBC's largest professional development program area.

Extension was also a pioneer in the field of early childhood education in British Columbia. Child study as a field of scientific inquiry had grown in the United States during the 1920s and 1930s, with Canadian universities McGill and Toronto also participating. Academics in Canada and the United States popularized psychological theories that emphasized the role of environment in shaping personality and maintaining healthy, happy, and "normal" children.[25] By 1940, UBC was offering an undergraduate course in child psychology that considered these new theories and practices of "mental hygiene."[26]

Interest in child rearing in British Columbia rose during and following the war for two reasons: first, mothers were drawn into the workplace to boost war production or to re-place men who were serving overseas, creating a sudden demand for childcare facilities (which required licensing after 1938); second, the birth rate was rising by war's end with the advent of the baby boom, and parents were seeking educational opportunities for their children. As parents tapped into the kindergarten movement with its child-centred pedagogy of learning through play, Extension responded in 1941 with a study group course in child psychology.[27] In 1945, Extension collaborated with the BC Parent-Teacher Federation to study ways to assist "co-operative play schools," and subsequently produced educational materials and hosted conferences. Extension followed with a study-group course on "Co-operative Play Groups for Children Under Six" and continued in the 1950s with annual short courses for pre-school workers. Working closely with the Vancouver Co-operative Play Groups Association and the British Columbia Pre-School Education Association, Extension provided many valuable educational services including, in 1956, a twelve-week "Co-operative Leadership Training Course" to develop leaders and managers in early childhood education.

In 1962, Friesen reported that pre-school education was "coming-of-age in British Columbia" and noted a significant number of initiatives by his Department and the Faculty of Education. In that year, Extension reported offering fifty-two courses and workshops to 2,225 pre-school teachers and parents in Vancouver and across the province. The demand was prompted in part by new legislation permitting public kinder-gartens which, until 1960, were uncommon and poorly funded in most school districts. When the province amended the *School Act* to permit school boards greater freedom to establish kindergartens, with full government funding, the Vancouver School Board increased the number of its kindergartens considerably.[28] In the mid-1960s, primary responsibility for programming in early childhood education shifted from Extension to the Faculty of Education, which had launched UBC's Child Study Centre in 1959, and housed the Department of Early Childhood Education.

*The Education of Your Pre-School Child: A One-Evening Program for Parents of Pre-School Age Children and for Teachers of Nursery Schools and Kindergartens (1965)*

*How can parents prepare their child for school?*

*Can pre-school children be taught to read?*

*Should pre-school children be taught to read? At home? At kindergarten?*

*What is the value of 'creative play' in the home and in kindergarten?*

*What can nursery school and kindergarten contribute to a child's educational and personal development?*

## COMMUNICATIONS

In 1957, Extension established a "Communications Service" directed toward people working with or interested in the mass media. Television, having arrived in the Vancouver area in 1954, was rousing popular and academic interest, and Extension was willing to experiment. Friesen had hired an energetic young instructor in 1956 who was passionate about the implications of broadcast technologies for adult education. Alan Thomas was President MacKenzie's nephew, and had earlier worked with the Canadian Association for Adult Education (CAAE); he had professional contact with Friesen, CAAE President Roby Kidd, and media guru Marshall McLuhan, and was working on a doctorate in adult education at Columbia University.[29]

In collaboration with the British Columbia Association of Broadcasters, Extension developed a non-credit program of part-time study in radio, television, and film for students from across Canada. For five years, with ongoing financial support from the Association of Broadcasters, Extension organized evening courses, seminars, and conferences exploring "the possibilities of the new media" (radio, television, and film). Between 1959 and 1962, Extension held an annual "Summer School of Communications," delivering courses on communications and mass media theory, along with practical courses on the techniques of writing, speech, and film production.

In 1961, Extension organized a two-year certificate program in "Communication and Broadcasting." The certificate was composed of evening courses in "Speech for Broadcasting," "Commercial Writing for Broadcasting," "Film Production," and "Communications and Mass Media." In his 1962 annual report, Friesen remarked that "nearly all of the students either secured or advanced their position in the industry while participating in the program" (p. 17). Despite such strong results, Thomas returned to work at the CAAE in the summer of 1961, and the communications program ceased operations within a year.

## EVENING COURSES IN BUSINESS AND MANAGEMENT

UBC delivered its first evening course in "Business Management" in 1940. In that sixteen-week course, Professors Morrow and Currie from the Department of Commerce lectured on finance, marketing, and human resource management, with the objective "to acquaint the members of the class with the common problems of management that arise in all businesses." The Department of Commerce was then new and small, looking to expand at a time when UBC was still under financial restraint. Extension courses helped to meet some of the rising demand without having to depend on UBC for operating funds. Evening courses in "Business English," "Elementary Economics," "Commercial Law," and "Psychology in Business and Industry" were delivered for a couple of years until Extension took a brief hiatus from business management courses to focus on other wartime priorities.

*Summer School of Communications (1961)*

*Seminar on Communications*

*An investigation of basic aspects of communication theory and media study. The Seminar will draw heavily on the experience of participants in the exploration of the nature of political, economic, social and artistic characteristics and effects of the mass media and other forms of communications.*

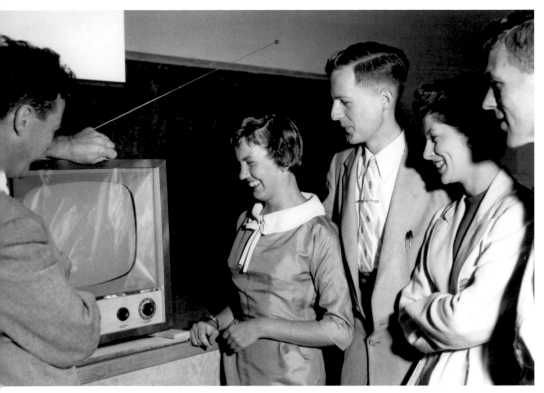

Returning to the field in 1947, Extension met post-war demand by expanding its evening courses in business and management. Extension offered three streams of study: business courses for the general public, typically instructed by UBC Commerce faculty; courses open to members of the Society of Industrial Accountants of British Columbia, leading to the designation of Registered Industrial and Cost Accountant (RIA); and a series of courses in traffic management for those interested in transportation via road, rail, sea, and air. Between 1948 and 1952, Extension offered an average of sixteen business and management evening courses each year, to an average of thirty-six students per course. In the 1950s, Extension offered a diverse and growing selection of evening courses in areas such as accounting, marketing, human resource management, industrial organization, investment, and personal finances. Extension delivered courses dealing with management in specific industries or sectors, such as "Freight Traffic Management" and "Municipal Administration." Extension sometimes provided customized programs for particular organizations, such as a non-credit correspondence course in "Supervisors' Training" for the Ocean Falls Company in 1954 and 1955.

By the early 1960s, UBC enrolled more than two thousand students each year in business and management evening courses, but Extension played a less prominent role. Most of these students took courses through the "Diploma Division" of the Faculty of Commerce and Business Administration, which had grown considerably following its establishment in 1956. By 1961, many professional business associations worked with the new Faculty

**Top left:** Radio and TV writing course, 1955. **Top right:** Speed reading course for executives, 1958. **Bottom:** Insurance short course, 1950. *UBCA 3.1/599.1, 1.1/8179-3, 3.1/1001.3*

to deliver continuing education programs. Extension still offered collaborative programs in Freight Traffic Management and in Purchasing, and delivered general interest courses such as personal investing, speed reading, industrial psychology, and the application of computers in business – a revolutionary new field.

Through the mid-1960s, Extension and the Faculty of Commerce continued to share responsibility for evening courses in business and management. The Faculty provided courses leading to certificates or diplomas in areas such as accounting, public administration, management, and real estate. Extension delivered non-credit courses in more general fields such as operations research, statistics, computers, law, and economics. The number of courses and participants remained high; in 1967 for example, over 1,500 people took part in Extension's non-credit business and management courses. On July 1, 1968, the Faculty of Commerce and Business Administration assumed control of all continuing education programming in business and management, although Extension continued to include management content in its programs for professional audiences, and to deliver interdisciplinary humanities and social science courses for business audiences.

The transfer of administrative responsibility for extension and continuing education programs from the Department of University Extension to the Faculty of Commerce and Business Administration foreshadowed a number of similar transfers from the Centre for Continuing Education to other professional faculties in the 1970s and 1980s. There were a number of factors behind these developments. As professional faculties at UBC developed their capacity for research and degree-credit teaching, they wished to further serve their alumni and other constituents through the provision of extension services and continuing education programs. The tendency for financially successful programs to be transferred to professional faculties was an indicator of successful and innovative work on the part of staff with Extension and the Centre for Continuing Education. This tendency began with business programs in the 1960s, and continued in subsequent decades with programs in education, agriculture, social work, law, engineering, and a range of other professions. The specific circumstances for each transfer of responsibility will not be elaborated in this book; however, the transfers reflected the academic and financial goals of the faculties involved, and were supported by policy developed by the UBC Senate (see Chapter Six). The successful development, incubation, and transfer of continuing professional education programs was one of the many important contributions of Extension and the Centre for Continuing Education to the UBC community.

## CONFERENCE SERVICES

From 1947 onwards, Extension made its Acadia Camp residential facilities available as a conference centre. Except for eight weeks each winter when the Youth Training School operated, the facility was used by a range of local, provincial, and national organizations

**TABLE 3.1:** Business and management evening courses, 1947-1952.

## COURSES FOR THE GENERAL PUBLIC

Business Finance

Economics in Practice

Economics and Public Policy

Investment Analysis

Marketing

Personnel Management

Public Utility Marketing

Purchasing

## COURSES FOR MEMBERS OF THE SOCIETY OF INDUSTRIAL ACCOUNTANTS

Accounting I

Accounting II

Advanced Cost Accounting

Business Mathematics

Fundamentals of Cost Accounting

Industrial Legislation

Industrial Organization and Management

for meetings, conferences, and other educational events. Extension administered the Conference Centre, and frequently provided marketing, registration, secretarial, and other support services. In the 1950s, on average, ten to twenty conferences took place each year at the Conference Centre, with a total of one thousand to twenty-five hundred participants. In 1958, Extension established a special office to administer this growing service which, in John Friesen's view, was of immense educational value for adults who did not have the time for a longer stay on campus.[30]

The demand for conference services continued growing into the next decade, such that between 1958 and 1965 Extension hosted an average of over seventy-five short courses and conferences each year, typically with over eighty participants at each event. The work of Extension often went beyond simply arranging the use of facilities, to include educational planning and evaluation. As an additional service, Extension began to publish conference proceedings – some seventeen in 1967 alone.

In 1969, UBC established a "Convention Office" as part of its Housing Administration department. The creation of the Convention Office released the Centre for Continuing Education from its conference administrative responsibilities so that it could operate, until 1974, an "Office of Short Courses and Conference Consultation." Under this arrangement, the Centre for Continuing Education provided advice to faculties and off-campus groups in the planning, management, and evaluation of their short courses and conferences, while the Convention Office organized accommodation, meals, student registration, and logistical operations.

## CERTIFICATE AND DIPLOMA PROGRAMS

Extension began delivering evening courses leading to educational credentials in the latter 1940s. In 1948, Extension offered four courses in accounting and business mathematics that carried credit toward the "Registered Industrial and Cost Accountant" certificate recognized by the Society of Industrial Accountants of British Columbia. However, like the three-year program in "Traffic Management" that Extension began delivering in 1947, the credential was not conferred by UBC. The first official reference to the potential for Extension to award UBC credentials was made in Shrum's 1953 annual report. At the end of a discussion of the non-credit evening course program, Shrum wrote: "it might also be noted that there is an obvious desire on the part of night class students to have some form of recognition attached to their studies" (p. 22). The following year, and foreshadowing developments in more recent decades, Friesen commented on the "rising demand for recognition of evening class training" (p. 10).

In 1951, Extension and the UBC School of Commerce offered special series of evening courses for the Chartered Life Underwriters' Association, the Canadian Retail Credit

*How to Invest your Money in Stocks and Bonds (1961)*

*The course describes and illustrates Canadian securities, investment terms, principles and procedures and their use in the wise investment of money. The ten lectures will cover the following subjects: Background for Investments; Bonds and Debentures; Preferred Shares; Common Shares; Financial Statements; Investment Management; Building the Investment Portfolio; Mutual Funds; Industry in B.C.*

Grantors' Association, the Certified General Accountants' Association, the Vancouver Board of Trade, and the staff of the Canadian Bank of Commerce. By 1955, a number of similar courses, restricted to members of particular professional groups, had developed into programs leading to a certificate or diploma from the sponsoring professional association. These "diploma courses" included instruction in accounting, marketing, banking, management, and sales, with the external association conferring a credential, the School of Commerce providing the instruction, and Extension assisting with promotion and administration.

The credentials offered in the diploma courses were not, however, UBC credentials. In his 1956 annual report, Friesen outlined the educational opportunities offered by his department in fields such as human relations, agricultural extension, community organization, and adult education, and suggested that "some of these training courses may well be broadened to warrant a certificate or diploma for the participants successfully completing the courses" (p. 6). Soon, Extension offered a formal certificate in two programs: the "Certificate Course in Communication and Broadcasting" which ran from 1960 to 1962; and the "Community Recreation Leadership Certificate" which ran in 1961 and 1962.

Although Extension advocated for, and experimented with, non-degree certificates as means of recognizing and encouraging the completion of extended programs of study, few were ever granted. The first ongoing certificate and diploma programs were the Diploma in Adult Education, offered in collaboration with the Faculty of Education beginning in 1966; the Diploma in Administration for Engineers, offered in collaboration with the Faculty of Applied Science beginning in 1968; and a Certificate in Criminology launched in 1969. In 1970, the Centre for Continuing Education introduced a Certificate in Early Childhood Education, and a couple of years later added an Instructor's Diploma for people teaching vocational subjects in schools, community colleges, and other institutions.

## EXTENSION CREDIT STUDIES

Until the late 1940s, Extension courses were separate from UBC's degree programs, with the modest exception of the Summer School of the Theatre. Some UBC departments had offered extra-mural credit courses since 1929, after considerable debate, with "directed reading" (correspondence) courses for credit joining them in a very small way in 1935. In 1944, there were problems with correspondence courses provided to the armed forces ("not a uniform success" claimed Dean of Arts Daniel Buchanan, possibly intending the pun), and the problems of consistency escalated following the war.[31]

At Senate's request, President MacKenzie formed a committee in April 1949 to investigate the matter. Gordon Shrum chaired the committee, which eventually proposed that Extension organize and administer evening and correspondence credit courses.[32]

*Economics 325: Labour Economics and Labour Problems (1955)*

*Labour problems arising out of the factory system and large-scale enterprise; insecurity, unemployment and discrimination; working conditions, hours and wages. History, structure and functions of trade unions; employers' policies and association; collective bargaining and industrial conflict; labour legislation and political action.*

The previous year, Shrum had argued in his annual report that there was "increasing demand for extra-mural courses which carry credit toward a university degree" (p. 1) and had recommended that UBC deliver credit courses in the evenings, as short courses, and as correspondence courses in selected subjects. Following Senate's approval of the proposal, Shrum announced that Extension was quite willing to provide "needed extension of the services of the University to those in the community who are less favoured by educational opportunities." He expressed the hope that the "high standard of achievement which has been maintained in the past" would continue.[33]

In 1950, Extension delivered four correspondence courses (English 200, History 304, Psychology 301, and Education 520) and two evening courses (Geography 201 and English 411) for degree-credit. The next year, three additional correspondence courses (Economics 325, Philosophy 100, and Geography 409) and four different evening courses (English 428, Slavonics 205, and Social Work 520 and 582) were offered. The seven correspondence courses remained unchanged for several years, unlike the evening credit courses which changed each year. In 1951, Extension distributed "Suggestions for Preparing Correspondence Courses" to faculty across campus, intended "to help those who are entrusted with the authorship of a course, and to establish reasonable standards of uniformity throughout all present and future correspondence courses carrying University credit" (p. 1). The booklet listed the "characteristics of a good correspondence course," outlined the standard style and format of courses, explained the examination process, and presented various rules and guidelines. In these years, UBC followed a policy that up to one year of credit toward the BA degree could be earned through correspondence study.

**Top left and right:** Conference proceedings (1962) and brochure (1969). **Bottom:** Dorothy Bennett marks correspondence courses, 1961. *UBCA 3.1/537*

By mid-decade, the number of correspondence courses offered by UBC had increased from seven to twelve, with new courses in History, French, English, and Economics. In his 1956 report, Friesen noted that the expansion of correspondence courses was "consistent with the wish of this Department...to make University courses available to as many British Columbians as possible, provided suitable safeguards are maintained against lowering the quality of instruction" (p. 8). But then growth stalled; Extension offered only fourteen credit correspondence courses in 1968, in Economics, Education, English (3), French, German, History (3), Philosophy, Political Science, and Psychology (2). Enrolment in correspondence courses rose from 257 in 1950 to 1,214 in 1965, but then dropped to 613 in 1968, remaining around that level until 1976. Reduced enrolments in correspondence courses reflected the greater availability of off-campus and evening courses in these fields.

In contrast, demand for additional extra-mural credit courses offered through Extension experienced significant growth over the years. Initially, extra-mural classes were held in the evenings at the Vancouver Normal School, a more central location than the Point Grey campus some ten kilometres distant. When UBC assumed responsibility for the pre-service education of elementary teachers in 1956, the Normal School closed and Extension moved most of its evening courses to the UBC campus the following year.[34] In 1956, the term "Extra-mural Courses" was replaced with the term "Lecture Credit Courses" to reflect the on-campus nature of most of these courses. The very substantial growth in enrolments between 1954 and 1957 (from 246 to 1,411) reflected two changes. Prior to 1955, UBC had offered only a limited number of senior-level extra-mural courses, catering to those students who required one or two liberal arts courses in order to qualify for graduation. In 1955, UBC introduced junior-level "Lecture Credit Courses." In addition, in 1956 the Faculty of Education began offering degree-credit

The University of British Columbia
EDUCATION-EXTENSION CERTIFICATE PROGRAM
in the EDUCATION OF YOUNG CHILDREN

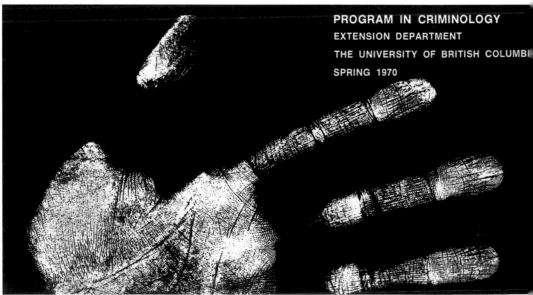

PROGRAM IN CRIMINOLOGY
EXTENSION DEPARTMENT
THE UNIVERSITY OF BRITISH COLUMBI
SPRING 1970

lecture courses off-campus. By 1959, the Faculty was delivering courses in eleven centres outside Vancouver. The Faculty of Arts also began delivering off-campus courses in 1959 and, for several years, assigned a faculty member from the Departments of English or History to live and teach on a full-time basis in Prince George during the academic term. More generally, however, off-campus instruction was provided by UBC faculty commuting from campus. By 1966, UBC used the term "Extra-Sessional Credit Courses" for off-campus and evening credit courses administered by Extension, whose enrolment stood at some 2,500 annually by that time.

Despite all this growth, John Friesen's annual reports regularly noted the demand for additional credit courses through Extension. In 1956, he wrote that the "time seems to have come when the day university will add an evening division to enable even more than are presently served to continue their studies either toward a diploma or degree or simply for the love of intellectual pursuit" (p. 4). In 1961, Friesen reiterated the call to enlarge extra-mural offerings in both Arts and Education, and even suggested that potential students would soon be demanding post-graduate courses in these and other faculties (p. 5). Although UBC offered numerous extra-sessional credit courses, they were not organized to allow part-time students to complete degree programs. Advocacy for the expansion of degree-credit programs for part-time and off-campus students would continue in the 1970s. Meanwhile, enrolment in extra-sessional credit courses continued to grow – from a total of about 2,500 per year in the first half of the 1960s, to a total of more than 3,500 per year in the first half of the 1970s.

## chapter summary

## SUPPORTING RURAL LIVELIHOODS AND URBAN CAREERS

*The Extension era (1936-1970) was characterized by transformative social and economic change – from urbanization and the shift to an industrial and service economy to the rise of women's participation in the labour market.*

*Founded on April 27, 1936, the Department of University Extension helped adult learners meet the challenge of transformative change by offering an expanding range of professional development opportunities in agriculture, home economics, fisheries, forestry, teaching, communications, and business.*

*From the outset, Extension's programs were interdisciplinary in nature, focussing on the practical problems of the communities they served rather than the traditional boundaries of disciplines. Noteworthy examples included the Youth Training Schools and the Educational Programme for British Columbia Fishermen.*

*In these early years, Extension set the foundation of a collaborative operating model that can be traced throughout the organization's history. Extension formed effective program partnerships with agricultural associations, women's institutes, co-operatives, professional associations, UBC faculties and departments, and a range of federal and provincial departments.*

# Music has always been the most generally beloved of the arts, for it satisfies two of man's most deeply felt needs

*– the need for the release of his emotions, and the need for self expression. In moments of highest exaltation or of deepest sorrow man has always turned to music – he has made music, he has danced to it, and he has listened to it. Here in Canada we are a young country, and we have not always been able to devote as much time to music as we could have wished. In recent years, however, we have taken great strides forward, both in making music and in appreciating it... With the rest of the world, we have joined the army of listeners who turn to the radio and to phonograph recordings for good music. Music and the appreciation of music are becoming part of our Canadian culture. The aim of this course in Music Appreciation is to enable those who take it to enjoy music more fully.*

Dr. Ida Halpern
From a passage she authored as part of a
study group course in Music Appreciation
(ca. 1945)

*Chapter Four*

# Fostering cultural enrichment

Robert England, UBC's first Director of University Extension, once stated that the aim of education was not primarily to fit people for specific vocations, but to give them a new zest in life.[1] Helping people understand themselves and the world in which they live has been a consistent goal of extension and continuing education at UBC. From the 1930s to the 1960s, Extension helped British Columbians understand and participate in the social and cultural world through a range of programs in the liberal and fine arts, providing public lectures, delivering courses and seminars, and circulating books, movies, and musical recordings. In the early years, when Depression-weary British Columbians had a particular need for "zest in life," extension lectures and film presentations provided education and entertainment to hundreds of thousands of participants annually. By the 1960s, evening courses in social sciences, humanities, and fine arts engaged thousands of people each year in wide-ranging programs of study. Although the content of liberal education changed over these decades, the programs described in this chapter shared the objective of fostering personal growth, greater understanding of the human and natural worlds, and the enrichment of cultural life in British Columbia.

## EXTENSION LECTURES AND RADIO PROGRAMS

Extension maintained the established tradition of UBC professors lecturing at off-campus locations. In 1937, Extension facilitated 201 lectures, most of which took place outside the Greater Vancouver area, to a cumulative audience estimated at 12,350 people. In addition to stand-alone lectures, "courses" of extension lectures touched on history, psychology, the natural sciences, classics, and agriculture. Most extension lectures were of general interest ("The Georgian Period" and "Life in Ancient Greece"), while some had a professional focus ("Marketing of Farm Products"). Well into the 1940s, Extension published bulletins to publicize its extension lecture service.

Popular extension lectures in the early years explored social and political issues, international affairs, and current events. Lectures were hosted by a range of groups, such as the Victoria University

Extension Association, the YMCA and YWCA, the British Columbia Penitentiary, community centres, and many other voluntary associations. The Vancouver Institute, having been brought under closer university influence in the early 1930s, remained a popular venue for UBC lectures.

Extension staff members soon recognized the pedagogical limitations of the public lecture format, and began to emphasize other educational strategies such as short courses and study-discussion groups. In his 1940 annual report, Shrum explained:

> There has been a decreasing stress in recent years on occasional Extension lectures given by members of the University staff. The Department has stressed instead short courses lasting usually two or three days, study groups, and occupational schools of two or three weeks' duration. In this way it is felt that a more lasting contribution can be made to the educational development of a community. The occasional lecture undoubtedly serves a useful purpose. It stimulates interest in the community in the subject being discussed by the lecturer, and it affords a valuable contact between the University staff and the people of the Province. It is because of these advantages that the Department has no intention of eliminating altogether this phase of Extension work. But the experience of the past few years has shown that where more intensive study is given to a subject, more lasting results are achieved.

Shrum also indicated that short courses and residential schools could be instructed by people other than regular members of UBC faculty, who were increasingly unavailable for extension work.

Although Extension shifted its pedagogical emphasis, extension lectures remained a prominent form of contact between UBC and its external communities. Typically, during the 1940s, nearly four hundred lectures each year were delivered to aggregate audiences of over forty thousand people. After 1950, Extension was less involved with lectures, but continued to match lecture requests from community groups to UBC faculty members. Extension organized "Capsule College" during the 1950s, an annual series of UBC faculty presentations to high school students and community leaders in the interior of British Columbia. From 1957 through 1970, Extension coordinated a "Speakers' Bureau" to facilitate off-campus lectures by UBC faculty members.

Radio broadcasts provided another dimension to extension lectures. Although educational radio broadcasts by UBC faculty had begun in the 1920s, the use of radio for educational programming increased significantly in the late 1930s and 1940s. In 1937, Shrum became the Chairperson of the British Columbia Regional Advisory Council of the CBC. In 1938, UBC built a sound-proof studio and Extension organized radio broadcasts (206 the first year) on farming, music appreciation, poetry, and other subjects. In the 1940s and 1950s, Extension coordinated listening groups for the Farm Radio Forum and the Citizens' Forum (see Chapter Five).

Extension used radio for educational purposes for many years. In 1960, it collaborated with the local Vancouver radio station CKWX to broadcast more than thirty educational

*Leisure hours should be golden hours opening doors to the world of art, drama, music and science. The University of British Columbia, through the Department of University Extension, offers men and women throughout the Province of British Columbia the opportunity of richer, intellectual experience, of sampling the best in art, music and literature, as well as in economics, history and science.*

*Extension Bulletin 4
Activities for Spring Term
1938*

programs in a series entitled "Sounds of the City." This fifty-five minute radio program sought to "explore the ways in which an independent radio station can make use of the rich and varied resources of its own community as a source of creative programming." CKWX, facing new competition from television, provided two grants of $12,000 to Extension to produce the shows, with additional funds from the Leon and Thea Koerner foundation of $1,750. "Sounds of the City" went on to win an award from the American magazine *TV Radio Mirror* for the "most original radio program in Canada in 1960." Bill Ballentine, the Director of Special Broadcasts with Extension (and former president of the UBC Radio Society), wished radio to be a "responsible voice" in the life of a community "interpreting to its listeners the enormous variety of their environment."[2]

In subsequent years, Extension worked regularly with the Canadian Broadcasting Corporation and UBC faculty members to produce series of radio broadcasts on timely issues. For example, in 1962, Extension produced series on "The Border in Question" (Canada-U.S. relations), "Asian Perspectives," and "The Heritage of our Law."

Television emerged as a medium for educational programming in Vancouver in the mid-1950s. John Friesen, noting the arrival of a local television broadcasting station in 1954 and the improvement of facilities south of the border, created a Committee on Radio and Television "to investigate the University's role in television and suggest ways of increasing the use of radio."[3] Extension then sponsored a one-day "Television Workshop" with over sixty delegates from organizations across British Columbia who discussed the effect of television on family life. Although Extension studied educational television and considered policy, it never made extensive use of that medium in the delivery of its own programming. Not until 1965-66 did Extension produce its own television program:

*The University has made a real effort to provide in some measure the opportunities whereby adults in even the remotest sections of the Province may keep in contact with the arts, with natural and social science, with political and economic developments, and, in short, with the life and thought of their provincial University. As a result, the University is becoming firmly established as the centre of the cultural life of the Province.*

Gordon Shrum, Director
Department of University
Extension
1938

Top: Building theatre sets, ca. 1964.
Bottom left: Pottery class, 1949.
Bottom right: Cliff Robinson's
"Painting for Pleasure" class, 1950.
UBCA 1.1/9961-1, 1.1/10112

twenty-six weekly, half-hour broadcasts on "Great Asian Civilizations" that reflected the growing interest at UBC in the other side of the Pacific.

## FINE ARTS

Programming in the fine arts was prominent in Extension. For decades, proponents of fine arts, particularly of music, had urged UBC to offer course credit in these areas. Student ensembles (such as the UBC Musical Society) were popular, and by the late 1920s the university provided some credit for music studies done under the auspices of a recognized conservatory. Some faculty members, such as English Professors Garnett Sedgewick and Ira Dilworth (who joined the CBC in 1938 and founded the CBC Radio orchestra), spoke about art and music to various audiences, but UBC did not play a strong role in the local arts community. In 1937, Robert England collaborated with organizations such as the Vancouver Symphony Orchestra, the Vancouver School of Art, and the Provincial Department of Education to deliver performances, courses, and lectures relating to drama, music, and the visual arts. In early 1937, the university received a Music Set – hundreds of records, music scores, reference books, and a state-of-the-art orthoponic phonograph – from the Carnegie Corporation which was unveiled, by formal invitation, before a "large and representative gathering of the music-loving citizens of Vancouver."[4] In addition to its work in music, Extension delivered afternoon and evening courses in "Art Appreciation" as early as 1937.

In the second half of the 1940s, Extension increased evening courses in fine arts to about five per year, and actively contributed to a new and lively artistic culture in Vancouver and the province.

The post-war renaissance of the arts was aided by people like Ida Halpern, an early and long-serving Extension instructor in music appreciation. A talented musician and musicologist from Vienna, Halpern and her husband fled Europe in 1938 and settled in Vancouver, where she became a music teacher and an active force in the local arts community. Halpern, like other Europeans who came to Vancouver at that time, found herself in a rather dull and parochial city. In the view of historian and UBC Professor Emeritus William Bruneau, these new Europeans were "a little impatient with the provincialism of Anglo-Saxon Vancouver and its comfortable ways."[5]

Halpern found post-war UBC to be changing for the better. A donation from a local brewer, Robert Fiddes, enabled President MacKenzie to launch a Department of Music in 1946 with acclaimed violinist Harry Adaskin as Head. With his wife, pianist Frances Marr, Adaskin used Extension courses for his mission to popularize classical music, and to enhance the "limited tastes of Vancouver audiences and the primitive state of music education in the province."[6] Nicholas Goldschmidt, Czech-born conductor of CBC's Opera Company and Musical Director of the Opera School of the Royal Conservatory of Music (Toronto), also came to teach at Extension during the 1950s. Although serious composers from British Columbia like Jean Coulthard found it difficult to obtain widespread public acclaim, recognition of local talent was part of the arts revolution encouraged by Extension.[7] At the same time, President MacKenzie was hiring new faculty members in the visual arts, notably architecture and painting.

By 1949, Extension was able to offer studio courses in painting and other visual arts, thanks to a donation by the local chapter of the Imperial Order Daughters of the Empire to provide workshop facilities.[8] These were crucial in developing local talent, and in providing teaching jobs for established artists. Some Extension instructors went even further to recognize local art: Ida Halpern, for example, soon began collecting and studying the music of west coast First Nations, while painting instructor Clifford Robinson published prints of native masks, figures, and artefacts.[9] Robinson also taught "Painting for Pleasure" classes for Extension.

Courses in music appreciation, art appreciation, and painting became the core of a vibrant program in the fine arts offered by Extension, sometimes in collaboration with other organizations like the Vancouver Art Gallery and parent-teacher associations. Saturday morning art classes for children were popular for over a decade.

Pottery and ceramics classes were also an integral part of Extension programming. Beginning in the late 1940s, local potters Hilda Ross, Mollie Carter, and Zoltan Kiss began teaching in the basement of the UBC library (in the corner of the Fine Arts

*How to Look at Pictures (1945)*

*This course is designed to assist the layman to understand and to judge fine pictures... Pictures to be considered will come under the following headings: Drawings and Prints; the British School; Impressionism and Post-Impressionism; the Expressionists; Water-Colour; Abstract Painting; the Critic Looks at Modern Canadian Painting.*

Gallery). There was no significant pottery or ceramics community in the province – Kiss recalled making his own potter's wheel from driftwood, and an electric kiln from a discarded refrigerator.[10] Soon after, Olea Davis joined Extension with degrees from McGill, the Ontario College of Art, and L'Ecole des Beaux Arts in Montreal, and convinced Gordon Shrum that they should have their own studio in a reconditioned army hut near the Conference Centre. In 1952, Extension opened its "pottery hut," and Davis coordinated the ceramics program at UBC for some thirteen years. Davis and other Extension instructors helped pioneer a robust ceramics community in the province, forming the British Columbian Potters' Guild in 1955.[11] Other arts – sculpture, batik, and weaving, for example – also found a home with UBC Extension. Instructors for Extension courses over the years were often local pioneers in their art who helped create a vibrant creative community: Bill Reid (sculpture and jewellery), William Koochin (sculpture), William P. Weston (painting), and Mary Boback (painting and printmaking) were among those who taught in Extension programs.

Fine arts courses were not limited to Vancouver residents. During the 1940s and 1950s, Extension provided dozens of British Columbia communities with study group courses in art and music appreciation, co-sponsored travelling art exhibitions, and sent out instructors for studio courses. When the UBC Board of Governors provided a special subsidy for extension programming outside the greater Vancouver area from 1960 to 1963, the number of fine arts courses held around the province increased substantially, only to fall when funding support was withdrawn.

During the 1950s, Extension continued to diversify and expand its evening courses in the fine arts, from about ten courses per year to eighteen. Nearly half of these courses were in the visual arts, with music, drama, and children's programs comprising the remainder. New evening courses included ceramics (1954), portraiture (1954), graphic design (1954), choral singing (1955), sculpture (1956), life drawing (1956), metal work (1956), interior design (1958), linoleum and woodblock printing (1960), and acting (1960). A new Extension Arts and Crafts Centre established near the Conference Centre in 1958 provided studios for painting and sculpture, as well as a special studio for children taking courses with Extension, or participating in research and teaching projects organized by the Faculty of Education.

The annual number of participants in fine arts evening classes in the Vancouver area peaked at nearly one thousand in the early 1960s, supported by a five-year grant from the Ford Foundation's Fund for Adult Education, through which Extension established and maintained a separate Liberal Arts Division. Annual enrolment declined to about 500 in the latter half of that decade. Overall, Extension delivered over 230 fine arts evening courses during the 1960s, attracting nearly 7,400 students in the visual arts (60 percent of enrolments), music (23 percent), theatre (11 percent), and children's programs (6 percent).

*Pottery for Beginners (1955-56)*

*A practical and lecture course, intended for beginning students. Instruction will include consideration of wheel-throwing and other forming techniques, with consideration of glazes, craftsmanship and standards in ceramics.*

## DRAMA AND THEATRE

Drama was another important component of UBC programming in the fine arts. Gordon Shrum later claimed that when he became Director of Extension, he did not want people to think that his background as a physicist made him unsuitable for the position, or that he would simply program talks on science and technology. Consequently, he hired Dorothy Somerset in 1937 to develop programs in theatre. Somerset, Australian born but educated at Radcliffe College (Harvard) and in England, had been very active in Vancouver drama circles. She was a leading lady with the city's Little Theatre, and for several years had directed for the UBC Players Club, a popular student troupe.[12]

By 1939, Extension was actively supporting amateur theatre groups across British Columbia. Extension began with three-day dramatics courses in acting, directing, movement, voice, make-up, and scenery delivered at nine centres in the interior of British Columbia (expanded to week-long courses the following year), and soon added a "University Drama School of the Air" with radio broadcasts on CBC radio. Eighty listening groups across the province registered with Extension for this program, each receiving copies of plays and discussion guides. In 1940, the "Radio Drama Workshop" engaged

**Top left:** Painting class in the late 1960s. **Top right:** Music class, 1960s. **Bottom:** Dorothy Somerset and student prepare for *Back to Methuselah*, 1956. *UBCA 20.1/15*

190 listening groups across the province, and broadcast three plays by George Bernard Shaw. The University Extension Library also began circulating a collection of some 1,500 plays that had been assembled through donations and purchases. Over fifty amateur theatre groups across the province registered (at a fee of one dollar) to use the "Play Lending Library" in 1939. Extension compiled a catalogue of available titles the following year, and the number of registered groups increased from about 120 in the early 1940s to over two hundred in the early 1950s. Finally, Extension piloted a playwriting course in 1939, subsequently delivered by correspondence, and a study-group course in acting the following year. The level of interest in theatre remained consistent through the 1940s and into the next decade. In 1955, Sydney Risk delivered drama workshops in twenty-four locations around the province for over 700 participants. Similar workshops of three days to two weeks in length continued through the early 1960s, providing instruction in acting, directing, and stagecraft.

Extension also supported theatre by employing staff to advise local drama groups on producing plays, adjudicate various festivals, organize regional and provincial drama conferences, support non-governmental agencies in the arts (including the Vancouver Community Arts Council and the BC Drama Association), and serve in executive

**Top:** Summer School of Theatre presents scenes from *The Trojan Women* on the steps of Main Library, 1955. **Bottom left:** Dorothy Somerset and students reviewing script *Back to Methuselah*, 1955. **Bottom right:** Dance workshop, 1959. *UBCA 3.1/1076, 1.1/2751, 1.1/8236.2*

positions with national and regional organizations (such as the Dominion Drama Festival and the Canada Theatre Conference). Extension's "Theatre Advisory Service" was active from 1940 through the mid-1960s.

Although its instructors frequently worked with amateur theatre companies, Extension also helped spawn local professional theatre of high quality. Over the years, several pioneers of theatre in Vancouver worked with Extension. Sidney Risk, Joy Coghill, and Jessie Richardson (after whom the "Jessie Richardson Theatre Awards" for professional theatre in Vancouver are named) taught with Extension while launching professional theatre companies. Risk founded "Everyman's Theatre," Vancouver's first professional theatre company, and Coghill and Richardson helped found "Holiday Theatre," Canada's first professional theatre company for children.[13] With Dorothy Somerset, who began teaching in UBC's Department of English in 1946 and eventually became Head of the new theatre program in 1959, these theatre pioneers helped establish the Frederic Wood Theatre at UBC as a leading venue for theatrical innovation.

## SUMMER SCHOOL OF THE ARTS AND THE FINE ARTS FESTIVAL

One of the earliest fine arts programs of Extension was a six-week "Summer School of the Theatre," delivered in 1938 to eighty participants at UBC. The curriculum included instruction in acting, directing, improvisation, stage work, voice, make-up, costume, and movement, and the program culminated with a student performance of Euripides' tragedy, *The Trojan Women*. The summer school was repeated three times, paused for the war, and returned in 1945. In 1946, it was expanded into "junior" and "senior" sections, which carried undergraduate credit at UBC.

In the post-war years, the "Summer School of the Theatre" was joined by other activities in the fine arts. Music appreciation and painting began in 1946, and a course in photography began the following year. For twenty years, Extension organized a "Summer School of the Arts" on the UBC campus with over 260 people on average participating each year, primarily in theatre, painting, music, and photography. Other courses included Radio Script Writing (1946-47); Writing for Television (1953-55); Creative Writing (1948-50); Weaving (1948-52); Pottery or Ceramics (1949-55); Batik (1952-53); Children's Art (1954); Art History (1954); and Sculpture (1955).

In 1947, Extension piloted its first "Summer Festival of Art," with the exhibition of work produced in its painting and photography courses, and performances of plays by theatre students. In 1948, the "Summer Fine Arts Festival" expanded to include an exhibition of paintings from the Montreal Art Association and special concerts by guest performers. For many years, the Fine Arts Festival presented visual and performance art of summer students, and invited established artists of national and even international stature to

SUMMER FESTIVAL OF THE ARTS

JULY 25 to AUGUST 31 1955

at the
UNIVERSITY OF BRITISH COLUMBIA

OUTDOOR SCULPTURE EXHIBITION

SIR HERBERT READ—Lecture, "Art as Symbolic Communication"
Physics Bldg., Room 200          12.15 p.m.

HARRY AND FRANCES ADASKIN
Works for Violin and Piano by Mozart
Physics Bldg., Room 200          12.15 p.m.

SIR HERBERT READ—Illustrated Lecture, "Recent Development in Non-Figurative Art"
University Auditorium          8.00 p.m.

CBC VANCOUVER CHAMBER ORCHESTRA
Broadcast Concert
Brock Hall Lounge          7.20 p.m.

SIR HERBERT READ—A Poetry Reading
University Auditorium          8.00 p.m.

SIR HERBERT READ—Lecture
"The Creative Experience in Poetry"
Physics Bldg., Room 200          12.15 p.m.

exhibit or perform. For example, in 1952, the summer festival welcomed such visiting luminaries as Nicholas Goldschmidt (who acted as the music director for eight years); Leonard and Reva Brooks, the acclaimed painter and photographer, respectively; Edith Heath, the first non-architect to win an American Institute of Architects Gold Medal for her architectural tiles; Hal Painter, the eminent San Francisco tapestry weaver; and Helen Ellis, a leading local weaver.[14] Observers praised the summer arts festivals at UBC as contributing to the artistic leadership of the city, region, and even the country. Reasons for success: strong community interest and enthusiasm for the arts, good administration, good teaching, good location, and support from the UBC administration – the Board of Governors offered to underwrite deficits from 1955 to 1957 to allow the festival to expand, although this financial support proved to be unnecessary.[15] The success of UBC's summer festival provided a catalyst for the first Vancouver International Festival of the Arts in the summer of 1958.

Extension continued to organize a Summer School of the Arts until 1965. Courses expanded to include dance and high school band programs, and special events coordinated with its Summer School of Public Affairs (see Chapter Five). Total enrolment in the early 1960s averaged nearly five hundred participants each year. The final Summer School of the Arts was held in 1965, as the UBC Board of Governors had asked Extension to discontinue the program, and as degree-credit courses in drama and opera had expanded in the summer session and replaced non-credit offerings. Following this setback to programming in the fine arts, Extension re-introduced summer programs in arts and crafts in 1968.

## SOCIAL SCIENCES AND HUMANITIES

Programming in the social sciences and humanities has always been central to the evening classes offered by UBC. In 1937, Professor Garnett Sedgewick from the Department of English delivered a fifteen-week Shakespeare course on Monday evenings at the Vancouver Normal School. In the subsequent two decades, Extension offered a small number of evening courses in the humanities and social sciences each year, taught by members of UBC faculty.

Until the late 1940s, Extension typically offered two or three evening courses per year in the humanities and social sciences, primarily in the areas of English composition, literature, economics, and psychology. In the latter 1940s and early 1950s, courses in these fields increased to four or five per year, with additional programs delivered throughout the province using a study-discussion format.

Evening programming in the social sciences and humanities grew substantially at UBC in the 1950s, with the addition of courses in philosophy, religious studies, history, sociology, and anthropology. By the 1960s, more than one thousand students each year were taking courses that reflected contemporary concerns.

The most popular courses during the 1960s were related to psychology, sociology, and anthropology, with 42 percent of the total enrolment of 10,680 during the decade; history, philosophy, and religious studies accounted for 31 percent; English composition and literature, 15 percent; and other disciplines such as economics, political science, linguistics, communications, and such new fields as women's studies, Asian studies, and urban studies attracting 12 percent of student enrolment. Beginning in 1967, significant numbers of non-credit liberal arts courses were delivered during the daytime at the Vancouver Public Library.

It is important to note that, since the 1950s, the liberal arts at UBC have included the exploration of the natural sciences. Extension regularly presented popular evening courses on scientific concepts and in the philosophy of science. One couple, Hildegard and Werner Hesse, attributed their life-long passion for birding to a three-year evening program they took starting in 1956; years later, they left a sizeable bequest to UBC for ornithological research.[16] In the autumn of 1966, Extension offered a series of courses under the heading of "Science Programs." A promotional brochure for these courses claimed that:

> Science is the burning idea of the 20th Century, comparable in its impact on men's minds to the flush of democratic enthusiasm of the late 18th Century. To understand the world we live in today, it is necessary to have some appreciation of what science is all about. The courses in the Science section of this brochure aim to acquaint the layman with some of the issues and advanced knowledge relating to the scientific revolution transforming our world.

Courses inspired by this rationale continued to be popular in the 1970s and 1980s.

As part of its programming in the humanities, Extension provided courses to improve people's writing skills. Since 1915, UBC had always emphasized the importance of strong

**Left:** A panel discussion from an Asian Studies course in the 1960s. *UBCA 3.1/594*
**Right:** Brochure for an Extension liberal studies course, 1964.

language skills in English, particularly writing. Clarity, eloquence, wit, and literary skill were the marks of a properly-educated person, whether exercised in the workplace or in more cultural activities.[17] Many people outside the university agreed, and as occupations requiring good communication skills grew, so too did the demand for writing courses.

The earliest Extension writing program at UBC was a sixteen-week evening course in "English Composition" delivered in 1938. Offered in collaboration with the BC Branch of the Institute of Chartered Accountants, its aim was to provide "training in the use of clear and precise English." Evening courses in "Business English" or "Practical English Composition" followed, offered every couple of years. Creative writing courses began in 1947 with an evening course entitled "Writing for You" and a four-week intensive course delivered during the summer of 1948. Thirty-six participants enrolled in the full-time summer program, which was repeated in the summers of 1949 and 1950. Creative writing

Pierre Trudeau (L), guest speaker at Extension's Summer School of Public Affairs, 1960s.

as a serious field had just arrived at UBC with the English Department's appointment in 1946 of Earl Birney, an alumnus and by then a two-time Governor General's Award winner for poetry (1942, 1945). Birney returned to his alma mater on condition that he be permitted to teach a creative writing course, the first such credit course at a Canadian university.[18] In 1949, Extension developed a non-credit correspondence course in creative writing, while the evening course became a regular feature during the 1950s and 1960s.

## LANGUAGE AND TRAVEL PROGRAMS

Extension began providing language courses in 1944-45, when it offered evening classes in Russian and Spanish, reflecting a fascination at UBC and in the general public with countries recently in the political spotlight. In 1946, a class in conversational French was added. Courses in French and Spanish were offered at least once every year during the 1950s, joined by regular courses in German after 1955 and Italian after 1957, no doubt reflecting the influx of immigrants from Germany and Italy. Introductory courses in other languages came and went. Russian was taught four times in the late 1950s, and both Hebrew and Chinese were offered in 1960.

Language programming expanded in the early 1960s, and then declined as Extension coped with budget cutbacks and new priorities. Over the decade, 3,295 people enrolled in 169 evening language courses, with just over half of these in French courses, a further one-fifth in Spanish courses, and most of the remainder in German, Italian, and Russian. As interest in Asia rose, Extension began to deliver evening classes in Japanese in 1962. Courses in other languages such as Arabic, Greek, Norwegian, Polish, Swedish, and Ukrainian appeared intermittently during this decade, but Japanese was the only language other than French to become a regular part of Extension's evening course program.

While language programs helped introduce Vancouver residents to diverse cultures, study tours of other countries promised first-hand exposure. Extension's first travel study program was directly linked to language programming; in 1955, Extension offered a course entitled "Spanish for Beginners and a Spring Tour of Mexico." After a sixteen-week evening course in Spanish, students were invited to join a conducted tour of Mexico City, Cuernavaca, Taxco, and the Toluca Valley.

Study-tours soon became a regular programming item. A nine-week evening course on "Travel in Western Europe" in 1956 concluded with an optional tour. Study travel courses to Europe were repeated in 1957 and 1959. In the 1960s, as air travel became more widely accessible, Extension increased its tours, which were usually organized by an external travel agent. Over the course of the 1960s, trips to Europe, Japan, and Latin America were the most popular. Although data regarding the number of participants on the tours are not available, enrolment in the evening courses themselves was quite popular, with forty to fifty participants in each class.

*Canadian Universities' Tours to Mexico, the Orient, Europe, and South America (1961)*

*Better international understanding is one of our great social imperatives. Today's smaller world requires bigger men and women who, through study and first-hand observation, can achieve a greater appreciation of the attitudes and conditions of their world neighbours.*

*To help meet this challenge, a number of Canadian Universities, through their Departments of Extension, are offering travel-study tours designed for adults.*

## EXTENSION LIBRARY SERVICE

*Visual Aids Catalogue – Introduction (1938)*

*Visual aids have an educational value now so universally recognized that they are becoming part of every school and educational organization. This recognition is based upon scientific experiments which have demonstrated that pictures, still or in motion, when properly used, make learning easier, stimulate interest and greatly aid the memory.*

In addition to organizing public lectures and courses, Extension promoted the liberal arts throughout British Columbia by circulating educational resources, beginning with a library service in 1936. The University Extension Library gradually built up a collection of books on subjects relating to Extension's programs, including agriculture, biography, education, literature, history, art, music, drama, co-operatives, science, and the social sciences. Although intended initially to provide resources for students in non-credit extension programs, the library service soon grew popular among British Columbians without access to a local library. Beginning in 1938, Extension published and distributed catalogues of its books and plays, and extended borrowing privileges to individuals and organizations across the province. Two years later, the Extension Library acquired some one thousand different pamphlets for use in evening classes or study groups, or for loan or sale at a nominal fee.

Beginning in 1952, the Extension Library Service was restricted to people living in communities without local library service, people having physical mobility impairments, and students in courses offered by Extension. As a result, the proportion of volumes sent to rural and inaccessible locations increased, providing a much valued service in selecting and shipping books. Extension library staff often received notes of thanks. One Kemano resident on British Columbia's north coast wrote, "Thank you so very much...this service is indeed a boon to those of us who live under more or less isolated conditions." In 1955, UBC Head Librarian Neal Harlow commented that, "Miss Edith Stewart, as Extension Librarian, interprets the world of books to a self-selected and omnivorous clientele, and she matches books and people with a sure hand." [19] The number of books circulated by the Extension Library grew to more than ten thousand per year by the end of the 1940s, and to more than twenty thousand per year by the end of the 1950s.

In the late 1950s and early 1960s, the number of public borrowers declined as other library services across the province improved. Nonetheless, the total circulation of the Extension Library remained high due to the increasing number of correspondence students using the services. In 1964, UBC discontinued its general library service for off-campus borrowers, and restricted the Extension Library to registered drama groups and students in correspondence courses. By the late 1960s, Extension no longer provided a library service, although the main UBC Library continued to maintain a collection for students in distance education courses.

## MOVIES, SLIDE SHOWS, AND RECORDS

In 1938, Extension began circulating audio-visual resources to support educational presentations in various communities. Beginning with slide shows, Extension soon

# AUDIO VISUAL SERVICES

films • slides • filmstrips • recordings • equipment

DEPARTMENT OF UNIVERSITY EXTENSION, THE UNIVERSITY OF BRITISH COLUMBIA

circulated moving picture films as well as necessary equipment. Slide shows and movies were often provided by the Dominion Government Motion Picture Bureau, the National Parks Bureau, the National Film Society, the Film Department of the British Council, and a number of commercial firms. By 1944, Extension had a library of five hundred movies and eight hundred film strips for circulation among Farmers' Institutes, Women's Institutes, parent-teacher associations, Boards of Trade, Youth Training Clubs, and other organizations. For several years beginning in 1939, Extension also provided courses in the use of audio-visual resources for educational purposes. The first cinematography course attracted more than fifty students and led to the establishment of the British Columbia Institute of Cinematography.

Beginning in 1941, Extension collaborated with the National Film Board (NFB) and the Canadian Council of Education for Citizenship to organize monthly educational film circuits throughout the Lower Mainland and Vancouver Island, the Okanagan Valley, the Kootenay District, and the North Coast regions. Where necessary, the NFB paid for projectionists who often faced challenging travel and living arrangements. Attendance grew quickly; the first year, Extension distributed films to 396 organizations in 254 communities, and estimated the aggregate attendance at all films to be over 400,000. The typical program on these monthly circuits consisted of a feature film, a short educational film, and a short film of local or general interest. NFB films shown at that time often encouraged Canadians to support the war effort, in preparation for a new era of democratic participation at home and abroad.[20]

The circulation of slide shows and movies continued after the war, serving both entertainment and educational functions at a time when commercial television had not yet been established. Extension also coordinated local "Film Councils" and the "BC Circulating Exchange" to help community groups access and select appropriate movies. Thirty-five Film Councils had been established in the province by 1948, the year the NFB and Extension co-sponsored a Film Council Conference.

**Top left:** Extension's Audio Visual Services brochure, 1959. **Top right:** Using a slide show to illustrate an Extension lecture, 1960s. **Bottom:** Movie being shown in an Extension course, 1960s.

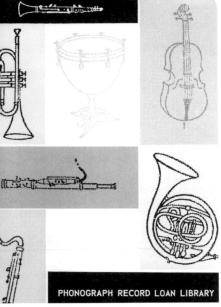

By the mid-1950s, Extension's Audio Visual Services unit served as either provincial library or co-ordinating agency for films produced or distributed by the United Nations, the federal Civil Defence agency, the NFB, the Canadian Film Institute, and the Industrial Film Council of British Columbia. In these years, Extension circulated over fifteen thousand movies per year.

In January 1941, Extension initiated a service to loan phonograph records to individuals and music appreciation groups across British Columbia, from UBC's Carnegie Music Set. The borrowing catalogue provided seven categories of records available for loan:

1. Orchestral Selections Available from the Carnegie Music Set
2. General Music Collection
3. Folk Dances
4. Selections by Various Instruments of the Orchestra
5. Selections Illustrating the History of Music
6. Songs and Dramatic Readings from Shakespeare
7. Dialect Records

Borrowers paid one dollar annually for the privilege of borrowing up to seven records at any one time for a maximum of three days. The Extension library shipped the records to relatively remote parts of the province and to servicemen in military stations. Borrowers paid all mailing costs, and any damages to records taken out in their name; breakage

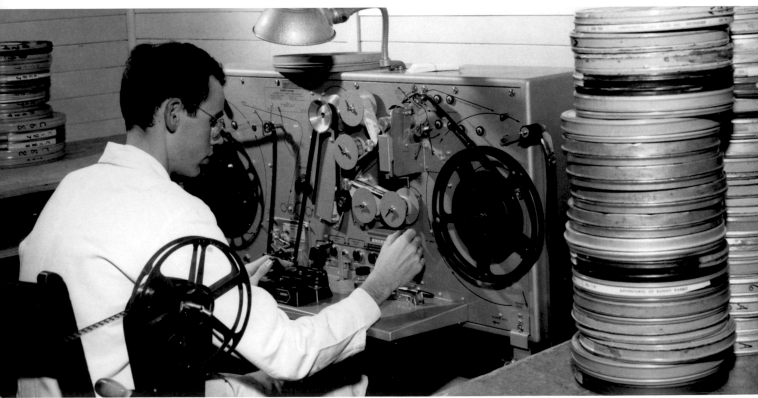

during shipping was common.[21] In 1944, Extension acquired a collection of folk dance and square dance records to help "community groups in planning recreational programmes." The next year, Extension expanded its collection again, this time to assist teachers and other adults responsible for children and youth programs. The circulation of phonograph records grew substantially, peaking at over 10,000 records in 1955.

In the 1960s, given the greater commercial availability and affordability of movies and records, Extension reduced its circulation of these resources. In 1964, UBC required the Recordings Library to operate on a cost-recovery basis, and within two years Extension had stopped providing this service and redirected its support to faculties and departments on the UBC campus. Extension continued to operate a film library, loan films to organizations across British Columbia, and serve as an agent for the NFB and other film sources, through the late 1960s. In 1968, it loaned 3,575 films. However, by the early 1970s, the Centre for Continuing Education had withdrawn from the business of loaning films.

*chapter summary*

## FOSTERING CULTURAL ENRICHMENT

*The Extension era (1936-1970) was shaped by transformative cultural changes, including the rise of mass media, a growing number of people travelling internationally, and increasing immigration to British Columbia of people from around the world.*

*Relying heavily on UBC faculty members as extension lecturers and evening class instructors, the Department of University Extension delivered an expanding range of cultural enrichment offerings in partnership with external agencies, including community-based and voluntary organizations, arts groups, charitable foundations, radio and television stations, and the National Film Board.*

*In addition to extension lectures and radio offerings, program innovations over this period included the introduction of fine arts, drama, theatre, social sciences, humanities, language, and "Summer School of the Arts" courses. After all, as Robert England (UBC's first Director of University Extension) stated, the aim of education is not primarily to fit people for specific vocations, but to give them a new "zest in life."*

*Modest fees were typically charged for these programs to encourage access by a broad range of adult learners. In addition to these fees, offerings were supported by substantial grants from organizations such as the Carnegie Corporation and the Ford Foundation.*

# During a 1947 Workshop in Group Discussion Techniques, Mrs. Peter Amy described "What the discussion leader expects from her group" as follows:

*Be ready to take part in the discussion, in preparing assignments or making reports. ■ Be willing to listen to the other person's point of view intelligently and sympathetically. ■ Be willing to share ideas and information, and to express an opinion. ■ Avoid trying to dominate the discussion - ask for suggestions as to how to deal with a member who wants to "hog the floor." ■ Avoid being aggressive in stating an opinion. Do not be ashamed to acknowledge a change of mind, and heart, if convinced by another's argument. ■ Do not hesitate to ask for an explanation of some point not understood before the discussion gets away from you. It shows you are listening intelligently. ■ Do individual study between meetings. The value of group discussion depends to a large extent on the work which individuals do on their own. ■ The leader expects members to be punctual, to attend regularly, to be friendly, informal and considerate of new or timid members.*

Mrs. Peter Amy
Member of the Parent-Teacher Federation
(1947)

## Chapter Five

# Cultivating public-minded citizens

A central goal of extension and continuing education at UBC has been to help people participate actively in public affairs. During the Depression, for example, Extension organized public lectures regarding the crisis and its potential resolution, while during the Second World War Extension organized study groups to examine the war and problems of post-war reconstruction. Over the years, Extension staff members offered three enduring types of programs to promote civic engagement and to encourage responsible forms of citizenship: study groups to discuss the liberal arts and key social issues; evening courses, public lectures, and conferences relating to important current events; and training for volunteers and professionals involved in human and social service work, including the emerging field of adult education.

## STUDY GROUP PROGRAMS

Shortly after its founding, Extension encouraged study groups as a means of bringing citizens together to discuss current events and topics of social and cultural interest. In 1937, the fledgling department formed ten study groups, and encouraged other groups formed by parent-teacher associations, the League of Nations Society, and consumer co-operatives. The study group program expanded rapidly. By 1939, UBC supported 179 study groups across the province, and offered numerous courses to such groups, including: British Columbia History, Practical Psychology, Modern Literature, History of the Theatre, Economics and Public Affairs, International Relations, and Co-operatives. In 1941, additional courses in child psychology and nursing were developed for study groups organized by the Parent-Teacher Federation and the Registered Nurses' Association.

UBC provided pamphlets and reference books, but leadership came from within the groups themselves. Although participants developed subject knowledge, they also practised citizenship and critical thinking skills through leading and participating in the groups. In his 1940 annual report, Gordon Shrum suggested that:

*Since an active member of a study group is forced to clarify his own thoughts, to hear and examine the ideas of others, and to assist in the formulation of group conclusions, it is felt that membership in a study group is an extremely valuable form of adult education. (p. 11)*

*Suggestions for Managing Study Groups (1938)*

*It is not necessary to seek a large membership – ten interested members make a better group than twenty-five indifferent ones. All the members should be encouraged to participate in the discussion. After the topics have been chosen a leader for each topic should be selected. Under normal conditions it is expected that one topic as outlined will be sufficient for one meeting.*

During the Second World War, Extension gave increasing attention to study groups, believing that "There is no better training for effective democratic citizenship."[1] In 1942, UBC provided study group courses on British Columbia history, modern literature, sociology, psychology, and fine arts. Extension also developed specialized study-discussion courses on co-operatives and credit unions for the Educational Programme for British Columbia Fishermen. Some 259 study groups across British Columbia registered to follow one or more of these courses in 1942.

The number of study groups grew during the 1940s, peaking at 441 in 1947. UBC's study group courses were used by universities in Alberta, Saskatchewan, Manitoba, and Quebec. In 1946, Extension reported that agencies in other provinces had purchased over seven hundred sets of "Child Psychology for Parents," over four hundred sets of "Marriage and Family Life," and over seventy sets of "Public Speaking." By the end of the decade, Extension offered course materials to study groups on subjects relating to public affairs, family life, and the arts:

- Marriage and Family Life
- Child Psychology for Parents
- Co-operative Play Groups
- Understanding Adolescents
- Home Decoration
- Public Speaking
- Acting
- Art Appreciation
- Music Appreciation
- Modern Literature

- Dominion-Provincial Relations
- Know Your Government
- Mainsprings of World Politics
- The Changing Far East
- East and West of Suez
- The United Nations
- Economic Planning of the UN
- Canadian Immigration Problems
- Co-operatives
- Credit Unions

In the late 1940s and early 1950s, the study-discussion method declined as Extension focussed more intensively on evening courses, conferences, and correspondence courses.

Two of Extension's study group programs were distinguished by their use of radio to transmit course content. During the 1940s and 1950s, Extension coordinated the National Farm Radio Forum and the Citizens' Forum within British Columbia. The Farm Radio Forum began in 1941 as a collaborative venture of the CBC, the Canadian Federation of Agriculture, and the Canadian Association for Adult Education. Over the winter months, the CBC broadcast a weekly, half-hour program on topics related to agriculture and rural life – topics chosen by a national planning group composed primarily of farmers from across Canada. Before each broadcast, listening groups were given discussion points and supplementary literature, such as the weekly "Farm Forum Guide" and the pamphlet

series "Planning for Plenty." Each week, groups reported back highlights of their discussions to the provincial office, which forwarded the highlights to the national office for use in subsequent broadcasts.

Although Farm Radio Forum received international acclaim, it was less successful in British Columbia than elsewhere in the country. Over one hundred and eighty groups participated during the first two years, but then group numbers steadily declined until only ten groups participated in 1955. Historian Gordon Selman suggests several reasons why the Forum was less popular in British Columbia than elsewhere: British Columbia's rural population was scattered and less involved with farmers' organizations than elsewhere; radio reception was poor in many areas; national topics often did not fit local circumstances; and field work was inadequate – it was simply too difficult to provide live, personal support to far-flung groups in rugged British Columbia.[2]

While the Farm Radio Forum addressed issues facing farmers, the Citizens' Forum used a similar format to foster Canadian identity and promote discussion of important social, political, and economic issues. Launched in 1943 as a joint venture of the CBC and the Canadian Association for Adult Education, the British Columbia section began with the support of over seventy organizations. As with the Farm Radio Forum, Extension coordinated local discussion groups across British Columbia.

The Citizens' Forum was not quite the success that its idealistic leaders had hoped it would be, but for years it averaged some four hundred study groups across Canada. In British Columbia, response in the first two years was strong, with over one hundred groups participating. In 1946, it dropped to thirty-eight groups with 216 participants and

slowly slipped to twenty groups with 129 participants in 1955. With such controversial topics as growing American influence over Canada, the merits of communism in China, corporal punishment for children, and the challenge of achieving peace, the Citizens' Forum occasionally drew criticism from conservative sources. Indeed, in 1950, Roby Kidd, the Associate Director of the Canadian Association for Adult Education, was compelled to circulate a lengthy memorandum to the Citizens' Forum provincial offices defending the Forum against accusations that it was "conspiring to attack free enterprise," that its speakers were disproportionately "left-wingers," and that its public meetings were "packed" with "communist or left-wing sympathizers."[3] UBC's Department of University Extension facilitated the Farm Radio Forum and the Citizens' Forum into the late 1950s.

## LIVING ROOM LEARNING

Although study-discussion groups had declined in the 1950s, they experienced a renaissance in 1957 when the Ford Foundation's Fund for Adult Education provided Extension with a three-year grant to launch an ambitious "Study-Discussion Programme in the Liberal Arts." Dubbed "Living Room Learning," the program followed earlier examples at several American universities which, in the context of the Cold War, were intended to help people in the "free world" develop their abilities to function as democratic citizens – less likely to succumb to threats posed by communism or McCarthyism.[4] A Living Room Learning brochure illustrates this sentiment:

*These special study-discussion programs devoted to the liberal arts are in the highest sense the most practical form of education you can get in a free society. This is truly education for freedom. For within the group itself – even as you discuss the great ideas of today and past times – you will be experiencing in miniature the essence of the democratic process.*

The formal goals of Living Room Learning were to help participants understand their culture; to think independently, critically, and objectively; to develop tolerance for alternative ideas and opinions; and to enhance communication skills.[5] Extension provided course outlines and resource materials (typically books or audio recordings) to local discussion groups, and trained group leaders. Round-table discussion, through which participants exchanged their thoughts about readings and topics, was the primary teaching and learning method.

Leadership for Living Room Learning was organized by Knute Buttedahl, an idealistic young Canadian of Norwegian descent who had been active in labour and human rights issues, and had a degree in commerce from UBC.[6] The program expanded in the late 1950s to involve more than 1,300 participants each year, in over one hundred local groups of six to twenty-four participants, in more than forty communities. For ten weeks beginning in September and February, Living Room Learning groups discussed current events, humanities, social sciences, and the arts in more than twenty courses developed by UBC or other agencies (the Fund for Adult Education, the American Foundation for Continuing Education, and the Canadian Association for Adult Education).

In 1961, Extension advertised the following Living Room Learning courses:

- World Politics
- Canada and World Affairs
- Russian Foreign Policy
- The Ways of Mankind
- Great Religions of the World
- Introduction to the Humanities
- Understanding our Economy
- The Challenge of Modern Living
- Shakespeare and his Theatre
- Looking at Modern Painting
- Music that Tells a Story
- Discovering Modern Poetry
- Transition and Tension in Southeast Asia

Financial support from the Ford Foundation ended in the autumn of 1960. President MacKenzie thanked the Fund for Adult Education for supporting Living Room Learning at UBC, which continued to subsidize the program until 1964, at which time the Board of Governors reduced funding to Extension, and the program was discontinued due to financial restraint. Efforts to revive the program in the latter 1960s were not successful.

*The Ways of Mankind (most popular Living Room Learning course)*

*This is an examination of the greatest wonder of the world: man himself, and the drama of the many cultures he has created. Your life, your feelings, your ideas will be placed into the framework of the world's culture; your attention will be drawn to situations ranging from the ethics of an African tribe to the problem of a corporation executive's wife; you will get a new look at our values and social mores.*

## PUBLIC AFFAIRS COURSES AND CONFERENCES

Current events courses were an early and ongoing part of Extension at UBC. In 1937, Professor F.H. Soward of the Department of History taught "Some Problems of the Post-War World" as a series of fifteen lectures on Thursday evenings. Through such courses, Extension enabled citizens to discuss key events relating to developments such as the Great Depression, the Second World War, post-war reconstruction, the Cold War, nuclear weapons, the United Nations, and international politics. During the 1940s, Extension typically provided one or two evening courses per year, attracting over sixty students per course, on average.

In the following decade, evening courses in public affairs both increased in number, and diversified in content. Over thirty "Public Affairs" courses and weekend workshops were advertised during the 1950s, some of which took a more specialized look at particular issues. Community organizations could also host Extension's Supervisor of Citizenship and Public Affairs for presentations or consultation on, for example, disarmament, Indian affairs, communism, and Africa.

The 1960s brought an even greater expansion, with nine public affairs evening courses delivered each year to fifty participants per course, on average. Topics reflected the major issues of the decade, from the civil rights movement in the United States to the development of communism in China.

Evening courses were joined by summer programs in public affairs in the post-war years. Workshops in international or intercultural relations took place annually from 1945 to 1950, and a series of six lectures on "Latin American Life and Culture" was offered in the summer of 1947. Between 1953 and 1959, Extension staff worked with the United Nations Association to deliver an annual, five-day seminar on the United Nations for high school students. In 1956, this event brought ninety-six high school students from across British Columbia to the UBC campus. Shorter seminars on the United Nations were also delivered for adults.

Conferences on current events and public affairs also joined the summer programs from the latter 1950s to the latter 1960s. For example, in 1957, Extension co-sponsored a conference of the Citizenship Councils of British Columbia, and a five-day seminar with the title of "Japan – 1957." At the time, people of Japanese descent were returning to the coast following their forced migration and internment during the war; UBC began designing its famous Nitobe Gardens in 1959 to symbolize the new, more diverse, and accepting society that educational leaders envisioned. For a decade beginning in 1958, Extension delivered an annual "Summer School of Public Affairs," combining a number of workshops pertaining to current events with a major seminar focussed on the following countries and regions of particular interest:

*Current International Problems (1948-49)*

*This course will deal with contemporary problems of the international scene such as the future of the United Nations, peace-making in Europe and the Far East, the Palestine issue, the Marshall Plan, Communism and the West, the foreign policies of the Great Powers and Canada, the future of the British Commonwealth and current international events.*

the emergence of
CHINA

新中國

AUGUST 29 – SEPTEMBER 3, 1965
UNIVERSITY OF BRITISH COLUMBIA

AFRICA

and
THE
UNITED
NATIONS

- 1958: Malaya
- 1959: India
- 1960: Africa South of the Sahara
- 1961: Israel
- 1962: The Middle East

- 1963: Latin America
- 1964: no seminar
- 1965: China
- 1966: India
- 1967: The Soviet Union

A large five-year grant from the Ford Foundation's Fund for Adult Education awarded to UBC in 1960 went to support programming in public affairs and the liberal arts. The Ford Foundation grant helped expand evening courses and daytime seminars and assisted with two multi-year projects designed to promote "education for public responsibility," one in collaboration with the BC Provincial Council of Women, and the other in collaboration with the BC School Trustees' Association. Two other multi-year programs began in 1962, with financial support from the federal government. The Indian Affairs Branch funded Extension to offer leadership development education to chiefs and councillors with First Nations communities in British Columbia. The Citizenship Branch provided funding for three-day workshops on "Leadership and Community Responsibility" for leaders of regional and provincial voluntary organizations. Although varied in their audiences and substantive content, these four multi-year projects all endeavoured to build leadership capacity in communities and voluntary organizations.

**Top left:** William C. Holland giving a public affairs course on India, 1959. **Top right:** Brochure for course on China, 1965. **Bottom:** Brochure for a seminar on Africa and the United Nations, 1965.

## EDUCATION FOR HUMAN AND SOCIAL SERVICES VOLUNTEERS AND PROFESSIONALS

Although most of its civic engagement work involved providing public affairs programs to the general public, Extension also organized educational activities for parents, community volunteers, and people whose working lives were dedicated to helping others. In many regards, such initiatives were similar to the professional programs described in Chapter Three. However, they are included in this chapter because they were very often delivered to parents and community volunteers rather than paid professionals, and because the professionals who took these programs were dedicated to working with individuals and communities on issues of social and political significance.

Educational programming relating to human and social services was one of Extension's earliest activities, part of a much broader expansion of social services education at UBC. Until 1927, when Toronto social worker Laura Holland wrote a scathing report of the social services available in Vancouver, "community welfare" in the city consisted mainly of orphanages and industrial schools for delinquent children. UBC hired its first sociologist in 1929 and launched a diploma program in social service, which struggled for years with inadequate funding.[7] As part of UBC's new commitment to "scientific" social work, Extension in 1940 hired Marjorie Smith (formerly a stenographer in Extension) to develop programs in social services.[8] Smith became a valuable senior member of the staff, earning a Master of Social Work degree from UBC, and was considered by Shrum to be "a young woman of outstanding ability not only academically but as a leader in group and community work."[9]

**Top:** Marjorie Smith, coordinator of human and social services programs, 1951. *UBCA 1.1/12926* **Bottom:** Brochure for Extension program in social welfare, 1959.

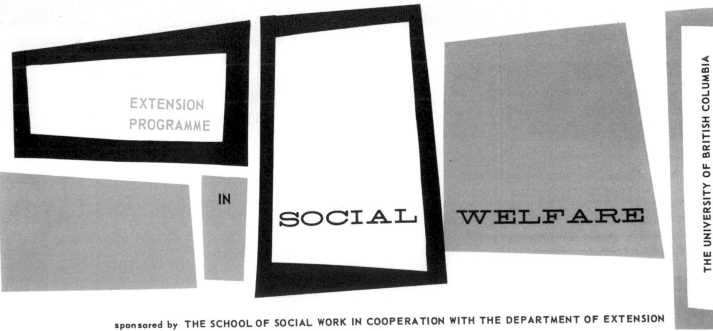

EXTENSION PROGRAMME IN SOCIAL WELFARE

THE UNIVERSITY OF BRITISH COLUMBIA

sponsored by THE SCHOOL OF SOCIAL WORK IN COOPERATION WITH THE DEPARTMENT OF EXTENSION

Parenting education was an early topic of interest responding to a new focus on child development and its critical role in building a better society. In 1941, Extension developed a study-group course in "Child Psychology," which was used by hundreds of local discussion groups, many of which were associated with parent-teacher associations (PTA), throughout the 1940s. In 1944, Extension organized a "Parents' Institute" in collaboration with the Parent-Teacher Federation of British Columbia.

Two-day Parents' Institutes became annual events, typically attracting between 150 and 200 participants through the 1940s and 1950s. Topics ranged from "Teen-Agers Today," and "Co-operative Play Schools," to "Modern Trends in Education." Beginning in 1947, the main conference was for many years followed by a three-day "Workshop in Discussion Group Techniques" aimed at building the skills and experience of PTA leaders and members.

In 1951 and 1952, the Parents' Institute was joined by a "Parent-Youth Conference" at which about fifty high school students met parents "to discuss problems of mutual interest." Such parent-youth events were repeated several times in the next decade. By the mid-1950s, Extension was organizing numerous "Group Development and Leadership" workshops for parent-teacher groups each year.

In 1948, Extension established a formal "Parent Education" program. In that year, activities in Extension included acquiring and circulating films on child development; developing and distributing educational kits for PTA meetings; distributing eight hundred copies of study group courses relating to child psychology and family life; registering four hundred parents for six lectures on the subject of child psychology; hosting a two-week course in pre-school techniques for twenty-five women; and hosting the annual Parents' Institute. In subsequent years, Parent Education staff members provided educational services and advice to parent-teacher associations, and distributed pamphlets and discussion-group courses on parenting issues. In 1950, Extension reported that more than 2,100 people participated in more than forty parent education meetings.

In 1953, Extension changed the name of its "Parent Education" service to the "Human Relations Service." The scope of Extension's activity expanded to include mental health and group development. Extension continued to work closely with parent-teacher associations and with the Vancouver Association of Co-operative Play Groups, and expanded its efforts to work with other agencies in the fields of education, health, recreation, social services, business management, and labour.

The Human Relations Service provided numerous workshops on leadership and group development each year, and organized conferences and seminars on issues ranging from intercultural relations and social work, to community recreation and parenting. In 1953, it delivered a series of sixteen lectures on various aspects of life in Canada to recent immigrants. Co-sponsored by the Vancouver YMCA, the Civic Unity Council, the Federal Department of Citizenship, and the Canadian Labour Congress, the lectures attracted

*Group Development Workshops (1955)*

*The purpose of these workshops is to help participants become more effective as group members and leaders by developing their understanding of themselves and others, and their skills in working with groups.*

about seventy immigrants and leaders from local ethnic groups. From 1954 through 1957, Extension hosted an annual five-day seminar in human relations in conjunction with the Summer School of the Arts (see Chapter Four).

In the late 1950s and early 1960s, Extension changed the name of the unit working in this field two more times, but continued to provide workshops on group development and leadership to individuals and organizations in the public, private, and not-for-profit sectors. It also continued to provide education and advice to parents, staff, and leaders involved in pre-schools.[10] In the early 1960s, Extension expanded its work into new areas of the human and social services, including gerontology, public health, community planning, and mental health.

From 1963 through 1970, Extension organized numerous educational events in community planning. The first was the "Okanagan Community Planning Tour" held in Penticton, Kelowna, Vernon, and Kamloops in 1963, which engaged UBC faculty members and professional planners in a series of public lectures, meetings, and consultations with local officials and members of the general public. Over 1,500 people in the Okanagan participated in these community planning events over a period of about three months. In subsequent years, Extension organized numerous community planning events and initiatives across British Columbia – from an annual "Short Course on Community Planning" and seminars for professional planners, to public forums and the provision of advice to local governments and voluntary organizations involved in various aspects of community planning. Throughout the 1960s, community planning and urban affairs programs involved hundreds of British Columbians each year.

## BUILDING THE FIELD OF ADULT EDUCATION

Extension had a special interest in adult education as a field of professional practice and scholarship. In the early years, UBC's influence on developing the field of adult education was primarily through the engagement of the Director of the Department of University Extension with local, provincial, and national organizations of importance to the education of adults. Robert England corresponded with Ned Corbett, the charismatic former Director of Extension at the University of Alberta, who had become founding Director of the Canadian Association for Adult Education. In 1944, Shrum reported being "actively associated" with the Canadian Association for Adult Education, the Canadian Youth Commission, the NFB, the Vancouver Institute, the Adult Education Committee of the Vancouver YMCA, the Provincial Nutrition Committee, the National Farm Radio Forum, the National Council of Citizens' Forums, and the Regional Committee of the Canadian Legion Educational Services. Professional service work by directors and other members of Extension staff contributed significantly to the development of adult education in Canada.

UBC's first credit course in adult education taught by Roby Kidd (front row, second from left), 1956. *UBCA 3.1/442*

In the mid-1950s, Extension became increasingly involved in both formal and non-formal education for adult educators. John Friesen, as one of the first Canadians to hold a doctorate in Adult Education, envisioned professional careers awaiting people with specialized preparation as "adult educators." Soon after he arrived at UBC, Extension co-hosted the "First Conference on Adult Education in British Columbia," bringing together representatives of over fifty organizations to share information, exchange ideas, and promote networking among adult educators.

Thanks to the academic respectability of adult education in the eyes of President MacKenzie, the new Dean of Education, Neville Scarfe, and other social scientists at UBC (who saw adult education as applied sociology), John Friesen was able to arrange for a new course during UBC's annual Summer Session. In July 1956, Friesen's friend

**Right:** Robert England, John Friesen, and Gordon Shrum (L-R), the first three Directors of UBC Extension, meet to celebrate 25 years of service to adult learners in British Columbia, 1961. *UBCA 62.1/3*

Roby Kidd, then the Director of the Canadian Association for Adult Education, taught "The Administration of Adult Education Programmes," to thirty-six students – some of whom received graduate-level degree-credit from UBC for completing the course.

Kidd's course provided encouragement to launch a graduate training program for educators of adults, supported by the Faculties of Education and Agriculture. Beginning part-time in 1957, the program expanded in 1960 when Coolie Verner was hired as UBC's first Professor of Adult Education, and UBC awarded its first MA in adult education. Thanks in part to Verner's leadership, the graduate degree program grew slowly until, by 1970, it was quite secure. Canada's first graduate program in adult education has continued to the time of writing this book, despite several administrative changes.[11]

In the early 1960s, Extension delivered a number of non-credit seminars and workshops for instructors and administrators responsible for the education of adults in various settings. For example, in 1963, Extension organized a week-long seminar on "Programmed Learning for Adults" and a week-long workshop for "Night School Directors." The following year, in collaboration with the Vancouver School Board, Extension held an evening course in "Teaching Adults – Methods and Techniques." In 1966, Extension offered four non-credit workshops for adult educators, and developed a non-credit Diploma Program in Adult Education in collaboration with the Faculty of Education.

Less formally, Extension hosted visitors wishing to learn directly from the renowned work of department staff. In his 1956 annual report, Friesen noted that adult educators from Indonesia, Japan, Pakistan, Great Britain, Chile, and the West Indies had visited his

department to learn about "plans, programs, and methods" (p. 6). Such visits continued for many years. Extension staff also visited other provinces and countries on occasion, to support the development of adult education. The most ambitious example of such work was a project in India. From 1964 through 1968, with funding from the Canadian External Aid Office, members of Extension worked in India to build the capacity of the University of Rajasthan to develop and deliver university extension programs.

In the 1970s, the Centre for Continuing Education collaborated with the Faculty of Education to offer an ambitious range of non-credit courses for instructors and administrators in the field of adult education. The Diploma Program in Adult Education continued throughout the decade, and, for several years beginning in 1973, the Centre hosted an annual "Chautauqua-by-the-Pacific." Named after travelling educational shows that visited small towns in rural United States and Canada in the early 1900s, Chautauqua-by-the-Pacific attracted educators from across British Columbia and beyond to UBC for a week-long series of workshops, lectures, and special events. Over the course of the decade, UBC delivered an average of twenty-eight non-credit workshops and courses each year, in the field of adult education, with an average of twenty-five participants per course. Such events included those relating to teaching practices ("Group Leadership" and "Effective Instructional Techniques"), those relating to program planning ("Program Evaluation in Adult Education" and "Identifying Community Needs and Preparing Program Objectives"), and those relating to various domains of adult education ("Programming with Older Adults" and "Training in Industry"). In the 1980s, the Faculty of Education assumed full responsibility for professional development programs for adult educators.

*In the field of non-credit programming, UBC's continuing education activities have a reputation second to none among the universities in Canada and each year many visitors from home and abroad visit our Centre to discuss our curriculum, methods, and organization.*

*Gordon Selman, Director
Centre for Continuing Education
1973*

## CULTIVATING PUBLIC-MINDED CITIZENS

*The Extension era (1936-1970) was a time of transformative political change, encompassing major events such as the Great Depression and Second World War, and movements such as those for civil rights, feminism, and decolonization.*

*During this period, the Department of University Extension increased its capacity for offering educational programming that focussed on major current events, social issues, and geographic regions. Extension also organized programs for those whose working lives were dedicated to helping others, such as human and social services professionals.*

*Extension study groups (and later "Living Room Learning" groups) brought citizens together to discuss topical issues while developing critical thinking abilities, and openness for new ideas and opinions.*

*Extension was instrumental in building the field of adult education through active involvement with the Canadian Association for Adult Education and a range of other organizations with adult education mandates. In 1956, John Friesen (then Director of University Extension) arranged for UBC's first credit course in adult education to be taught by Roby Kidd, one of Canada's preeminent adult educators.*

# Over the past 20 years, Joyce Craig has enrolled in many French language conversation courses with UBC Continuing Studies.

Although UBC Continuing Studies offers French courses in the daytime, evening and on weekends, she usually enrols in the Saturday morning classes as they have a relaxed, social atmosphere. As Joyce describes, "we call ourselves le Club du Samedi here at UBC...even the professors call us the Saturday morning club. There's lots of fun. We joke, we laugh at each other. We're here because we really want to be here. It's really enjoyable to go to Montreal or Quebec City or Paris and be able to actually converse with people in their language. When people hear my accent and try to speak to me in English, I tell them: I'm here to speak French."

*Chapter Six*

# From Extension to
# UBC Continuing Studies,
# 1970-present

## FROM EXTENSION TO CONTINUING EDUCATION

The transition from the Department of University Extension to the Centre for Continuing Education at UBC was consistent with developments at other major universities in western Canada.[1] All four provincial universities had established extension departments by 1950. These departments were responsible for a range of educational programs for adults not enrolled in traditional on-campus study. When the provincial governments founded new public universities in the 1960s and 1970s, those universities soon established continuing education units of their own.

As at UBC, universities in North America generally used the term "extension" prior to the 1960s, while they have tended to use the term "continuing education" since the 1970s. These terms are not synonymous. Extension connotes teaching, research, and service practices that connect university faculty members with people who are not in attendance on campus as full-time students. Continuing education connotes the delivery of educational programs to people having already obtained a certain level of education. Instructors include a wide range of experts, from full-time faculty and alumni, to professional practitioners and community-based resource people. Although extension work occurs today, and continuing education work took place in the period prior to 1960, there has been a shift in focus from extension to continuing education, even among those institutions that retained the term "extension" in their organizational chart.

In the earlier era, extension was typically a function in which universities invested taxpayers' resources in the provision of services to members of the public, although participants were often charged a modest fee for participation. In the contemporary era, continuing education is a function that universities increasingly seek to operate on a near cost-recovery basis, where tuition paid by participants or their employers generates the majority of revenues. Although complete cost-recovery has never consistently been achieved by continuing education units in western Canada, the public sector financial model of the extension era has been replaced, at most universities, with an expectation that continuing education units derive the majority of their operating resources from tuition revenues and external contracts.

In addition to having different financial models and modes of delivery, extension and continuing education tend to serve different types of learners. In western Canada, extension programming in the past often reached rural audiences, and was designed for people with modest levels of initial education. In contrast, contemporary continuing education participants in western Canada typically live in cities and already possess some post-secondary education. Women now constitute a strong majority of learners in most continuing education programs, although men still outnumber women in certain professional fields, such as those related to computer science and engineering. The shift in the gender composition of continuing education students reflects both changing rates of labour market participation, and the evolution of the substantive focus of continuing education programming – an evolution to be described in Chapters Seven through Nine.

## THE CENTRE FOR CONTINUING EDUCATION

In 1969, at Gordon Selman's request, UBC appointed a Senate Committee on Continuing Education to review and make recommendations regarding the university's policy framework for extension and continuing education. In May 1970, the committee submitted four major recommendations:

1. The University recognize its responsibility in regard to continuing education and provide adequate support through policies concerning academic promotions and building plans;

2. The University observe certain budgeting principles aimed at strengthening continuing education programs;

3. Continuing education be conducted by the Centre for Continuing Education (to replace the Department of University Extension) and by Faculty Divisions of Professional Continuing Education (such as those operating in the Health Sciences and Commerce); and

4. There be a President's Co-ordinating Committee on Continuing Education.

UBC Senate approved the recommendations, and the Board of Governors approved all of them except the second.[2] Eventually, the Board of Governors adopted the principle that the direct costs of continuing education programs should be recovered from external sources, with UBC providing support for costs relating to facilities and administration, and perhaps start-up money for new projects.

In 1971, the Centre for Continuing Education annual report claimed that its activities differed from those of the Department of University Extension primarily with regard to "an increased focus on professional continuing education, more complex and sequential general education courses, and greater integration with the campus' other academic bodies" (p. 1). In 1971, two policy and governance bodies were created to oversee

*Professional continuing education is now a specialty program operation. In the past, few courses were planned on a sequential and systematic basis. Various courses of this type are now in existence, more are being planned and a number of non-degree credit certificates and diplomas are being offered.*

*Jack Blaney, Acting Director
Centre for Continuing
Education
1970*

continuing education at UBC: the Council for the Centre for Continuing Education, and the President's Co-ordinating Committee on Continuing Education. The Council formulated and reviewed general program policy for the Centre, while the Co-ordinating Committee promoted coherent campus-wide policies, since other units, notably in areas of business administration and health and human services, operated significant continuing education programs on their own. Consistent with UBC's "democratization movement" of the late 1960s, the Centre's Advisory Council consisted of faculty members from across campus and other stakeholders, including continuing education students. It proved to be less than effective, however, and was changed into a Senate standing committee a few years later.[3]

With a renewed mandate and governance structure, the Centre for Continuing Education set to work from its new offices in Carr Hall (and later Duke Hall), formerly part of the Roman Catholic St. Mark's College on the northern edge of the UBC campus. Space at UBC was in short supply during the late 1960s as baby-boomers swelled undergraduate numbers. Programs of the Centre were increasingly delivered through conventional, classroom-based courses in academic subjects, although innovation was still encouraged in relation to "urgent community problems and areas of unique interest to adults."[4] Classes were largely held at UBC, but downtown locations like the public library also were used.

Centre for Continuing Education staff in the mid-1970s.

Gordon Selman, as the first Director of the Centre for Continuing Education, felt that the Centre in the early 1970s suffered benign neglect from senior administrators, and even, occasionally, outright hostility from Deans intent on having their faculties administer their own continuing professional education programs.[5] Despite his best efforts, for example, Selman could not expand the degree-completion opportunities for part-time adult students, although the university began to enrol more part-time women, older adults, and visible minorities in its daytime degree-credit programs.

University continuing education in British Columbia received an important boost in 1974, when the province's recently elected New Democratic Party passed a new *University Act*. The Act mandated universities in the province to "provide a programme of continuing education in all academic and cultural fields throughout the province," although with a proviso that these services were subject to available resources. The Act also permitted student and staff representation on the Board of Governors, and the unionization of employees. After several tense meetings and votes, the UBC Faculty Association, however, emerged as a "special bargaining unit" rather than a certified union. The Faculty Association admitted program directors from the Centre for Continuing Education as a special class of faculty member (librarians were admitted along similar lines); five years later, Association negotiators managed to reach an agreement with the university on terms for "confirmed appointment," providing tenure for program directors.[6]

Gordon Selman's departure as director in 1974 coincided with the appointment of a new UBC President, formally installed in 1975. Douglas Kenny, a former UBC psychology professor and Dean of Arts, was intent on expanding research and professional education at UBC, as well as creating a more professional and efficient central university

**Left:** Douglas Kenny, UBC President (1975-1982). **Centre:** John Edwards, Director of the Interior Program, mid-1970s. *UBCA 41.1/2605, 5.1/826* **Right:** Pauline Gensick, Centre for Continuing Education staff member, 1970s.

administration. He wished to maintain ties between alumni and UBC as the number of people in the traditional age cohort for university studies went into decline, and to re-establish UBC's presence in the province's interior where Simon Fraser University and the University of Victoria were assertively promoting their continuing education programs.[7] The Centre for Continuing Education launched a new Interior Program from a Vernon office, where John Edwards organized lecture series, conferences, and the occasional short course in the Thompson-Okanagan and Kootenay regions. To Edwards, the program served as "a very basic attitudinal and informational change-agent amongst the public on behalf of post-secondary education."[8]

Kenny publicly expressed significant interest in promoting continuing education at UBC. In his 1976 *President's Report*, he reflected upon the importance of community engagement to a university's reputation:

> Many factors contribute to the reputation that a university enjoys in the community generally and in the academic world. No university will be highly regarded if its curriculum remains static and its graduates are ill-prepared for their chosen fields of work, if it is unable to attract research grants to allow faculty members and graduate students to explore new areas of knowledge, or if it is unwilling to place its vast expertise at the disposal of the community. (p. 6)

To demonstrate how assertively UBC was working to ensure that it served communities throughout British Columbia, Kenny wrote that "nearly 70,000 persons had contact with the University in the 1975-76 academic year" through extension activities, and that there was "scarcely a major or medium-sized centre in the province" that did not "benefit from UBC in one way or another" (p. 10).

In his president's reports from 1976 through 1983, Kenny consistently highlighted continuing education, along with teaching and research, as a core function of UBC. His continuing education reports summarized participation of tens of thousands of British Columbians in the programs of the Centre for Continuing Education and those organized by faculties in fields such as health sciences, commerce, social work, agriculture, education, and forestry. In his 1983 report, Kenny proudly claimed that "UBC sponsors and actively promotes one of the most extensive university continuing education programs anywhere in the world" (p. 27).

In 1974, UBC appointed a senior faculty member, Walter Hardwick, to oversee not only the Centre, but also all of the university's continuing education work.[9] Hardwick was a great supporter of educational innovation, but little came from this attempt at administrative centralization, since Hardwick soon took a leave to become the Deputy Minister of Education in the recently elected Social Credit government.[10] The Centre for Continuing Education reverted to earlier administrative arrangements, with a Director answering now to the Associate Vice President (Academic) instead of a Deputy President.[11]

*It is perfectly evident that there is no one geographical or social and educational community with which the university can or should safely identify. The university must create its own community, a community that will change steadily with all the pain and discomfort that that implies.*

Dr. Alan Thomas
Former Director of the
Communications Service
with the Department of
University Extension
1971

With Hardwick's departure, Jindra Kulich became Director of the Centre for Continuing Education. Kulich, Czech born, had worked for UBC's Department of Extension and the Centre for Continuing Education for many years, had earned a Master's degree at UBC in adult education, and frequently wrote on historical and contemporary developments in European adult education. Like his predecessors, Kulich had strong views regarding the role of adult education in maintaining a democratic civil society, and he ensured that the more profitable courses supported the less profitable, such as those in fine arts and current affairs. To many staff, Kulich helped to create a pleasant and collegial "family" atmosphere. Camaraderie ran high among full-time staff in many areas; people worked hard, but lunchtime parties with creative themes were not uncommon.[12]

Administrative and programming changes in continuing education at UBC reflected the significant social changes taking place in British Columbia in the 1970s. Both Kenny and Kulich expressed an awareness of such social changes. In his 1979 *President's Report*, Kenny wrote:

> The breadth and depth of our continuing education programs reflect the rapidly changing world in which we live. The revolution in communications, the growth of the women's movement, the incredible increase in the rate at which new knowledge accumulates, the desire of our citizens to improve themselves intellectually and economically, the increased amount of leisure time that is available to people – all these factors have contributed to the expansion of continuing education programs offered by the University. (p. 23)

Also in 1979, Kulich reported that his professional staff had unanimously adopted a "Statement of Roles and Goals for the Centre for Continuing Education." That statement began with the assertion:

> Since the citizens, organizations and institutions of British Columbia have become increasingly aware that learning is an important ingredient in their lifelong growth and development, their demands and needs for continuing education programs and services are growing and changing. To a greater extent than ever before, they also realize that they must have access to a variety of learning resources available in the province if they are to participate effectively in influencing the social, economic and political forces that govern their lives.

In his final *President's Report* (1983), Kenny argued that in the coming decades, "a continuation of lifelong learning will be more important than ever, not solely on grounds of principle, but for the pragmatic reason that we are entering an era in which no individual can count on having completed his or her formal education" (p. 27).

Despite the encouragement of continuing education in President Kenny's reports, the Centre's operating grant did not consistently grow in these years; in fact, UBC reduced its allocation to the Centre several times in the 1970s and 1980s. One observer later described the response of the university administration as "all possible assistance short of actual help."[13] The downturn in the economy in the early 1970s, which led to high inflation and unemployment in British Columbia, made matters worse. Kulich warned as

*Lifelong learning is generally accepted as a cornerstone of academic life. Continuing Education is, as it should remain, an important activity for UBC... It is one of the most successful means for UBC to maintain an active link with the community, benefiting both faculty members and participants.*

*Report of the Task Force on Continuing Education 1989*

early as 1975 that the Centre would have to be ruthless in cancelling programs with low enrolment, streamline its offerings, and increase fees to cover costs.[14] In 1981, he wrote that "non-credit general continuing education is not afforded the share of university resources and government support it needs and warrants."[15]

Nonetheless, program directors at the Centre still enjoyed freedom to be creative and innovative, as long as any losses could be subsidized by the more financially stable programs, and the Centre prospered.[16] "We were like an octopus – when one arm was cut off, we had seven more. And we quickly re-grew the lost arm," recalled Phil Moir, Program Director at the time.[17] Another program director during the 1970s described the Centre's structure as "free-flowing, creative, flexible, but not anarchic – if that is possible."[18] Programmers tapped into provincial and federal grants, delivered well-attended general and professional programs, participated in special events, and developed programs specially designed for women, older adults, Aboriginal people, and elected municipal officials.[19] By the end of the 1970s, computer technology was popular enough to warrant a serious push into the field, but the programs had to operate on a strict cost-recovery basis. Instructors were competent and committed, using a range of venues at the university, in Vancouver libraries, Pacific Centre Mall, and, after 1977, in a second-storey office downtown on Robson Street.[20] Increasingly, staff members and program directors were female, consistent with the rise of the women's movement and the Centre's support for it through such initiatives as the Women's Resources Centre (see Chapter Nine).

**Left:** Gordon Selman, Centre for Continuing Education (CCE) Director (1967-1974). **Centre:** Anne Ironside, first coordinator of the Women's Resources Centre (1972) and Acting CCE Director (1988-1991). **Right:** Jindra Kulich, CCE Director (1974-1988). *UBCA 5.1/2775, 44.1/14*

**Top:** Kay Pennant, 1970s. **Bottom left:** Estella Overmyer with her son, late 1970s. **Bottom right:** Office staff members Roberta Crosby and Linda Shelton, 1975.

The financial circumstances of UBC worsened in the early 1980s, as the inflationary squeeze of the 1970s led to a world-wide recession. Enrolments began to decline, particularly in professional programs, partly because companies could not afford to send their employees to educational programs. Kulich warned repeatedly that program areas had to avoid deficits and that programming, regrettably, would have to go "where the dollars are."[21] As the 1980s advanced, the financial problems of UBC increased as the government began reducing public expenditures and adopting "market solutions" to economic problems, following a trend in England and the United States. Public education in British Columbia seemed particularly under siege, and critics charged that the provincial government was not using federal transfer payments for their intended purpose of supporting post-secondary institutions.

The government's restraint program announced in the summer of 1983, which sparked widespread protests and strikes, imposed a five percent cut on the UBC operating budget for 1985. UBC's new president, George Pedersen, and his bursar, William White, began to review the Centre's programs to ensure that they were not being subsidized by the university, and even to see whether they could generate additional revenue.[22]

Kulich suggested an external review of the Centre, so that, at the very least, cuts would be informed and consultative.[23] The Faculty Association had no agreement with the university regarding termination in a situation of financial exigency, but Kulich vowed to avoid lay-offs and held several meetings to discuss alternate ways to meet an impending cut to the budget. He then set about forming closer ties with academic departments as recommended by the external review.[24]

Matters came to a head early in 1985. As departments across the university prepared to defend their programs from sizable cuts, George Pedersen resigned out of frustration with the lack of timely government information about the university grant (and to accept the Presidency of the University of Western Ontario). When the budget cuts were announced, several units across UBC were hit hard – programs were combined and eliminated, and staff and faculty were laid off, provoking angry responses from faculty and students.[25] The Centre for Continuing Education lost several positions, important programming areas such as conference management, and the Interior Program. The Centre survived despite deep cuts to its operating grant that year.[26] Along with prior attrition, its full-time staff size was reduced to that of fifteen years earlier, and its freedom to pursue innovative program objectives was in question.[27]

When David Strangway accepted the position of UBC President later in 1985, he looked for ways to make UBC a research university "second to none" without additional government support. This meant competing nationally for the best faculty and students, and providing them with top quality facilities. As a consequence, it meant reducing costs and increasing non-government revenue in various ways, including fundraising, corporate and philanthropic partnerships, and sales of services. He was remarkably successful, although critics were uncomfortable with the commercial activities on campus, the closer relationships with business and industry, and the growing power of the President's Office.[28]

President Strangway visited the Centre for Continuing Education early in 1986, expressing his vision of UBC as an elite institution, and asking how the Centre would fit such a vision while becoming financially self-sustaining.[29] Kulich suggested that the latter was neither practical nor desirable: at about 86 percent cost-recovery, the Centre was at its maximum and besides, the Centre should be seen as an integral part of the university's continuing education system wherein some areas might subsidize others.[30] Several staff members, however, were pessimistic about whether their program areas would ever recover full costs.[31]

In the end, the Centre for Continuing Education came under increased pressure for cost-recovery and then revenue generation. Kulich sought professional marketing advice to make that transition before stepping down in 1987, remaining as a Director of Special Programs. Anne Ironside, who had trained as a social worker and biologist before joining

*The University of British Columbia can be counted upon to provide educational leadership, and to share its expertise and resources as Canada responds to the challenges and opportunities of internationalization.*

*David Strangway*
*UBC President*
*1988*

the Women's Resources Centre as its first coordinator in 1972 (see Chapter Nine), served as Acting Director for several years while senior administrators decided on the new direction for continuing education across the university. Ironside, an inspiring advocate of life and career planning and educational access for women, attempted to persuade UBC's administration to adopt policies more supportive of the Centre, but was only partially successful. President Strangway recognized continuing education and the Centre in the 1988 UBC mission statement "Second to None," but at the same time insisted that these services would have to adopt a more business-like approach and recover the costs of their provision.

In 1989, President Strangway formed a Task Force on Continuing Education to guide the future organization of continuing education at UBC. This committee of eleven UBC faculty members (including one Centre for Continuing Education program director) and a team of external consultants reported in October 1989, with several recommendations: UBC should adopt a semi-centralized model that included an Associate Vice President to oversee all of the university's continuing education operations, while permitting the faculties to run their own continuing education programs. The Task Force noted that university continuing education was both a legal requirement and a social responsibility, not "a luxury to be dispensed with in tough times, or an ancillary service that derives its justification from its link with another more highly valued activity." In addition, thought the Task Force members, the ability to pay should not be the sole criterion when choosing a program; more profitable areas should help support others.[32]

Members of the Centre were reasonably pleased with the Task Force's recommendations.[33] Others at UBC, however, were quite unhappy with the report. The Task Force representative from the Faculty of Commerce and Business Administration provided a dissenting opinion, criticizing the report harshly and suggesting that complete decentralization of all continuing education to the faculties was the most efficient and effective approach, and one that had already been proven. During late 1989 and early 1990, the President's Office received several strongly-worded letters from Deans and Department Heads opposing the Task Force report and its recommendations.[34]

President Strangway was not easily moved. In March of 1990, he sent a brief memo to a Community Advisory Committee on Continuing Education outlining the position of the professional faculties which favoured the decentralized model.[35] The committee, which included John Friesen, was not impressed, denouncing what it saw as a professional, academic bias that completely ignored community interests or needs. They wanted to see a broad approach to continuing education that encouraged cooperation among faculties, provided room for experimentation, and represented the university as a whole. The outline of the decentralized model, the committee thought, was "an inward-looking draft document that shows more concern for academic *amour propre* than for public education."

This response seems to have confirmed President Strangway's decision to adopt the Task Force recommendations; UBC was engaged in a massive fundraising effort, and public support was very important.[36] In May, he prepared a report for Senate, intended to end "two years of turmoil" surrounding continuing education. The proposal assured Senate that academic standards for credit courses would continue to rest with Senate, and that a Senate advisory committee would play an important role in establishing standards for non-credit courses. Strangway then sent the Community Advisory Committee a copy of his Senate report; both Friesen and the committee chair responded with enthusiastic support.[37]

**Left:** Walter Uegama (L), Associate Vice President, UBC Continuing Studies (1991-1999), shares a laugh with David Strangway (R), UBC President (1987-1997), while viewing progress on construction of the new Continuing Studies Building, 1997. **Right:** Madeline Olding shares program information at the Vancouver Public Library, mid-1990s.

## UBC CONTINUING STUDIES

In 1991, UBC appointed Walter Uegama as Associate Vice President (Continuing Studies) to oversee the Centre for Continuing Education, the Office of Extra-Sessional Studies, and UBC Access Guided Independent Study (later to become Distance Education and Technology). Soon thereafter, these three units were merged into what became known as UBC Continuing Studies. This new unit was more like an academic faculty, whose Associate Vice President joined the Council of Deans. Uegama was also charged with overseeing continuing education in the faculties and providing incentives for expansion. He was well-suited for the new role, as he held both a doctorate in higher education and a Master of Business Administration. As well, he had considerable professorial experience at the University of Windsor, and administrative experience with Selkirk College and the Open Learning Agency in British Columbia. His fluency in Japanese was also useful to UBC's internationalization efforts, as he came to play important roles in exchange programs with universities and colleges in Japan. Soon, he had reorganized UBC Continuing Studies programs into five divisions that represented distinct educational markets (Academic Performance; Career and Corporate; General Public; Credit Programs; and International).

This new framework was intended to facilitate effective programming, improve student services, raise the visibility of UBC Continuing Studies, improve staff engagement and morale, and generate adequate revenue to cover program costs and staff salaries. Efficiencies would be found by centralizing some activities, and decentralizing others that required specialized programming or subject-matter knowledge found within a particular division. Competition from other universities, colleges, and private providers had intensified, making organizational efficiency and careful marketing important for success. However, Uegama also kept something of a philosophical tie with his predecessors by recognizing that the university had an important role to play in culture, citizenship, and community development. Programs would continue in these areas if there was sufficient interest, even if they provided no net profit.[38] Nonetheless, a number of program directors and instructors were unhappy with the new business-like approach sweeping UBC and other Canadian universities which, in their view, seemed to value sales of educational commodities over the provision of socially relevant educational experiences. Others found that the new structures sometimes interfered with their classroom preparation. In some program areas, however, the changes were hardly felt at all.[39]

**Left:** Spanish Coordinator Patricia Martin with students in the Buchanan D Building in the 1980s. **Right:** Instructor Dinorah Dugas with students in Spanish language class at UBC Robson Square, 2000s.

In addition to making administrative changes, Uegama expressed a renewed vision of continuing education in the context of a changing province. In his triennial report for 1990-93, Uegama argued that there was a "symbiotic relationship" between UBC and the people of British Columbia, and that continuing education was an important "link between academic research and the community" (p. iii). He cited the mandate of continuing education at UBC – "to build a broadly-based program of credit and non-credit offerings that will draw on the strengths of the University of British Columbia and match them to demand and opportunities" – and argued that the continuing education offerings of UBC were "of exceptional quality, timeliness, and scope for the province, nation, and world" (p. 1).

Uegama eloquently expressed the links between social change and people's need for lifelong learning, in his 1995 annual report:

> Our societal landscape is undergoing rapid transformation. A dichotomy of conflicting features confuses any analysis of what's happening. We see globalization but cocooning, transnational economic organizations but tightly targeted local markets composed of niches. Corporate supply and profit are unparalleled but accompanied by huge reductions in the workforce. There is the expanding wealth of a few while poverty increases globally. Clearly, the need to be informed, individually and collectively, has never been greater. (p. iii)

In more recent years, UBC Continuing Studies has identified a number of key social, economic, and technological trends that influence its educational programs and services. Key trends have included the aging of the Canadian population, growing demand for post-secondary credentials, increasing concerns regarding environmental sustainability, public health and globalization, and rising demand for education among overseas students and mature adults in the workplace.

In the context of such major changes in British Columbia, UBC Continuing Studies stated in 1996 that its mission was to link the university to the world by:

• Identifying and meeting lifelong learning needs;
• Extending the educational and intellectual leadership of UBC to the community;
• Anticipating and fulfilling social, cultural, and labour needs; and
• Acting as a model of educational innovation in the university.

During the mid-1990s, UBC Continuing Studies pursued this mission while deriving an increasing proportion of its revenues from sources other than the UBC budget. Some program areas were clearly contributors "to the overall fiscal health of UBC Continuing Studies," while others were not.[40] On the whole, however, even after paying for the full cost of overheads, new facility development, and renovations, UBC Continuing Studies was close to breaking even. These were years of significant change to both business processes and educational programming. Marketing and other aspects of the administration of educational programs became increasingly the domain of professionals

*Continuing education structures are externally oriented, engaged with professional associations and community-based organizations, attentive to regulatory frameworks...[and] responsive to changing urban (and provincial) demography.*

*Report of the External Review Committee of Continuing Studies 2007*

with specialized training. Instruction in English as a Second Language (ESL)[41] and other languages expanded significantly, online learning became increasingly important, and a large number of new certificate programs were introduced. The expanded delivery of non-degree-credit credentials reflected both an effort by UBC Continuing Studies to position itself in a distinctive niche at UBC, and increased demand among British Columbians who, like other Canadians, were finding educational credentials to be increasingly necessary to obtain good jobs. Although many program areas were maintaining themselves financially, Uegama's "five year plan" for the late 1990s relied strongly upon the success of distance education, English language courses for international students, and collaboration with industry and professional faculties to provide professional development certificate programs. Programs were designed to be market sensitive, changing with demand and circumstance.

Perhaps paradoxically, UBC Continuing Studies began focussing on residents in metro Vancouver while simultaneously addressing a more global clientele. Between 1990 and 1995, the province of British Columbia created "university colleges" in the Kamloops, Kelowna, and Fraser Valley regions, established the University of Northern British Columbia in Prince George, and expanded regional colleges to serve interior residents. UBC was better suited to respond to social and economic developments particular to the Vancouver region, such as Pacific-rim immigration and new high-tech industries. As well, UBC Continuing Studies supported social movements focussed on women, First Nations, older learners, and environmental sustainability.

Balancing the local focus was more attention to global demand for education. Writers in *The Economist* recognized Vancouver by 1995 as an international city, while UBC itself was welcoming international students, international research cooperation, and international investment as never before, especially from Asia-Pacific countries.[42] UBC was not alone: international education was becoming important to a number of educational institutions in many countries. UBC Continuing Studies courses in languages and cultural understanding escalated in number and enrolment during the early 1990s, and the activities of the English Language Institute grew.[43] At the same time, new developments in computer and communications technology played a huge role in expanding distance education. In 1995, UBC hired Tony Bates, a renowned pioneer in distance education techniques, as Director of the new Division of Distance Education and Technology.[44] CD-ROM and then the Internet became key new media in providing distance education across the province and beyond.

In April of 1997, an external review team found UBC Continuing Studies to be doing well overall. The team did, however, make several recommendations to improve administrative organization and information systems, communications with campus partners, self-assessment, and institutional funding. The reviewers felt that a re-introduction of a small budget from the university might improve the morale of some staff and restore the fine

*Universities help shape our civil society by emphasizing the importance of democratic rights and freedoms, and by educating global citizens who are politically, culturally, and socially aware. Universities also provide solutions through research, discovering knowledge and creating new technologies that can bring hope to millions who may be suffering from poverty, malnutrition, or disease.*

*Martha Piper*
*UBC President*
*2002*

arts, science, and culture courses that had recently been lost.[45] In 1999, UBC transferred responsibility for extra-sessional degree-credit programs away from UBC Continuing Studies; the loss of revenue from this reorganization made budgetary support from central administration even more crucial for UBC Continuing Studies. In 2003, the Distance Education and Technology unit gained its independence as faculties developed their own capacity to use new technologies. Of course, UBC Continuing Studies continued to make use of the Internet for online instruction in many of its non-credit programs, using a variety of software to provide innovative and responsive curricula.

In 1997, Martha Piper replaced David Strangway as president, and introduced a new strategic plan – *Trek 2000* – the following year. UBC Continuing Studies adjusted its organization and programs to fit the five "pillars" outlined in this new plan: People, Learning, Research, Community, and Internationalization. During Piper's nine-year presidency, UBC expanded in several ways: the number of students, faculty, and staff grew; new "high tech" classroom space was added, and older buildings were renovated; UBC researchers acquired substantial funding for research of international significance; the university opened a new centre in downtown Vancouver; and international engagement with students and research partners increased. The "entrepreneurial" policies established in the early 1990s continued unabated, partly due to a provincial funding freeze of university budgets in 1994 followed by sizable reductions of federal transfer

**Top:** Vancouver in the 1990s. *Photo: Yolande Morin.* **Bottom:** Martha Piper, UBC President (1997-2006). *UBCA 44.1/2133*

payments to support health and education, and a freeze of student tuition for several years. In these circumstances, UBC's administration seemed particularly adept in the "business" of higher education despite the difficulties caused by student crowding and cuts to services. While some members of the UBC community remained critical of the business ethos and considered UBC to be at its limits of growth, campus development (including controversial market housing projects) proceeded at a fast pace.[46]

*Trek 2000* prompted a minor re-organization of UBC Continuing Studies, and the re-naming of some program areas. Perhaps most significantly, however, the President's Office re-established a small budget for UBC Continuing Studies in 1999 to assist with programming in areas such as public affairs, arts and humanities, and the Women's Resources Centre, reflecting President Piper's commitment to community engagement.[47] Jane Hutton, Director of the Career, Corporate, and Community Division for many years, was a strong advocate for this funding, which was essential after the loss of revenue from Extra-Sessional Studies. After a short time serving in an acting capacity while Walter Uegama was on leave, Hutton became the Associate Vice President (Continuing Studies). A graduate of UBC (Psychology and Library Science), Hutton had

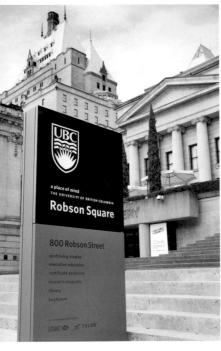

**Top left:** Jane Hutton, Associate Vice President, Continuing Studies (2000-2007). **Bottom left and right:** UBC Robson Square, downtown facility hosting programs since 2001.

provided forward-looking leadership in computer programs during the 1980s, and strong divisional leadership during the 1990s, which earned her praise from external reviewers. When she took over as Associate Vice President, UBC Continuing Studies was suffering from the collapse of speculative Internet companies (the "dot-com bust") that was stifling demand for previously well-attended applied technology programs, an unexpected downturn that had serious repercussions. But there were positive developments as well. Because of *Trek 2000's* emphasis on community, UBC Continuing Studies finally found a new home in downtown Vancouver. Hutton made a persuasive business case to UBC administrators: rental of various downtown spaces for classrooms and the Women's Resources Centre was expensive, and provided sub-optimal exposure for the university. Hutton played a large role in finding an appropriate and substantial off-campus location, and in 2001, UBC Robson Square opened with space for UBC Continuing Studies in the heart of downtown Vancouver.

Internationalization, another focus of *Trek 2000,* was addressed through courses and programs involving languages, ESL, and intercultural communication, which remained strong program areas in the new millennium. The continuation of international travel programs, often oriented toward language learning, also furthered the university's internationalization objectives. However, enrolment was subject to intense competition and an unpredictable international market. For example, international student enrolment in ESL programs dropped suddenly in 2003 after the outbreak of severe acute respiratory syndrome (SARS).

Following custom, the University instituted an external review of UBC Continuing Studies before Jane Hutton left her position. The reviewers had much to praise: excellent, dynamic leadership; generally collegial working relationships among peers, academic units, and community groups; high-quality and diverse programming; an ethos of cooperation; and sincere community and civic-minded outreach. But there were a few weaknesses as well. The student information system was inadequate, and the various units within UBC Continuing Studies were seen as a little too independent, with administration too decentralized. UBC Continuing Studies relied on a few programming areas for the bulk of its revenue, leaving it vulnerable should these areas falter. There were also concerns about the institutional arrangements under which UBC Continuing Studies operated. Unlike other institutions, UBC seemed to the reviewers to require excessive amounts of consultation with faculties, which had the power to commandeer successful UBC Continuing Studies programs. As well, UBC Continuing Studies was barred from programming in certain fields. The resolution of these problems, the reviewers noted, would enhance an excellent operation.[48]

*Ensuring that our great university is well connected with our many communities is at the core of continuing education belief and practice.*

*Open Minds: Continuing Education in Review 2005*

Judith Plessis, another well-respected UBC Continuing Studies program director, succeeded Hutton in 2007. A long-time instructor and program leader, Plessis was a scholar in modern languages, literature, and film, having studied in France (Université de Nantes) and the University of British Columbia, where she earned a doctorate in comparative literature and became a faculty associate with the UBC Centre for Women's and Gender Studies. For twenty-five years Plessis had provided teaching and administrative leadership in UBC Continuing Studies language programs, particularly French, and she took office at a time of stability for UBC Continuing Studies. Plessis oversaw continued growth and innovation in her first years as Executive Director, UBC Continuing Studies.

In 2009, three years after Stephen Toope replaced Martha Piper as president, UBC presented a new strategic plan, *Place and Promise: The UBC Plan*. It outlined nine commitments: student learning, research excellence, community engagement, Aboriginal engagement, alumni engagement, intercultural understanding, international engagement, outstanding work environment, and sustainability. UBC Continuing Studies was well-aligned with this strategic plan, having recently adopted a new mission statement:

> UBC Continuing Studies is an academic unit that inspires curiosity, develops ingenuity, stimulates dialogue and facilitates change among lifelong learners locally and internationally. We anticipate and respond to emerging learner needs and broaden access to UBC by offering innovative educational programs that advance our students' careers, enrich their lives and inform their role in a civil and sustainable society.

UBC and the province were changing, and UBC Continuing Studies looked for opportunities to participate in those changes. UBC Continuing Studies enjoyed significant accomplishments in providing meaningful educational experiences to many people. Staff members won awards for courses, certificates, and marketing initiatives; UBC Continuing Studies hosted the 2009 Canadian Association for University Continuing Education conference, with influential speakers like former Vancouver Mayor and provincial Premier Michael Harcourt. It had recovered from economic downturns, changes in government priorities, and international crises. It even survived disruptions related to the Winter Olympics held in Vancouver in 2010, for which it gave up half its programming space in UBC Robson Square for use as the international media centre.

The next three chapters describe the major continuing education programs delivered by the Centre for Continuing Education and UBC Continuing Studies in the last forty years, showing how they responded to new developments in the economy, technology, arts, recreation, and current affairs, while adhering to UBC's longstanding commitment to support people's economic, personal, and political lives.

Professor Stephen Toope, UBC President (2006-present). *Photo: Martin Dee*

UBC Continuing Studies staff photos: **Top left:** Judith Plessis and Mary Holmes. **Middle far left:** Beth Hawkes. **Middle left:** Mackie Chase. **Bottom left:** Pauline Gensick, Ines Lin, Marie Esnault, Dorie Gray. **Top right:** Lisa Chau, Mike Weiss, Linda Fung. **Middle right:** Peter Moroney and William Koty. **Bottom middle:** Jo Ledingham and Jane Hutton. **Bottom right:** Nichola Hall.

In her spare time, she's the lead singer of a 15-piece big band called Paper Moon, but by day Rochelle Grayson has her fingers on the pulse of the rapidly changing social media landscape.

*Since 2008, Rochelle has been nominated as one of Canada's Top 100 Most Powerful Women by the Women's Executive Network and named one of Business in Vancouver's Top Forty under 40. With an MBA in Finance and Business Policy, Rochelle brings her knowledge and real-world experience to the courses she teaches in the UBC Continuing Studies Award of Achievement in Social Media program. "Students are tested to think through why and how social media can benefit their business or organizational goals. Most importantly, they learn how to find the answers to the fast-changing questions that are commonplace in business today. I also hope to provide them with realistic expectations of what can be achieved through social media."*

*Chapter Seven*

# Educating adults for the knowledge economy

Just as Extension had done from the 1930s to the 1960s, the Centre for Continuing Education and UBC Continuing Studies have devoted considerable attention to helping people make a productive and enjoyable living. However, the nature of professional education in recent decades has differed from that which took place during the Extension era, due to social, technological, and institutional change. As the provincial economy diversified, and as faculties took on direct responsibility for continuing education work in a number of well-established professions, the Centre for Continuing Education and UBC Continuing Studies adapted by providing educational programming in areas of emerging economic importance: information technologies; intercultural communication; niche occupations in industries ranging from film and television to health and human services; and specialized aspects of business management, such as project management, business analysis, and the integration of new technologies in marketing. In recent years, professional programming has increasingly focussed on programs of study leading to certificates – a development reflecting the growing importance of educational credentials in the labour market.

## AGRICULTURE, FORESTRY, AND FISHERIES

In the early 1970s, the Centre for Continuing Education operated extension programs in primary industries. In agriculture, UBC continued to provide education to those directly involved in food production. The province's agricultural output was on the rise, particularly in poultry, greenhouse production, and specialty crops. Family farms, still the dominant form of ownership, became increasingly mechanized and profitable, with agricultural revenues climbing from $209 million in 1971 to $1.8 billion in 1998.[1] The Centre for Continuing Education and the Faculty of Agricultural Sciences delivered short courses – most often with a focus on cattle, poultry, pigs, dairying, bee-keeping, and greenhouse production – throughout the 1970s. Two annual conferences that had been established by Extension were maintained during the 1970s. The "Stockmen's Conference," operated in collaboration with the BC Cattlemen's Association and the provincial Ministry of Agriculture, was held for the nineteenth consecutive year in 1979. The "Roadside Development

Conference," which became the "Highway Environment Conference" in the early 1970s, was held for the twelfth and final time in 1975.

Federal funding for UBC extension work with fishermen was discontinued in the early 1970s, and the Centre for Continuing Education subsequently focussed its fisheries education program on topics of interest to the general public in Vancouver. After 1972, the fisheries program became primarily a series of lectures held at the Vancouver Public Aquarium. Popular topics included "Ocean Life of British Columbia" and "Aquatic Mammals."

In forestry, the Centre for Continuing Education collaborated with the Association of Professional Foresters to provide professional development courses in areas ranging from ecology and environmental management to log transportation and the economics of forest products. In the late 1970s and early 1980s, the Centre for Continuing Education also offered a Diploma in Administration for Foresters. During this period, the scope of the work of the Centre for Continuing Education with people engaged in primary industries was extensive: between 1971 and 1976, an average of nearly eight hundred participants each year took part in the Centre's agricultural programming. The average number of participants in fisheries and forestry programs was just under three hundred, and just over 325, respectively.

In addition to providing continuing professional education programs in primary industries, the Centre for Continuing Education delivered an increasing number of evening courses and lecture series for members of the general public in Vancouver. Courses such as "Gardening for Apartment Dwellers," "Care of Houseplants," and "Gardening through the Seasons" were consistently popular in the 1970s, as were courses on foods and nutrition. Gardening and food courses for the general public attracted an average of over five hundred participants each year in the first half of the 1970s.

By 1980, the Faculty of Agricultural Sciences and the Faculty of Forestry had taken responsibility for the continuing education of professionals in their respective fields. The faculties continued to collaborate with the Centre for Continuing Education, but the Centre's own programming relating to the primary industries shifted to education for the general public. However, in the late 1990s, UBC Continuing Studies collaborated with Agricultural Sciences once again to provide a Certificate in Turfgrass Management, and with UBC's Institute for Resources, Environment, and Sustainability to provide a Certificate in Watershed Management. UBC Continuing Studies also administered a Certificate in Garden Design, which involved the UBC Botanical Garden, and a Certificate in Management of Aquaculture Systems in collaboration with Malaspina University College in Nanaimo.

*With the growth of professional schools and the increased demand for general and specialist education, the University has done everything it could to respond to the needs of professional organizations and the expressed needs of the public at large. I think it is safe to say that there is scarcely a single faculty, school or department in the University that is not somehow involved in general and specialist continuing education for our citizens.*

*Douglas Kenny*
*UBC President*
*1979*

## EDUCATION, LAW, AND SOCIAL WORK

The largest continuing professional education programs of the Centre for Continuing Education in the 1970s were undertaken in collaboration with the Faculty of Education, the Faculty of Law, and the School of Social Work. The scope of these programs was extensive, with an average of over 5,600 professionals enrolling in courses and conferences each year. Education dominated, accounting for about 60 percent of enrolments, followed by law, which accounted for about 33 percent. Until 1979, the Faculty of Education and the Centre for Continuing Education continued to deliver an "Education–Extension Program" to serve the continuing professional education needs of teachers, educational administrators, and others working in school systems, community colleges, and early childhood education settings. Certification for the province's elementary teachers had only recently required a university education, and the 1970s was a time of pedagogical and organizational experimentation in the public schools – creating a high demand for continuing education. The Education–Extension Program included short courses, evening classes, special lectures, and conferences, and emphasized fields such as vocational education, early childhood education, and education for children with special needs. The program helped teachers to develop knowledge and skills in various components of the K-12 curriculum: English, social studies, science, mathematics, art, languages, and physical education. It also offered professional development opportunities for school librarians, guidance counsellors, and teachers or specialists wishing to develop expertise in educational media, educational psychology, or the evaluation of learning. The Instructor's Diploma (formerly the Vocational Instructor's Certificate) and Certificate in Early Childhood Education, which had funding from the province, enrolled particularly large numbers of students; in 1976 there were 466 and 275 candidates actively pursuing these two credentials, respectively.

The Centre for Continuing Education helped to organize travel study programs for educators, which sometimes carried academic credit. The academic merit of the first degree-credit trip, to Britain in 1970, was met with suspicion by various advisory councils, but while administrators were deliberating on the appropriateness of the venture, the trip proceeded. The second trip, guided by Neville Scarfe, the Dean of Education, had more institutional support. Subsequent trips included a tour of English and Scandinavian facilities for people with physical and mental disabilities, at a time of protest against residential institutions for these populations and a rising interest in de-institutionalization and educational mainstreaming. A series of trips to examine schools and early childhood education in the Soviet Union and the Ukraine began at the end of the decade.[2]

In 1979, UBC's Faculty of Education assumed direct responsibility for continuing professional education for practicing teachers and educational administrators, including the various diploma programs. The Centre for Continuing Education continued to offer evening courses of interest to many teachers, as well as the Certificate in Early Childhood

Education and the Instructor's Diploma; the former was phased-out beginning in 1982 and the latter a few years later when the province cut its funding.[3]

In addition to its work with school teachers and educational administrators, the Centre for Continuing Education worked with UBC faculty members and community-based organizations having educational functions. Between 1976 and the early 1980s, the Centre helped the UBC School of Librarianship to offer two or three workshops or conferences each year for professional librarians. In the mid-1980s, a general interest course on museum management led to a special project with Vancouver's police department to help them establish their own museum.[4] Beginning in 1987, the Centre cooperated with the UBC Faculty Association and the President's Office to establish "Teaching and Academic Growth" – an educational service to help faculty develop stronger instructional skills.[5]

In the 1970s, the Faculty of Law collaborated with the Centre for Continuing Education to offer continuing legal education to lawyers and others with an interest in the legal profession. Part of this development can be attributed to the social movements of the 1960s, which sought greater public participation in the legal system, and to the shift of UBC's Faculty of Law away from an emphasis on commercial law.[6] UBC provided short courses in many aspects of legal practice, from courtroom proceedings and office management, to the review of legislation. Continuing legal education included courses in areas such as criminal law, civil law, business law, contracts, taxation, family law, and real estate. From the outset, the Law Society of British Columbia and the provincial chapter of the Canadian Bar Association actively collaborated with the Centre. In 1977, these organizations, along with the new Faculty of Law at the University of Victoria, formed the Continuing Legal Education (CLE) Society of British Columbia. For two years the CLE Society was head-quartered within UBC's Centre for Continuing Education, and administered by staff of the

FAMILY LAW CONFERENCE

education of young children
new directions and ideas

Centre. The CLE Society became independent in 1979, and the Centre's role in continuing legal education declined over time. The Certificate Program in Criminology, which largely enrolled police officers, was developed into a set of correspondence courses and then discontinued in the mid-1980s, due to low enrolment and funding cuts.[7]

In collaboration with the School of Social Work, the Centre for Continuing Education engaged in two basic forms of programming in the early 1970s. First, the Centre provided opportunities for practicing social workers without a professional degree to achieve professional recognition under the "Registered Social Workers Act" of British Columbia. Social services were expanding as a number of health services moved from institutional to community settings amidst public demands for accountability. The "Social Work Registration Program" comprised three courses: The Social Service System, Human Behaviour and Social Environment, and Basic Social Work Methods. Second, the Centre delivered numerous workshops and evening courses relating to human relations, some of which were influenced by the rise of humanistic psychology. Such courses ranged from those of interest primarily to social workers (crisis intervention) to those of interest to professionals in a wide range of organizational settings (intercultural communications, working with groups, and aging). In 1974, the School of Social Work assumed direct responsibility for the continuing professional education of social workers, but the Centre continued to offer courses into the 1980s on a range of topics from art therapy and therapeutic story-telling to sexual abuse and mental illness counselling.[8]

After 1974, the work of the Centre for Continuing Education in the field of human relations took two main forms. The Centre continued to offer a range of general interest courses in the social sciences and humanities which helped professionals and members of the general public to understand themselves and others better (see Chapter Eight). Additionally, the Centre established new programs for professionals working with older adults. This work began with a major project in "Housing for Older People" funded by the Central Mortgage and Housing Corporation. From this starting point, the Centre for Continuing Education began providing gerontology courses for a range of professionals working in settings relating to health, social services, recreation, education, religion, and housing. By the 1980s, work in this area had evolved again when the Centre introduced educational programming for seniors themselves, and courses and services on retirement planning (see Chapter Nine).

*Exploring Creativity with Young Children (1974)*

*This course is designed for kindergarten and preschool teachers and parents who are interested in pulling together past art experiences and looking at them from a creative point of view.*

## ENGINEERING, ARCHITECTURE, AND COMMUNITY AND REGIONAL PLANNING

Although several UBC professional faculties and schools began operating independent continuing education units in the 1970s, the Faculty of Applied Science, the School of Architecture, and the School of Community and Regional Planning worked closely with the Centre for Continuing Education until 1990. Continuing professional education programs for engineers and community planners had been established in the 1950s and 1960s, and the Centre for Continuing Education continued to employ a professional engineer as a program director until 1990. In the early 1970s, nearly 1,500 people per year participated in courses and conferences organized by the Centre for Continuing Education in the fields of engineering, architecture, and planning. Continuing education for engineers generally took the form of seminars and conferences, which typically addressed particular domains of engineering (chemical, civil, or mechanical engineering), specific sectors employing engineers (mining, construction, manufacturing, and environmental work), and the development of general skills (statistical analysis, computing, and business management). In 1978, the Centre provided support for the 86th Annual Conference of the American Society for Engineering Education held at UBC, the third time it was held in Canada.[9]

*Contract Law for Engineers (1974)*

*The purpose of this two-day seminar is to familiarize the participants with some of the more fundamental areas of commercial law which are relevant to their professional activities.*

In addition, the Centre continued to administer the Diploma in Administration for Engineers that had been established by the Faculty of Applied Science and Extension in 1968. The diploma program included courses in business management, project management, statistics, computers, report writing, and contract law. In the latter 1970s, this diploma program was expanded, through collaboration with engineering schools at the universities of Alberta, Calgary, and Regina, and by the addition of a parallel Diploma in Administration for Foresters.

Throughout the 1960s, Extension had helped organize an annual "Short Course in Community Planning" for elected municipal officials, administrators from municipal and regional governments, and professional urban or regional planners. In the 1970s, the Centre for Continuing Education collaborated with the School of Community and Regional Planning, and the Planning Institute of British Columbia, to deliver numerous evening courses and workshops of interest to these audiences. The provincial government in 1977 was considering a number of "megaprojects" such as coal mining and hydro development in the province's north-east, and thought that local municipalities were not prepared; the Centre was looked upon favourably to assist.[10] These continuing professional education events focussed on both rural and urban settings, and included topics relating to particular systems (transportation, land use, and housing), processes (budgeting, research, and management), and places (specific communities and regions).

Beginning in 1972, the Centre for Continuing Education worked with the UBC School of Architecture and the Architectural Institute of British Columbia to offer professional development workshops and courses for architects. These events covered technical aspects of architectural practice and the management of architectural firms.

During the 1980s, enrolment in continuing professional education programs for engineers, architects, and community and regional planners declined substantially. The

# Certificate in Site Planning

The University of British Columbia
School of Community and Regional Planning
and
Planning Programs, Centre for Continuing Education

CONTINUING EDUCATION IN
**COMMUNITY AND REGIONAL PLANNING**
Autumn 1972 Programs

prolonged economic recession in the mid-1980s reduced demand from these audiences, and financial constraint at UBC led the Centre for Continuing Education to reduce levels of staffing dedicated to them. In the context of challenging economic conditions, continuing professional education in these fields shifted to short courses with direct economic return on investment, and to the provision of programs that led to credentials for those completing them. For example, UBC developed a "Certified Professional" program for architects, structural engineers, and building inspectors working with the City of Vancouver; UBC also offered a "Certificate in Site Planning" for urban and regional planners. By 1990, full responsibility for continuing professional education in engineering, architecture, and planning had been transferred from the Centre for Continuing Education to the relevant faculty and schools.

## CONTINUING PROFESSIONAL EDUCATION AFTER DECENTRALIZATION AT UBC

When the Centre for Continuing Education was established in 1970, professional faculties were encouraged to establish divisions of continuing professional education, and the provision of such education gradually became more decentralized. By the end of the 1970s, continuing professional education units had been formed in the health sciences, business, education, social work, agriculture, and forestry. The Faculty of Law undertook its continuing professional education work primarily through the Continuing Legal Education Society of British Columbia. Other faculties and schools, such as those serving professionals in the fields of engineering, architecture, home economics, librarianship, and community planning, continued to deliver continuing professional education programs through the Centre for Continuing Education through the 1980s.

By the early 1980s, the scope of continuing professional education provided by faculties and schools at UBC had grown to an average of about thirty-thousand enrolments per year in total, primarily in the health sciences and business, but also in education, law, agriculture, forestry, and social work. Increasingly, the Centre for Continuing Education and subsequently UBC Continuing Studies focussed their continuing professional education programs on interdisciplinary areas not served by UBC faculties. Some of these programs were developed and delivered in collaboration with other UBC faculties and schools, and some were undertaken independently or in conjunction with external professional associations.

## COMPUTER SCIENCE AND INFORMATION TECHNOLOGIES

Although Extension had offered courses dealing with computers in the early 1960s, the development of the relatively affordable microcomputer in the mid-1970s brought increased educational interest in the new technology. In 1979, Jane Hutton established a distinct programming area in the Centre for Continuing Education to deliver computer science courses, seminars, and lectures. The timing was prescient: 1979 was the year that the first truly successful word-processing program (WordStar) and the first business-friendly spreadsheet program (VisiCalc) were released, moving the microcomputer from hobby interest to business tool. IBM was about to release its own microcomputer,

**Top left:** Computer class for seniors, 1980s. **Bottom left:** Calendar of computing courses, 1980. **Bottom right:** Jane Hutton at the computer, with colleague Vicki Ayerbe, mid-1980s.

Managing Change
Computing for
the New Decade

Winter/Spring 1980
UBC Centre for Continuing Education

which would catapult the personal computer into a central role in the business world. In its autumn 1979 program guide, the Centre for Continuing Education introduced its new Computer Science program by noting that:

> *The computer is a tool; a vehicle for moving facts and ideas. It allows us to make rapid connections among disparate sets of data, to access data from remote places, and to review enormous quantities of information in a short period of time. The technological breakthroughs and growth of the computer industry have had a profound influence on our home life, work environment, and the larger society in which we live. This fall, the Centre for Continuing Education will begin presenting a series of programs directed toward the continuing professional education of computer users and administrators. The series will also offer general level education for people interested in computing for business and hobby. (p. 16)*

The Centre offered computer programming courses in FORTRAN, PASCAL, and COBOL, as well as technical courses in word processing, computer graphics, and data networks. Further, it introduced a course entitled "De-Mystifying the Computer" for members of the general public. Hutton recruited bright young instructors with business experience who were at the forefront of using the new tools.

In the early 1980s, most courses were either of a general, introductory nature ("Computers Explained" and "Acquiring Keyboard Skills and Computer Confidence") or related to programming in languages such as BASIC, PASCAL, or C. Before long, specialized courses in graphics and music were also offered. Courses attracted a range of ages and interests, from complete beginners motivated by curiosity or fear, to early adopters of technology who were already computer-savvy. For the early years, lab courses were taught in the basement of the Computer Science Building, then expanded three-fold into a portable facility before moving to a specially designed and professional space in the old Bookstore.[11] Through the 1980s, the Centre for Continuing Education broadened its educational programming in computer sciences, hosting periodic conferences for medical practitioners, lawyers, and other professionals who required computer skills. In 1983, as technology developed, the Centre obtained a microcomputer laboratory (twenty-five donated Victor 9000s) and expanded its delivery of hands-on workshops and courses.

Hutton was less interested in computers per se than she was in information management, including the potential of the new digital information to influence the fine arts. In 1983, she and colleagues at the Centre for Continuing Education, encouraged by Director Jindra Kulich, staged the first International Conference on the Digital Arts (Digicon '83), hosting some four hundred professional artists and visitors from as far away as Japan and South Africa. Among the thirty eminent speakers were the producers of the movie *Tron*, one of the first films from a major studio to use extensive computer graphics; Robert Moog, the inventor of the Moog synthesizer; musician and music producer Todd Rundgren; David Em, one of the first digital "painters"; jazz musician Herbie Hancock; and Ed Emshwiller, Dean of the School of Film and Video at the California Institute of the Arts and bearded guru of computer animation. Dance and choreography presentations

*Programming in PASCAL (1980)*

*PASCAL is rapidly gaining wide acceptance as a tool for the development of sophisticated, highly reliable production software in the industrial, commercial, engineering and scientific communities. The entire language will be presented, as well as several common extensions. The emphasis will be on the application of PASCAL to various diverse problem areas, concentrating on how PASCAL's data structures and control structures lend themselves to the problem at hand.*

were held in Vancouver's Queen Elizabeth Theatre, as was the first ever concert with three musicians in three continents, linked via satellite. Despite some technical problems staging the concerts, the conference was an exciting forum in a new field of creativity. In 1985, the Centre staged a follow-up, Digicon '85, in partnership with the International Computer Arts Society (ICAS), which was equally successful – even making money, which was donated for fine arts scholarships.[12]

Programming in computer science and information technologies expanded dramatically during the late 1980s and into the 1990s as the technology became less expensive, faster, more powerful, and more user-friendly through developments like graphical user interfaces, email, and the World Wide Web. As the commercial centre of British Columbia, metro Vancouver had established itself by 1993 as an important location for high-tech industry. Large businesses located in the region had long used computers, but now small and medium-sized ones did as well; many jobs began to require basic computer familiarity, while others required extensive computer skills.[13] Not surprisingly, enrolment rose quickly in both credit courses in computer science and non-credit courses offered by UBC Continuing Studies. Home and recreational users also took a greater interest in the new high-tech developments, as indicated by a wave of technological newcomers attending courses in the early 1990s.[14]

During this time UBC Continuing Studies continued to provide leadership in emerging information technology by hosting new and innovative conferences, introducing visionary thinkers to the broader high-tech community. The MULTICOMM Conference in 1993, which attracted over two hundred participants, focussed on the emergence of multimedia CD-ROM technology and featured computer legend Ted Nelson, who coined the terms hypertext and hypermedia in the 1960s and conceptualized Project Xanadu, a worldwide hypertext network that predated the World Wide Web by some twenty years. The following year, MULTICOMM '94 attracted over three hundred participants and hosted guest speaker Nicholas Negroponti, co-founder of the MIT Media Lab and author of *Being Digital*.

Another successful and innovative conference hosted by UBC Continuing Studies in 1994 was the Writers' Retreat on Interactive Technology and Equipment (WRITE) offered in partnership with the then Emily Carr College of Art and Design. Held less than a year after the release of Mosaic, the first popular web browser, WRITE focussed on the emerging electronic publishing industry and broke new ground by forefronting the link between the Internet and content. Featuring Internet pioneer Howard Rheingold, WRITE '94 attracted nearly three hundred delegates from across North America and as far away as Europe, providing a showcase for established and up-and-coming artist-technologists. WRITE '95 brought additional leading-edge artists and technologists to Vancouver, including celebrated author Ray Bradbury, technology forecaster and director of The Institute for the Future, Paul Saffo, award-winning computer animator, Robert Abel, and numerous leading-edge Internet content developers.

*UBC Certificate in Multimedia Studies (1999)*

*The UBC Certificate in Multimedia Studies is for learners who are interested in developing, publishing or presenting digital media. This includes those working in the corporate sector, publishing, entertainment, the arts, the social service sector, health care, design, technical services, and the small business sector.*

The MULTICOMM and WRITE conferences reinforced the innovative leadership of UBC Continuing Studies in high-tech education and sparked numerous successful technology programs, including the Certificate in Multimedia Studies, Certificate in Internet Publishing, Certificate in Internet Systems Administration, and the Certificate in Internet Marketing. UBC Continuing Studies also launched the first web-based online course in Canada in the spring of 1995 with "Mastering Cyberspace: A Guide to the World Wide Web." The course integrated key Internet technologies such as web-based multimedia content, threaded online discussions, student-to-student and student-to-instructor email, and online interactive quizzes, all of which were to become standard pedagogy in e-learning. The course also proved the viability of delivering online courses to a worldwide audience with participants from as far away as Australia and Egypt.

Owing primarily to the popularity of Internet courses, and to serve students better, UBC Continuing Studies began delivering computer courses in downtown Vancouver at the newly established Roundhouse Community Centre located on the former Expo '86 lands on False Creek. In 1997, the two formed a partnership to manage a multimedia lab, which could be used to deliver hands-on computer training to twenty students at a time. UBC Continuing Studies provided computer hardware and software in exchange for use of the space. During the day and weekends the Roundhouse Community Centre hosted public programs, and on weekday evenings UBC Continuing Studies offered courses. The arrangement lasted until the establishment of the UBC Robson Square campus in 2001 in the heart of downtown Vancouver, at which time most information technology courses moved to the new location.

In the 1980s and early 1990s, the number and range of computer science courses offered by the Centre for Continuing Education increased substantially. In 1994, 119 course

**Left and centre:** Brochures for computer-related programs, 1990s. **Right:** An earlier program in computing, 1964.

sections were offered in the autumn semester, in areas ranging from word processing and spreadsheets to graphics, multimedia, and the Internet. Enrolment in these courses came to be significant. In 1995, UBC Continuing Studies reported that 4,353 students registered in its public computer science programs. The "high-tech bubble" of the late 1990s swelled course enrolment even more, while its collapse a few years later resulted in much lower enrolments and unit downsizing at UBC Continuing Studies.[15] Only 3,557 students enrolled in a more streamlined number of courses in 2006.

**Right:** Keeping up with computer applications – a mainstay of the past decade.

**TABLE 7.1:** UBC Continuing Studies selected IT programs, 1999-2009.

## 1999: "COMPUTERS AND TECHNOLOGY PROGRAMS"

Mastering Software Skills

Communications

Multimedia Studies

The Internet

Information Systems

## 2004: "HIGH TECH CAREERS"

Essential Software Skills

Design and Authoring

Internet and Multimedia

Databases

Systems and Networks

Security

Programming

Software Engineering

Industry Certifications

## 2009: "BUSINESS AND TECHNOLOGY MANAGEMENT"

Business Analysis

Multimedia and Web Design

Web Analytics

Web Intelligence

Network Administration and Security

Web Programming

Software Engineering

Industry Certifications

Technology Support

Social Media

UBC Continuing Studies offered programs that explored the social and economic impacts of computers in people's lives. For example, the three-part series *Living Online: Connections to the Future* opened up dialogue between technology experts, visionaries, and the general public to explore the impact of new technologies on how people worked and lived. Such events, which blended professional content with social issues and political consequences, provided an example of engaged and interdisciplinary programming.

In the late 1990s and early 2000s, UBC Continuing Studies increasingly emphasized programs relating to applied uses of information technology, rather than introductory courses (see Table 7.1 on p. 144). At the same time, the target audience shifted toward young, early career professionals and those interested in such new specializations as computer gaming, web design, and movie special effects, all thriving new industries in the Vancouver area.

In addition to stand-alone courses, UBC Continuing Studies developed and delivered numerous information technology certificate programs. The first was the Certificate in Multimedia Studies, established in 1995. By 1999, UBC Continuing Studies offered seven different programs of study leading to a certificate in the information technology field. UBC Continuing Studies offered many of these programs and courses in cooperation with UBC's Department of Computer Science, the Sauder School of Business (Faculty of Commerce and Business Administration), the Faculty of Applied Science, and the British Columbia Institute of Technology. Several of these programs won awards in the 1990s and the early 2000s for innovation and high quality, and most by this time were offered at the new UBC Robson Square location.[16]

## INTERCULTURAL COMMUNICATION AND INTERNATIONAL DEVELOPMENT

Just as British Columbia's economy and culture have become more dependent upon information technologies in recent decades, so too have they become more dependent upon the movement of people, ideas, and goods across international boundaries. In response to the globalization of economic and cultural life, UBC Continuing Studies developed important programs for people wishing to develop their knowledge and skills in communicating and doing business across cultures.

When UBC's new Asian Studies building opened in 1981, Premier Bill Bennett noted both the cultural and commercial value of the university's trans-Pacific interest.[17] In 1982, as part of a larger Canada/China Language and Cultural Program, the Canadian International Development Agency (CIDA) established five centres in universities across Canada to support technology exchanges between Canadian and Chinese professionals in a wide range of sectors. The Centre for Continuing Education was identified as the place on

*Introduction to Web Analytics (2010)*

*Successful organizations are leveraging the power of web analytics to realize the full potential of their websites, as well as to develop and maintain deeper client relationships that create measurable value to their business. In this course you are exposed to the key concepts, techniques and practices of web analytics.*

the UBC campus to host this project and CIDA provided funds to establish the "Pacific Region Orientation Centre" (PaROC). PaROC's mandate was to provide on-arrival and pre-departure orientation, as well as preparation and support for Chinese and Canadian experts participating in shared technology transfer projects and educational exchanges. PaROC focussed much of its work on communication strategies and cultural training for Chinese professionals and scholars coming to Canada to study or work under the auspices of CIDA. PaROC operated under the leadership of Helen Vanwel, John Redmond, and later, Mackie Chase, for the twelve years of the bilateral project.

In 1993, the CIDA project was completed and the Canadian orientation centres closed. However, PaROC had been so active and connected with so many individuals and organizations in BC, Canada, and China, that the director, Mackie Chase, and her colleagues did not wish to lose that knowledge base for UBC with the loss of federal funding. At that time, UBC and British Columbia were establishing stronger and more numerous cultural, academic, and economic ties in Asia, and UBC Continuing Studies took the risk of establishing the "Intercultural Training and Resource Centre" (ITRC) to provide programs and services to broader audiences than had been served by PaROC. With a one-year "start-up" budget from UBC Continuing Studies to cover the costs of the director and one staff member, the ITRC re-engaged with faculties, international corporations, the British Columbia Council for International Education, the Canadian Bureau for International Education, and foreign governments. After a year of small contracts and modest returns, the ITRC accepted an unexpected request from Executive Programmes in the Faculty of Commerce to provide academic preparation, business culture, and language programs for a group of visiting Korean executives. The executives had originally planned to take communication courses in Hawaii, but their organizer neglected to obtain study visas and the cohort was re-routed to Vancouver and UBC. The success of this program helped to assure the ITRC's future.[18]

The ITRC provided a range of intercultural training programs both independently and in partnership with other UBC faculties, including the Sauder School of Business, Faculties of Applied Science, Arts, Education, Forestry, Law and Medicine, and the School of Community and Regional Planning. The range of programs for undergraduate students, graduate students, faculty, and corporate and government groups included executive business courses; workshops on intercultural communication; briefings for Canadians departing for international work, and for people from various Asian countries arriving for work in Canada; and professional development seminars for intercultural and international educators, including international graduate students working as Teaching Assistants and some new international and visiting faculty at UBC. The International Teaching Assistant (ITA) course, after its inception in 1987, provided instructional skills training for international graduate students across all faculties at UBC. This program supported them to adjust effectively to the Canadian academic context and student expectations of effective instruction. The program has also prepared participants for delivery of

professional seminars and presentations in a North American context. Initially supported by CIDA, this program was funded by the UBC Teaching and Learning Enhancement Fund until 2011 for three to four classes of graduate students each semester.

In its 1995 annual report, UBC Continuing Studies stated that ITRC programs "focus on the skills needed by professionals to communicate effectively in a global economy," and "integrate language and intercultural communication skills with professional content" (p. 14). Custom-made programs for international clients included academic content and social and professional exchanges with Canadian counterparts. Each program was designed to meet the particular requirements of the learners and to impart a more subtle understanding of intercultural communication in all of its dimensions. The ITRC worked extensively with public, private, and non-governmental organizations to provide training programs and consulting services relevant to intercultural communication. In 1996, the ITRC delivered forty-six contract training programs, ranging in duration from one day to fourteen weeks. In 1997, the ITRC developed a Certificate in Intercultural Studies, and broadened its focus from customized training to include the delivery of workshops and courses for members of the general public.

**Left:** Japanese language instructor Megumi Oba with student, 2005.
**Right:** Sally McLean and Indy Batth facilitating an intercultural studies workshop, 2009.

In the late 1990s, with support and encouragement from Walter Uegama, the ITRC was renamed the Centre for Intercultural Communication and expanded its gaze southward to include Mexico and South America, a consequence of the economic "meltdown" in Asia.[19] In its fall 1999 program guide, UBC Continuing Studies stated that this centre provided "expertise to enhance the performance of individuals working in international and multicultural organizations" (p. 27). The Certificate in Intercultural Studies, launched just before the name change, provided courses in various aspects of intercultural relations: communication, problem-solving, negotiation, team-building, and knowledge exchange. The Centre for Intercultural Communication provided seminars for people moving overseas to work, for professionals making presentations to international or multicultural audiences, and for a wide range of organizations looking to enhance the productivity of employees working in culturally diverse settings. The Korean government began sponsoring programs for Korean students seeking a cultural and communication experience in English while studying for credit at their home institutions. Through the "Global Academics" program introduced in 2002, UBC Continuing Studies has also facilitated internship experiences for international students in Vancouver.

As immigration consulting grew into a popular but unregulated new industry across Canada, immigration lawyers and consultants asked UBC to provide an educational program in this field. The Centre for Intercultural Communication responded in 2000 with the Immigration Practitioner Certificate Program, taught by local immigration lawyers and immigration case workers and initially offered in partnership with Seneca College in Toronto. In 2007, UBC Continuing Studies developed its own unique program, the

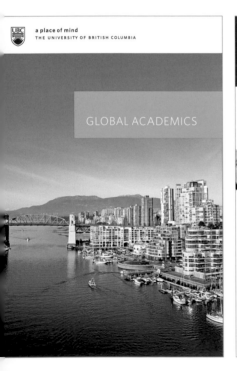

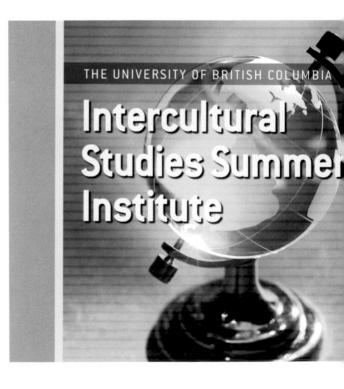

Certificate in Immigration; Laws, Policies and Procedures, with both online and face-to-face instruction. As of 2010, 509 people had successfully completed the program and demonstrated some of the strongest success rates on the regulatory exam for immigration consultants.

In 2004, a year after UBC launched its Global Citizenship Project as part of its new emphasis on internationalization, UBC Continuing Studies added a Certificate in International Development to its work in the field of intercultural communication. In its fall 2004 program guide, UBC Continuing Studies described the Certificate in International Development as "designed for professionals in health care, education and training, engineering, project management and humanitarian assistance, and others who want to add international development knowledge and intercultural expertise to their skill-sets" (p. 42). The certificate program included courses providing general knowledge of the field ("Introduction to International Development" and "Skills in Intercultural Communication"), along with those dealing with particular fields of work ("Issues in International Health Delivery" and "Education and Development"), and those addressing pertinent skills and processes ("Project Planning and Proposal Writing" and "Evaluating International Development Work"). Together, intercultural communication, international development, and immigration consulting were significant fields in which UBC Continuing Studies provided professional education in the new millennium.

## NICHE OCCUPATIONS AND SPECIALIZED PROFESSIONAL PROGRAMS

Information technologies and intercultural relations were the largest professional programs delivered by UBC Continuing Studies between 1990 and 2010. In addition, UBC Continuing Studies developed and delivered several programs to provide professional education in niche occupations or in specialized fields of business and technology management. Notable examples included work in the film and television industry, health and human services fields, teaching languages to adults, and in Internet marketing, e-business, project management, and environmental sustainability.

UBC Continuing Studies began delivering courses for people working in the film and television industry in the early 1990s, as British Columbia solidified its reputation as "Hollywood North" because of its geographical and financial appeal to movie makers, not to mention a low Canadian dollar and a large local community of skilled professionals. In the fall of 1991, the Centre advertised twenty-two courses dealing with various aspects of film and television: producing, directing, financing, marketing, distributing, entertainment law, writing, casting, filming, sound recording, editing, make-up, and costuming. By 2004, UBC Continuing Studies had established a Certificate in Entertainment Administration, designed for people with an interest in working in the

*UBC Certificate in Intercultural Studies (2010)*

*You examine specific cases, analyze your own experiences and collaborate with fellow students as well as online facilitators to reach a higher level of competency in interacting with people from diverse backgrounds.*

*Karen Rolston, Director*
*UBC Continuing Studies*
*Centre for Intercultural*
*Communication*

film and television industry. In its fall 2004 program guide, UBC Continuing Studies described the certificate program as "designed to teach the essentials of film and television administration, including producing, distributing, marketing and funding of entertainment made in Canada for an international audience" (p. 60). Students could complete the Certificate in Entertainment Administration on a full- or a part-time basis, or take individual courses from the program without enrolling in the certificate. By 2009, the curriculum had expanded to include courses in digital media and recent advances in post-production technology.

From the 1930s to the 1960s, Extension had worked with UBC faculties and schools to develop and deliver continuing professional education for people working in health and human services. In the 1960s and 1970s, this work was increasingly organized independently by Continuing Education in the Health Sciences, and the School of Social Work. The Centre for Continuing Education remained active in this field in the 1980s and 1990s, primarily through the counselling work of the Women's Resources Centre (see Chapter Nine). In the latter 1990s, UBC Continuing Studies renewed its involvement in the field of health and human services, a field which appeared set to expand in British Columbia when the provincial government introduced a new Ministry of Children and Families in 1996. UBC Continuing Studies once again facilitated the delivery of professional development courses for social workers, mental health workers, and rehabilitation professionals with such titles as "The Power of Visualization," "Perspectives on Working with Couples," "Narrative and Solution-Focussed Brief Therapies," and "Relevance of Dreams in Therapeutic Practice." By 2009, UBC Continuing Studies offered certificate programs in the following health and human services fields:

• Aboriginal Health and Community Administration (see Chapter Nine)
• Peer Counselling
• Practice Education for Health and Human Service Professionals

As with programming in information technology and entertainment administration, the certificate programs in the health and human services reflected demand for occupational skills.

The instruction of languages to adults was another niche occupation in which UBC provided continuing professional education. In the 1970s, the Centre for Continuing Education began providing a small number of specialized professional courses in teaching languages to adults. Initially, such courses were oriented toward people instructing a wide range of languages. By the early 1990s, the focus of such courses shifted to specialize in ESL teaching methods.

In addition to providing education and training in niche occupations, UBC Continuing Studies expanded its collaboration with the Faculty of Commerce and Business Administration in the 1990s. Often, the new courses and programs combined elements

*I really enjoyed the good feeling in the classroom. The instructors put great care into planning and organizing the ateliers, classes and optional activities.*

*Participant*
*UBC Continuing Studies*
*Language Program*
*1992*

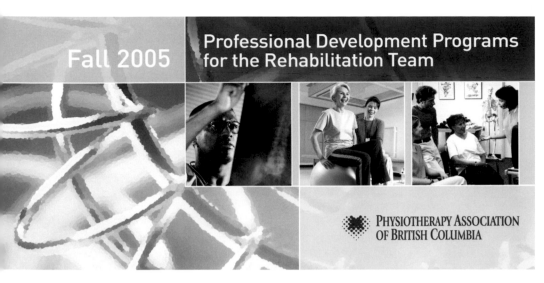

of business administration and information technologies. By 2009, UBC Continuing Studies offered two programs of study leading to certificates in collaboration with the Sauder School of Business (Business Analysis, and Integrated Marketing Strategy) and two programs of study leading to certificates in collaboration with the Faculty of Applied Science and the Sauder School of Business (Program Management, and Project Management).

## WRITING PROGRAMS AND ACADEMIC DEVELOPMENT

In 1967, Extension and the Faculty of Education established a Reading and Study Skills Centre. This Centre provided individualized programs for UBC students and adult members of the community to improve their reading, writing, and study skills for academic, professional, or personal reasons. In 1970, the Centre for Continuing Education reported that about 1,500 people had used the Reading and Study Skills Centre since its establishment, of whom about two-thirds were UBC students. In 1969-70, the Centre for Continuing Education established a Writing Improvement Program to assist students and adults with composition and essay writing. Throughout the 1970s, the Reading and Study Skills Centre provided courses and consulting services to UBC students and adult learners. Annual enrolment in "Reading Improvement" and "Writing Improvement" courses grew to more than five hundred participants during the early 1970s.

Although most of these programs were delivered on the UBC campus, and primarily to UBC degree-credit students, some were offered as in-house training programs to organizations in the Lower Mainland. In 1976, the renamed "Reading, Writing and Study Skills Centre" moved into its own army hut and acquired a full-time instructor/coordinator. The Centre expanded its programming to include courses in study skills, grammar, spelling,

**Top left:** Brochure for rehabilitation courses, 2005. **Top right:** Brochure from film and entertainment program, 1998. **Bottom right:** Brochure for the peer counselling program, 2000s.

technical writing, and vocabulary development, and began delivering a correspondence course in reading comprehension in 1977. Independent studies courses in writing, study skills, and library research skills were added in the late 1970s.

The Reading, Writing, and Study Skills Centre operated throughout the 1980s, serving UBC students and members of the general public wishing to develop their learning and communication skills. The Centre delivered an increasing variety of courses, which by the mid-1980s included those dealing with reading rate and comprehension, grammar and sentence structure, essay writing, business writing, editing, vocabulary development, spelling, study skills, public speaking, and freelance writing. The Centre continued to offer correspondence courses in reading and writing, and to deliver in-house training for companies and government agencies wishing support for their staff members' reading and writing skills. The Reading, Writing, and Study Skills Centre also provided workshops and tutorial support for students in their preparation for the English Composition Test, introduced by the English Department in 1974, and required of undergraduate students in most faculties.

By 1988, Senate was considering higher standards for international undergraduate students, who, although small in number, were increasing.[20] Partly in response to the influx of international and immigrant students who used English as a second language, UBC introduced a new standard in 1992, the "Language Proficiency Index" that applied to most students regardless of their area of study. A writing centre created by the Department of English to assist ESL students (and others) was transferred to UBC Continuing Studies in 1993 to carry on as the Writing Centre, located first in the

**Top left:** Ramona Montagnes, who has led the UBC Continuing Studies Writing Centre since 1992. **Bottom left:** Signage post for the Writing Centre. **Bottom right:** Writing Centre brochure, 2006.

Auditorium Annex and then in Brock Hall. The UBC admissions office thereafter referred students who were unsuccessful with their language proficiency tests to seek assistance at the Writing Centre.[21] As competition for international graduate students increased in the 1990s, the university began considering conditional admission for outstanding applicants with small deficiencies in English proficiency, who would be required to spend several months at UBC studying English. This proposal was adopted by senate as university policy in 2007.[22]

The creation of the Writing Centre gave rise to a "Math Centre" in 1993, operated in cooperation with the Department of Mathematics. Some Math Centre courses had been offered previously by the Reading, Writing, and Study Skills Centre, while others, including a "Number Skills" course for mature students or adults wishing to develop their competencies in basic arithmetic and algebra, were developed by staff at the Math Centre. The new centres developed major, non-credit academic preparation courses known as "Writing 098/Writing 099" and "Math 012." These courses were open to UBC students and others, and involved a full semester of instruction and skills development. The courses prepared UBC students for success in their undergraduate careers, and they offered members of the general public an opportunity to build their writing and mathematical skills for academic or professional purposes.

In the late 1990s, UBC Continuing Studies significantly expanded the scope and range of services provided by the Writing Centre, and moved it to the Ponderosa Annex C building. Beyond courses in academic writing, grammar and style improvement, diverse offerings were developed in areas ranging from business and professional writing to personal and creative writing. In addition to delivering courses, the Writing Centre began in the late 1990s to provide free tutoring services for UBC students, online resources relating to grammar and composition, and customized, in-house training services to various business and government organizations.

*After Michael Katz's first lesson, I went home and couldn't stop writing, and haven't stopped since.*

*Evaluation from a student at the UBC Continuing Studies Writing Centre*
*2008*

## CREDIT STUDIES

In 1976, administrative responsibility for evening, off-campus, and spring or summer session degree-credit courses was transferred from the Centre for Continuing Education to a newly created Office of Extra-Sessional Studies, directed first by Norm Watt and then by Kenneth Slade. Until 1984, the Centre retained responsibility for correspond-ence courses, through an office known as "Guided Independent Study." The Guided Independent Study office administered correspondence courses taken for degree-credit, as well as correspondence courses taken as stand-alone courses or for credit within the Criminology Certificate and the Certificate in Early Childhood Education. In the late 1970s and early 1980s, the Centre enrolled about 1,500 students per year in Guided Independent Study courses.

After 1984, the Centre for Continuing Education delivered a small number of certificate-level and non-credit correspondence courses each year, but was no longer involved in the administration of degree-credit courses. In 1992, the Centre for Continuing Education, the Office of Extra-Sessional Studies, and Guided Independent Study ("UBC Access") reconnected in the new UBC Continuing Studies as recommended by the Task Force on Continuing Education in 1989. From 1992 to 1999, UBC Continuing Studies was responsible for degree-credit courses offered off-campus, in the spring and summer months, in the evenings, or through distance education. It was responsible for the development and delivery of distance education courses until 2003. In 1995, Guided Independent Study began moving to online delivery and changed its name to Distance Education and Technology. Part-time students were a primary audience for such courses, including those who might have preferred full-time studies but were compelled to work part-time to support themselves.[23] Full-time students from the Vancouver area also enrolled in extra-sessional and distance education courses, partly for convenience and partly because UBC classrooms during the 1990s were often at capacity because of provincial policies that tied funding to enrolment increases.[24] In the mid-1990s, annual enrolments in Extra-Sessional Studies and Distance Education and Technology averaged, respectively, just over twenty-one thousand and just under four thousand students. In 1999, the delivery of face-to-face, part-time credit courses was again decentralized to faculties. In 2004, Distance Education and Technology was moved out of UBC Continuing Studies and into the portfolio of the Associate Vice President Academic to better complement the faculty degree courses, and merged with the Office of Learning Technology the following year.

The delivery of degree-credit courses via distance education had changed dramatically at UBC between the 1950s and the 1990s. In the 1950s and 1960s, correspondence courses were delivered exclusively through printed course packages sent to students through the mail. Tutorial support and the evaluation of assignments were undertaken either through written correspondence or by means of telephone. New technologies steadily came into use. UBC delivered its first televised degree-credit course in 1976: "Fine Arts 125 – Pyramids to Picasso." By the early 1990s, UBC Continuing Studies was using a variety of media in its distance education courses, including print materials, audio and video-cassettes, audio teleconferencing, and television broadcasts via the Knowledge Network. Over the subsequent decade, UBC adopted new technologies in its distance education courses, such as video-conferencing, computer-assisted instruction, and the Internet. In the development, teaching, and revision of distance education courses, faculties and schools provided subject matter experts and instructors, while UBC Continuing Studies provided expertise in instructional design, educational technology, media production, editing, and project management. As with all innovations, there were mixed motives behind these new developments: they permitted experimentation to find new and more effective pedagogies, but administrators also saw the potential to cut costs and generate revenue in a financially-constrained environment.

UBC Guided
Independent Study
Courses 1977-1979

The University of British Columbia

**Top left:** UBC's Rose Garden, 2011.
**Top right:** Calendar for credit courses
taken through correspondence, 1977-79.
**Bottom:** UBC's Koerner Library, 2010.

UBC Continuing Studies played an innovative and leading role in the development and implementation of new technologies for education at UBC and elsewhere. Under the leadership of Dr. Tony Bates, well known distance education specialist, author, and consultant, Distance Education and Technology (DE&T) became nationally and internationally recognized for its leading-edge work in the distance education field. During this period:

- Large and ongoing international projects were undertaken in collaboration with institutions such as Monterrey Institute of Technology and Higher Education (Tec de Monterrey) in Mexico and the Open University of Catalonia in Spain.

- DE&T became a popular destination for international delegations of distance educators to learn about and discuss state-of-the-art practices in distance education. The DE&T director and senior managers were in demand for international consultancy contracts and as conference contributors.

- A number of large, three-year research contracts, funded through the federal Office of Learning Technology, were completed, as well as other shorter research projects with the Canadian Bureau of International Education and the Ontario Securities Commission. A collaborative research and professional development program – Managing and Planning Learning Technologies in Higher Education – involved both national and international partners.

- A new online certificate (UBC Certificate in Technology-Based Distributed Learning) was developed and delivered to large numbers, including international students. This initiative resulted in the ongoing Master of Educational Technology, based in the UBC Faculty of Education.

- DE&T adopted "WebCT" (Web Course Tools) developed by Murray Goldberg, a UBC instructor of computer science, to assist online instruction. WebCT subsequently became widely popular in many universities.

Tony Bates, Director, Distance Education and Technology, UBC Continuing Studies (1995-2003).
*Photo: Martin Dee*

In recent years, UBC Continuing Studies has developed a series of non-credit courses designed to assist adults to gain access to graduate programs of study by improving their

scores on various standardized examinations used in determining admission to such programs. Test preparation courses for the GMAT (Graduate Management Admission Test), GRE (Graduate Record Examinations), and LSAT (Law School Admission Test) have enabled hundreds of learners to gain entrance to their desired program of graduate studies. GMAT, GRE and LSAT test preparation courses were designed to offer a credible, in-house alternative to private companies operating on the UBC campus. In a related manner, the International Graduate Study Preparation Program has provided non-credit instruction designed to give international students the academic and cultural skills they require to succeed in graduate-level studies in North America.

*chapter summary*

## EDUCATING ADULTS FOR THE KNOWLEDGE ECONOMY

*The continuing education era (1970-present) was one of rapid social and economic change, which included the emergence of new information technologies, the internationalization of production and consumption, and the expansion of post-secondary education.*

*New program partnerships emerged with professional associations, customized training clients, and government funding agencies that focussed on the complex knowledge and skills required for effective professional practice in a range of fields: agriculture, forestry, fisheries, education, law, social work, engineering, architecture, and community and regional planning.*

*In parallel to the establishment of the Centre for Continuing Education in 1970, professional faculties were encouraged to develop divisions of continuing professional education and the provision of such programs gradually became more decentralized. Over time, the Centre for Continuing Education and later UBC Continuing Studies developed expertise recognized on a national and sometimes international level in applied technology, intercultural communications, and education in specialized fields such as sustainability.*

*Programs increasingly operated in a cost-recovery manner, deriving the majority of their operating revenues from students, their employers, and external sponsors.*

*If universities and colleges are successfully to adopt the use of technologies for teaching and learning, much more than minor adjustments in practice will be required. Indeed, the effective use of technology requires a revolution in thinking about teaching and learning.*

*Tony Bates*
*Managing Technological Change*
*1999*

# Justin Newell has been lecturing on art history and leading enrichment tours for UBC Continuing Studies since 1985.

*His knowledge of history, art, political events, and famous sights are woven into captivating (and as some students say, "incredible" and "outstanding"), easy to understand presentations on such topics as art in the age of Enlightenment, the birth of Impressionism, artistic portrayals of Roman and Greek mythology, and depictions of Biblical stories from the Old Testament. His tours have taken participants to Venice, Florence, Rome, and other art centres of the world. Also a practicing artist, he adjudicates art competitions and creates images in many media including watercolour, acrylics, oil, oil pastels, pencils, and mixed media. As well as his work for UBC Continuing Studies, Justin shares his expertise at community and seniors' centres, and aboard cruise ships where he is recognized as "one of the top special interest speakers."*

## Chapter Eight

# Understanding diversity in a global environment

Following the transition from the Department of University Extension to the Centre for Continuing Education in 1970, UBC continued to help people understand themselves and their world by providing an extensive program of continuing education in the liberal arts. Some programs from the Extension era, such as the circulation of books and audio-visual resources, were discontinued. Others, such as the delivery of evening courses and workshops in the humanities, languages, and fine arts, flourished. As was the case with continuing professional education, non-credit liberal arts programming at UBC gained momentum following 1970 as UBC's gardens, museums, galleries, and academic departments in the humanities, social sciences, and fine arts offered their own public lectures, demonstrations, exhibits, film showings, concerts, recitals, and readings.

During the 1970s and 1980s, the Centre for Continuing Education maintained a vibrant program of courses, lectures, and workshops in the humanities, social sciences, and fine arts. The number of participants in such activities increased from just under five thousand in 1972, to just under ten thousand in 1976, and then to over twelve thousand per year during the 1980s. Between 1990 and 2010, the overall number of participants in liberal arts programs delivered by UBC Continuing Studies declined somewhat. However, there was also a significant shift away from short, stand-alone public lectures and toward courses of longer duration. As a result, the overall amount of instruction provided in the liberal arts remained high. In the 1990s and early 2000s, there was also an important shift in the substantive focus of programming in the liberal arts: from the humanities, social sciences, and fine arts to programs in language and culture.

## FINE ARTS

During the 1970s, the Centre for Continuing Education offered numerous evening courses, workshops, and summer programs in the fine arts. Studio courses included painting, drawing, calligraphy, printmaking, photography, textile arts, sculpting, performance arts, and many others. Art appreciation courses included music, painting, theatre, and film studies. In the early 1970s, some 1,500 people per year took part in the Centre's fine arts courses. Many more participated in special events, such as festivals and exhibitions. For example, in 1976, nearly 1,500 people took part in a "Festival of Early Music" which has continued to this day as the noted Vancouver Early Music Festival, co-sponsored by the UBC School of Music. A recital by pianist Anton Kuerti in the summer of 1971 attracted an audience of 350, and "An Evening with Aaron Copeland" in the fall of 1972 attracted 850 attendees.

Between 1938 and 1965, Extension had offered intensive fine arts programming on the UBC campus during the summer months. By 1980, the Centre for Continuing Education had launched the "UBC Summer Program," providing a range of cultural and recreational opportunities for adults, children, and families. In 1981, the Summer Program enrolled a total of 4,150 people in 184 educational events. Summer Program administrators coordinated residential accommodation and on-campus childcare for participants, and invited families from across North America to visit UBC during the summer months. Although liberal arts programming in the summer months has continued to the present at UBC, the Centre for Continuing Education stopped administering and marketing the "UBC Summer Program" in the mid 1980s.

In the 1980s and early 1990s, the Centre for Continuing Education offered both art appreciation and studio-based fine arts courses and workshops. Courses in which participants created artwork included those in painting and drawing, dance, photography, graphic design, jewellery making, fabric arts, and working with glass. Courses in art appreciation or theory included those in music, the visual arts, interior design, and architecture. Beginning in the latter 1990s, UBC Continuing Studies lost access to studio space and offered few courses involving artistic production, focussing instead on courses in the theory and appreciation of art, architecture, and music.

## HUMANITIES AND SOCIAL SCIENCES

Courses and workshops in the humanities remained very popular throughout the 1970s under the direction of Sol Kort, a lively and innovative program director. Drawing on UBC faculty members and visiting scholars, Kort sought out provocative speakers to critique contemporary "industrial-technological consumer society" and to consider alternative ways of being or living.[1] In a provocative paper entitled "Toward Resuscitating the Liberal Arts: Re-Visioning the Humanities," written for a conference in 1986, Kort argued that the "new humanities" addressed:

> issues arising out of our unprecedented contemporary history and with disciplines not fully incorporated into most standard academic fare: the larger conception of paideia as lifelong transformation of the human personality (L. Mumford); the new psychologies – humanistic, transpersonal, and archetypal (A. Maslow, C. Rogers, F. Perls, R. Assagioli and J. Hillman); the new polytheism (D. Miller); creative mythology (J. Campbell); clinical philosophy (P. Koestenbaum); cybernetic

*During the fall I took the program titled Religion and the Transformation of Society... It was one of the most interesting, varied and well-prepared series of lectures I have yet attended... My congratulations to the Centre, to Dr. Hexham, and to the participating lecturers for giving us so much to think about.*

Participant
Centre for Continuing
Education Program
1980

*epistemology (G. Bateson); epistemological anarchism (P. Feyerband); wissenkunst (W. Thompson); the human potential movement; the ecological movement; the peace movement; the women's movement; the new economics (H. Henderson); the new politics or politeia (J. Houston) and last, but not least, heretical elements from the diachronic (classical) humanities. (pp. 1-2)*

Kort's programs were popular with many people in Vancouver, including those engaged in what we might consider counter-cultural or "New Age" movements.

Humanities programming in the 1970s took three basic forms: evening courses, workshops, and public lectures. Evening courses and daytime workshops typically touched on such areas as philosophy, religion and spirituality, literature, creative writing, natural sciences, life sciences, lifestyles and identities, and health promotion. Table 8.1 on p. 162 provides examples of course titles in each category. The 1973 annual report of the Centre for Continuing Education noted that:

*[humanities] courses for adults are attractive and thrive when they appear to offer one of three basic opportunities for learning: (1) to learn how to become more integrated as a human person; (2) to learn how the natural universe works, in both its physical and biological aspects; and (3) to learn how to alleviate anxiety and express concern about the inequities and frustrations of both individual and collective life in our advanced society. (p. 14)*

**Top:** Language class learning about cultures through song, late 1970s. **Bottom:** Student with instructor, artist Ranjan Sen, 1980s.

Most of these courses were offered on the UBC campus, but many were held at the Vancouver Public Library.

Public lectures organized by the Centre for Continuing Education often presented UBC faculty members and prominent intellectuals to large audiences. Maverick psychiatrist

**TABLE 8.1:** Selected titles from humanities programs, 1970s.

**TABLE 8.2:** Popular humanities lectures, 1971-76.

**Bottom right:** Noam Chomsky (L) giving a Vancouver Institute lecture introduced by Eric Vogt (R), 1976. *UBC 41.1/1971.5*

| FIELD | SELECTED TITLES |
|---|---|
| Philosophy | General Systems Theory and Thinking Dialogue on Man |
| Religion and spirituality | The Practical Wisdom of Tibetan Buddhism Social Action and the Spiritual Quest |
| Literature | Science Fiction Then and Now Russian Literature and Culture |
| Creative writing | Poetry Writing Workshop Creative Writing Workshop in Fiction and Non-fiction Prose |
| Natural sciences | A Space Age Look at the Universe A Natural History of the Forest |
| Life sciences | The Mind / Brain of Man Human Anatomy and Physiology |
| Lifestyles and identities | Yoga, Biokinetics, and Body Awareness Ways of Centering |
| Health promotion | Habit Control Seminar Vegetarian Cooking and Nutrition |

| YEAR | LECTURE (ATTENDANCE) |
|---|---|
| 1971-72 | Norman Cousins: Planetary Management (430) |
| 1972-73 | Thomas Szasz: The Myth of Mental Illness (900) |
| 1973-74 | William Kaufman: Relativity and Cosmology Updated (392) |
| 1974-75 | Theodore Roszak: The Crime of Dr. Frankenstein (420) |
| 1975-76 | Joseph Campbell: Psyche and Symbol (440) |

Thomas Szasz, for example, spoke before nine hundred people in 1972 on the "Myth of Mental Illness" at a time of growing public outrage toward institutions for the mentally ill and the developmentally delayed. Table 8.2 (see p. 162) identifies the most popular public lectures in the humanities in each year between 1971 and 1976.

Lecture series on various topics also remained popular, including: Quest for Liberation; Explorations in the Human Potential; The Humanities and Life Sciences; Mind, Morality, and Social Conscience; and Towards a More Familial Society. The 1977 annual report of the Centre for Continuing Education reflected upon the "New Age" character of its humanities programming:

> We seem to be in the midst of a major paradigm shift in our culture transforming our traditional outlooks into something not yet clearly discerned, something akin to a new animism which seeks participation rather than control of our universe... This is contrapuntal intellectual fare of a new order emerging for reasons not fully understood but obviously related to the accumulation of seemingly insurmountable and unprecedented problems, dilemmas and crises facing world civilization. (p. 13)

In the latter 1970s, the Centre for Continuing Education offered many courses dealing with diverse approaches to physical and mental well-being, including meditation, yoga, shiatsu, and physical fitness. Some members of UBC's Senate advisory committee on continuing education, however, debated the appropriateness of these subjects.[2]

In the 1970s, continuing education programming in the social sciences took a similar form to that in the humanities: evening courses; workshops; and public lectures. Each year, between seven hundred and one thousand people took part in some twenty to thirty evening courses and workshops. In some years, public lectures and special exhibitions drew several hundred additional participants. A 1975 program on maritime archaeology left a legacy in the form of the Underwater Archaeological Association of British Columbia, a still-active group of divers interested in exploring local waters for shipwrecks and other signs of past human activity.

During the 1970s, the social science courses that consistently attracted strong public interest were those relating to the anthropology and archaeology of Aboriginal people in British Columbia, the growth and decline of pre-modern civilizations around the world, and popular psychology. Various courses giving an economic or sociological analysis of current events were also popular (see Table 8.3 on p. 164). In 1976, the Centre for Continuing Education began joint programming with the newly opened UBC Museum of Anthropology, which housed an outstanding collection of artefacts from the South Pacific and northwest coast of North America. While most social science courses were held on the UBC campus, some included field trips. For example, courses in archaeology and anthropology were sometimes accompanied by field trips to First Nations communities, and courses in ethnobotany and geology sometimes included rafting.

*Anyone can get involved – the only prerequisite is a desire to learn.*

*Arctic art, self-help housing – clear through to Zen – these are a few typical subjects among hundreds of general interest courses offered annually.*

*UBC is for Everyone! Centre for Continuing Education Brochure 1980*

Although overall enrolment in the humanities declined somewhat during the 1990s, programmers and administrators worked to keep the tradition alive. UBC Continuing Studies has continued to work collaboratively with the Vancouver Institute, still one of the city's foremost outlets for lectures in natural and social sciences, humanities, public affairs, and arts appreciation.[3] In recent years, programmers have been able to expand courses in arts and culture. Over the past twenty-five years, the number of courses offered in history and literature has remained relatively stable, while courses in philosophy and religion have declined in favour of courses relating to food and culture.

In the first decade of the new millennium, UBC Continuing Studies developed two programs of study leading to certificates in the humanities. The first of these, established in the late 1990s, was the Certificate in Liberal Studies, intended as a structured way to broaden intellectual horizons and enrich understanding of the arts and humanities. The second program blurred the distinction between traditional liberal arts and popular interest in food and culture: the Certificate in French Regional Cuisine.

*These five weeks have changed my life, and I thank all the coordinators and monitors who put so much effort into making this program a huge success.*

*Participant*
*Summer Language*
*Immersion Program*
*2011*

## LANGUAGES

Non-credit programming in language learning expanded dramatically at the Centre for Continuing Education during the 1970s, in part because of federal funding in support of French instruction following the 1969 *Official Languages Act*. The Language Institute was created in 1969 when it offered its first residential program in English as a second language. Mary Frank MacFarlane was its first director, to be followed by David Browne in 1975. The creation of the Summer Language Bursary Program (SLBP) by the Federal Government in 1971 gave new momentum to the Language Institute. UBC was to teach

| FIELD | SELECTED TITLES |
| --- | --- |
| Anthropology and archaeology | The Pre-History of BC<br>Tsimshian Art and Myth |
| Pre-modern civilizations | New Light on Ancient Civilizations<br>Famous Cities of the Past |
| Popular psychology | Psychology of Sport<br>Current Topics in Psychology |
| Economic or sociological analysis | Education and the Counter Culture<br>Propaganda, Information,<br>and the Media |

TABLE 8.3: Selected social science courses, 1975.

English to students from Quebec, and French to Canadians from all provinces. The first SLBP program was offered in 1972 with two sessions in both French and English for a total of 330 students (including sixty-nine international students). In 1973, there were two six-week sessions in English and one six-week session in French for a total of about four hundred students (including eighty-six international students). In 1974, UBC received a two-year matching grant from the Federal Government to teach French to adults. In 1975, over twelve hundred students took language classes, either as part of a residential program or in daytime, evening or weekend classes. In addition to the SLBP and to a large summer intensive program for French teachers, classes were offered year-round in French on campus, downtown, in churches or at schools from Oakridge to Richmond. English and foreign language classes were also offered on campus throughout the year.

As the Language Institute expanded, the English and French programs diverged with the creation of the English Language Institute and French and Modern Languages, later renamed Language Programs and Services. David Browne remained the director of both programs while Jean-Guy Trépanier was the co-ordinator of the French programs. A formal division took place in 1982 at which time Don Mosedale assumed the directorship of the English Language Institute and Francis Andrew became Director of Language Programs and Services.

UBC Language Programs and Services (Language Programs) established a strong reputation teaching conversational courses using the communicative approach. The program

**Top left:** Institut de Français instructor orientation led by program director Francis Andrew, 1985. **Top right:** Students role playing in a French language class, 1990s. **Bottom right:** Instructor Luisa Canuto on the right with Italian language student.

Top left: French Immersion Program in Quebec City, 1999. **Bottom left:** Instructor Yolande Morin in front of exhibit of students' work from travel photography program, 2003. **Bottom right:** Brochure for study-travel program Photography and Language Immersion in France.

offered immersion weekends in British Columbia and travel programs to various destinations such as Mexico and Japan, and French institutes in Quebec (from 1982) and France (from 1986). Funding from the British Columbia Ministry of Education allowed immersion weekends to be offered in French, Japanese and Chinese to British Columbia school teachers in destinations such as Whistler, Harrison Hot Springs, Penticton and Kelowna. In 1986, with the draw of the Expo '86 world fair in Vancouver, UBC Language Programs organized a large conference for about twelve hundred language teachers from Canada and the American Pacific Northwest.

In addition to planning and delivering hundreds of intensive summer programs, language and socio-cultural immersion weekends, conferences, and year-round part-time programs, UBC Continuing Studies language instructors developed original language teaching methods for their UBC classes during the 1980s and 1990s. These published course materials were also used by other educational institutions. For example, several distance language learning programs offered in partnership with the Open Learning Agency helped adult students in remote areas of the province learn French and Spanish. Patricia Martin, UBC Continuing Studies' Spanish Coordinator for over twenty-five years, developed the successful audio-visual program, *Soleado*. After several editions and the supplement of a DVD and web component, *Soleado* is still used in educational institutions throughout North America.

In 1992, the Centre for Continuing Education reorganized and created the Academic Performance Division to encompass several program areas under the leadership of Francis Andrew. This growing division included Language Programs and Services, the Summer Language Bursary Programs, the Quebec Institute, and the Writing and Math Centres. In 1993, Language Programs and Services became a separate program area

PHOTOGRAPHY & LANGUAGE IMMERSION IN **FRANCE**

under the leadership of Judith Plessis, long-time French instructor and Languages Coordinator since 1986.

The functional language teaching approaches developed by Language Programs helped adults learn languages effectively for travel or business purposes. The number of courses and the number of languages offered continued to grow and flourish in the 1990s, with a team-oriented teaching staff of over one hundred part-time instructors. The UBC Certificate in Business Spanish, followed by UBC certificates in French and Italian, were approved by UBC Senate in the late 1990s and helped consolidate the academic reputation of UBC Continuing Studies language programs.

In 2001, Language Programs and Services expanded its programming and became Languages, Cultures and Travel (LCT). This new division included significant cultural programs such as French Regional Cuisine and Understanding Wine, as well as destination travel programs featuring UBC Continuing Studies instructors teaching opera, art history, photography, tango, and cuisine in travel destination locations in Florence, Munich, the south of France, Buenos Aires and Quebec. The Understanding Wine Program, developed in collaboration with the Director of the UBC Wine Research Centre (Faculty of Land and Food Systems), Hennie van Vuuren, and taught by professional wine instructors, received a national award for program excellence in 2008.

A turning point in the development of LCT was the decision to offer language courses at the new downtown campus, UBC Robson Square, starting in 2002. Total registrations in LCT doubled in the first few years of the downtown offerings, and reached about 3,500 students annually by 2006. Focusing on the successes of programming at UBC Robson Square and the language training needs in Vancouver as the city prepared to host the Olympics, LCT experienced another period of growth and new programming. Lang Sun, an expert linguist, experienced Mandarin instructor and specialist in French immersion programs, became program director of Asia Pacific Language and Culture programs. When Judith Plessis became Executive Director of UBC Continuing Studies in 2007, Lang Sun took over the supervision of the day-to-day operations of more than one hundred language and culture classes per term.

*I appreciate the opportunity to come to this beautiful city and increase my knowledge of French. This trip has been an enlightening one for me and has steered me in a new direction. I can't thank you enough.*

*Participant*
*Quebec City*
*Program for Teachers*
*1996*

## ENGLISH LANGUAGE PROGRAMS

As interest among Anglophones in learning second languages has grown in recent decades, so too has interest among speakers of other languages in learning English. Programming in English as an additional language at UBC began in 1961, when fifty-nine people enrolled in four "Workshops in English for Newcomers." Over the next three years, Extension offered one or two ESL evening courses each year, to between thirty-five and sixty-five students. In the mid-1960s, Extension did not offer ESL instruction. However, with the establishment of the "Summer Language Institute" in 1969, residential programs in ESL for Quebec university students followed. Enrolment in ESL courses expanded rapidly in the early 1970s, and by 1976 there were nearly four hundred students in full-time summer immersion programs, and nearly three hundred students in part-time courses.

The Summer Language Institute attracted many international students, as well as students from Quebec. The ESL instructors sought full-time, year-round work and looked for ways to expand the English side of the Language Institute.[4] In 1977, the Language Institute became responsible for ESL courses for foreign students preparing for degree-credit studies, and began to offer full-time immersion programs of six weeks, three months, and six months, as well as part-time "college preparation" programs. These were eventually joined by evening courses for teachers, businesspeople, and other members of the public wishing to improve their English skills through an innovative communicative approach.[5] With significant expansion of the full-time programs came personnel organization: English language instructors formed a bargaining unit of the Canadian Union of Public Employees in 1981.

By the mid-1980s, the English Language Institute (ELI), as it was called after 1987, offered Communications Programs, Academic Preparation, and Special Programs for Groups, administered from its headquarters in two refurbished UBC worksites constructed as engineering laboratories in 1925. One special program came as a result of Expo '86: two Saudis, on hand to set up the Saudi Arabia pavilion, were provided with a six-week "specially designed English program."[6] Various ESL programs attracted many students (enrolment in special group programs alone, which included summer language bursary programs for Quebec teachers and students, had risen from 150 in 1980 to 900 in 1987). In 1987, Jindra Kulich suggested to UBC administrators that the ELI deserved new quarters. A new building was still low on the university's priority list in 1990, despite additional growth in academic preparation enrolment due to immigration, UBC's internationalization push, and the explosion of ESL teaching in Vancouver.[7] The Institute moved to Duke and Carr Halls in 1993, but this was still less than satisfactory given the size, configuration, and age of the buildings.

With the reorganization of UBC Continuing Studies in the early 1990s, the ELI was placed in the newly formed "International Division" because of its important role in working with international students. The ELI underwent a review in 1995 to sort out a number of structural and morale problems caused by recent growth and personnel changes, and emerged with three program areas: Intensive English Programs for students seeking to become degree-credit students at UBC; University and Professional Programs for special groups; and College and School Programs for high school and college students.[8] Walter Uegama, acting on the longstanding desire to find better accommodation for the ELI, prepared a plan to set aside funds for a new, more appropriate facility. In 1997, thanks in no small part to leadership from Catherine Vertesi, who served as ELI Director at the time, the ELI moved to its own new building on West Mall, closer to the centre of campus.

THE UNIVERSITY OF BRITISH COLUMBIA

# ELI WORLD

NEWSLETTER     1999, VOLUME 16     30TH ANNIVERSARY ISSUE     UBC CONTINUING STUDIES

## 30 Years of Memories and Friendship

Since 1969 students have been coming to UBC to learn English. Over this time, there have been many changes to the classrooms, the teachers, the programs and the city of Vancouver. One thing that has remained the same is the ability of the English Language Institute (ELI) to foster friendships among students and teachers from around the world. After finishing their program, many students return home with good language skills and also with a greater understanding of other cultures gained through the international environment at the ELI. With over 35,000 former students, the ELI is truly a worldwide network of people connected by shared experiences and unique memories.

In the last 30 years, many students have written to the ELI describing how their experience in Vancouver shaped their lives in a memorable way. Rachel Casey has maintained her friendship for over 25 years and writes, "How can I forget Vancouver and UBC, and especially the summer of 1974? That is when Marie Woods and I met. We were in the same class with Mrs Rowan. Marie and I have been close friends ever since." (See photo.) Another student from long ago, Akiko Iwata (1977) writes, "Many things have happened since then, but I am always thanking God that the friendship I got there never passes away."

*continued on page 2*

*Top: Over the years the ELI has taught English to many groups from all over the world. Middle: ELI Teachers pose for a "classroom" picture in the 1970s. Bottom left: Students in 1976 take a break from class to socialize. Bottom right: Marie Woods Schlader and Rachel Casey met at the ELI in 1974 and have been friends for over 25 years.*

**Top left:** The new Continuing Studies Building on West Mall, home of the English Language Institute (ELI). **Bottom left:** ELI "alumni" newsletter celebrating the institute's 30th anniversary in 1999. **Top right:** Coordinator Bill McMichael with student. **Middle right:** ELI Director Don Mosedale with student. **Bottom right:** ELI class in the 1970s.

Since the 1980s, the Centre for Continuing Education and UBC Continuing Studies have delivered a wide range of English language programs and services. Such programs and services have varied over time in duration and level, but have included:

• Full-time immersion programs for people wishing to learn English for personal or professional purposes.

• Full-time immersion programs for students wishing to learn English to gain admission or better prepare for studies at UBC or other post-secondary institutions.

• Shorter immersion programs offered in the summer months for people such as high school students, professionals, and teachers of English.

• A "homestay" program designed to provide immersion students with accommodation and opportunities to practise English with local families.

• Examination preparation courses for students wishing to improve their scores on standardized tests such as the Test of English as a Foreign Language (TOEFL).

• Customized training programs for companies, institutions, or professional groups.

• Cultural enrichment activities for ESL students seeking social and recreational experiences that contribute to their language learning.

• Multimedia language laboratories and library resources for ESL students.

By the early 1990s, annual enrolments in full-time immersion programs exceeded one thousand, with students from over twenty-five countries participating. In 1996, UBC Continuing Studies delivered twenty-seven special group programs, to a total of about one thousand students. The number of international students studying at UBC had grown substantially (to over 2,200 in 1996), giving rise to increased demands for programs in English for academic purposes. The primary countries of origin for ESL students

Left: English Language Institute (ELI) Academic Director, Andrew Scales. Right: ELI Coordinator, Lyn Howes, 1980s.

have remained Japan, Korea, Taiwan, and China, although enrolment by students from Mexico, South America, and the Middle East has grown.[9]

A review of the ELI in the late 1990s suggested a redesign of the Immersion Program curriculum. This led to the creation of the Intensive English Program, which continues to offer instruction at well-defined language levels, from beginner to very advanced. New program managers accompanied the new curriculum, including Director Mike Weiss, Academic Director Andrew Scales, and Administrative Director Gwen Semenoff.

Some of the former program areas within the ELI were combined, while College Preparation and School Programs were eliminated. A new Language and Culture Program took the place of a variety of shorter Special Programs that had usually run during the summer. Most foreign institutions which formerly sent groups to the ELI embraced the Language and Culture Program as it resulted in a culturally more diverse student body and lower costs.

In 1999, Senate approved the highest level of the Intensive English Program as constituting an English language admission standard for undergraduate degree study. This was the beginning of a strategy to directly support the academic vision of the University, paving the way for what is now known as "conditional admission" – a program that enables academically outstanding students who do not yet meet the English language admission standards to gain full admission. Conditional admission for undergraduate study was approved by Senate in 2007 and for graduate study the following year.

In 2010, the university asked the ELI to collaborate with the Centre for Teaching, Learning and Technology to develop a program to provide academic support to UBC students who speak English as an additional language. The pilot began in the fall of 2011, with the capacity to accept up to five hundred students. Subject to the success of the pilot, the Academic English Support program is expected to be capable of helping an increasing number of students annually in future years.

*This is the best opportunity to learn English, travel, learn more about Canada and the English culture, make new friends from different parts of the country, and create a good network for future opportunities.*

*Participant
English Language
Program
2011*

## STUDY TRAVEL

The cultural globalization implied by increased interest in language learning has also created ongoing demand for study travel programs that take people to other countries. Building upon the efforts of the Department of University Extension, the Centre for Continuing Education and UBC Continuing Studies provided a wide variety of such programs. These programs included international trips of two to four weeks' duration to a range of destinations, and shorter "field studies" closer to home, often to areas of natural or cultural significance. The program directors responsible for these offerings had considerable freedom to choose their destinations and itineraries, and they often chose adventurous, out-of-the-way locations and travel arrangements.[10]

In the early 1970s, the Centre for Continuing Education delivered an average of three study travel programs each year, to locations in Europe, Asia, and Latin America, with an average of twenty-three participants per program. The number of destinations and participants continued to increase in subsequent years. Some international study travel courses were designed to give an introduction to the history, culture, and geography of the countries being visited. Other courses focussed on particular themes, such as archaeology, gardening, or educational systems. Typically, the travel portion of the program was preceded by a series of lectures or a workshop by an expert in the destination or theme of the trip, often a UBC faculty member who later led the tour. In 1984, 135 participants enrolled in a total of nine overseas tours, to Hawaii, Japan, China, the Ukraine, Belize, and Hungary. International study travel programs have continued to the present day, taking students around the world to learn about culture, history, or nature; specialized travel programs have been organized to provide an opportunity for language immersion.

In addition to international study travel, the Centre for Continuing Education began, in 1975, offering a range of "Field Studies" programs. Such programs usually took place within British Columbia, but sometimes ventured elsewhere in North America. The focus was typically on the biological and physical sciences ("The Chilcotin: Natural History by Canoe" and "Marine Biology Field Trip to Cherry Point"), and also on art and the theatre ("Shakespearean Festival Study Tour" and "Art Tour of New York") and, for a few years in the 1970s, on outdoor recreation and survival skills. Local programs were as short as a few hours, while others lasted up to ten days. In 1985, the Centre for Continuing Education offered nine field studies courses to places such as Haida Gwaii (the Queen Charlotte Islands), Mount St. Helen's, Wells Gray Provincial Park, and the Bamfield Marine Station. Participants appreciated the adventurous nature of some of the trips, which might include passage on a refurbished mine-sweeper with Zodiac transport to a site of particular interest. Natural history tours often attracted participants with environmental interests who were keen to visit areas of ecological importance. On one occasion in the mid-1980s, the Field Study participants landed their Zodiacs on a beach on South Moresby Island (Haida Gwaii) during an environmental protest; the area was subsequently protected as a National Park Reserve.[11]

Since the 1980s, UBC has offered field studies on themes ranging from ecology and anthropology to the fine arts. As with the international study-tours, field studies eventually ceased to be a separate programming area but the trips continued. Field studies programs and international study travel have offered unique opportunities for continuing education students to learn about the world through a combination of direct experience, knowledge shared by UBC resource people, and interaction with other students. As with other areas of education provided by UBC Continuing Studies, study travel has provided experiences that cross academic boundaries, reflecting an increased attention to interdisciplinary programming at UBC and elsewhere.

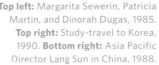

**Top left:** Margarita Sewerin, Patricia Martin, and Dinorah Dugas, 1985.
**Top right:** Study-travel to Korea, 1990. **Bottom right:** Asia Pacific Director Lang Sun in China, 1988.

*chapter summary*

## UNDERSTANDING DIVERSITY IN A GLOBAL ENVIRONMENT

*The continuing education era (1970-present) was marked by substantial cultural change, including transformations introduced by globalization, the rise of new media, and the evolution of postmodern forms of artistic expression and worldview.*

*Following the tradition of the Department of University Extension, the Centre for Continuing Education (1970-1992) and UBC Continuing Studies (1992-present) provided educational offerings designed to help people understand their globally-interconnected world. While the overall amount of liberal arts instruction remained high, there was a shift within it from the humanities and social sciences to languages and cultures.*

*Collaborative programming remained strong, with the introduction of new partners such as overseas universities. English language immersion programs for international students showed steady growth in support of UBC's internationalization efforts, paving the way for the introduction of UBC's conditional admission program. In this program, academically-outstanding students gain full admission to degree programs after successfully completing English language training through UBC Continuing Studies.*

# Paolo Bernasconi is putting his education and on-the-ground experience to good use as an online facilitator for the UBC Certificate in International Development.

*Designed for those working or planning to work in the field of international development, the program emphasizes the importance of understanding cultural differences in international development work and examines the many cultural challenges to development. "As an online facilitator, I provide feedback to participants, but it's also a learning experience for me as I often reflect on the exchange of comments and that helps me broaden my own understanding and awareness," explains Paolo. As an HR specialist with the United Nations Population Fund (UNFPA) based in New York and covering the Africa region, Paolo regularly travels to Africa to assist country offices with staffing matters and to ensure appropriate personnel are in place to carry out UNFPA programs.*

*Chapter Nine*

# Nurturing civic engagement

UBC has maintained a strong commitment to helping people participate actively in public affairs. After 1970, study-group programs and radio forums were no longer facilitated by UBC; however, the Centre for Continuing Education offered a growing number of workshops, evening courses, and public lectures and forums on current events and social issues. In addition to expanding such programs, the Centre opened up new areas of programming for particular populations. Although women, seniors, and Aboriginal people had always been included in the programming of the Department of University Extension, the Centre for Continuing Education began providing programs specifically designed to engage with these groups. In recent decades, university-community engagement has become a significant concern of academic departments and faculties at UBC, many of which have hosted public events, and developed programs to ensure dialogue between faculty members, students, and members of various communities.

## WORKSHOPS, COURSES AND EVENING LECTURES IN PUBLIC AFFAIRS

In the 1970s, the Centre for Continuing Education offered three major streams of public affairs programming, directed respectively toward women, the general public, and elected officials with local governments. In the early 1970s, annual enrolments in these three areas averaged about three thousand, twelve hundred, and seven hundred, respectively. At that time, the largest public affairs initiative was known as "The Daytime Program" which comprised a wide range of courses and lectures oriented primarily toward the learning needs of women (although this was not the initial intention).[1] The women's movement and the rise of feminist thought had been a significant aspect of the social upheaval of the 1960s, but except for the Daytime Program, launched in 1968, UBC was slow to respond.[2] Although the topics of individual courses were oriented toward professional or personal development, the Centre for Continuing Education was in fact playing a significant role in a major social movement. In its 1971 annual report, the Centre for Continuing Education stated that a major goal of the Daytime Program was "to provide resources for the many women feeling the impact of the radical redefinition of female roles and changing social expectations" (p. 22). Many of the courses within the Daytime Program were organized in collaboration with women's groups such as the Vancouver Women's Club, the National Council of Jewish Women, and the YWCA. Courses included those relating to personal growth ("Assertiveness Training for Women" and "The Literature of Self Discovery"), career development ("Introduction to Employment Interviewing" and "Human Relations in Management"), relationships ("Sex and Marriage" and "The Challenge of Being Single"), and the liberal arts ("History for Travellers" and "Selecting and Collecting Art"). Beginning in 1973, courses in the Daytime Program were joined by a series of courses delivered through the Women's Resources Centre.

In the 1970s, the Public Affairs Program of the Centre for Continuing Education organized both face-to-face educational events and television broadcasts, under the leadership of Gerald Savory, to promote citizens' awareness of, and participation in, key social and political issues. In its 1971 annual report, the Centre for Continuing Education stated:

> The underlying premise of the Public Affairs Program area is that each citizen should have a significant part to play in the political decision-making process and that it is one of the University's roles to assist citizens and elected representatives in their search for information and analysis relating to public issues. (p. 30)

Current events courses included a regular lecture series entitled "The International Scene" as well as lectures and courses relating to different regions (Africa, Asia, and Europe) and issues (pollution, Canada's foreign policy, and technology). In addition to current events, public affairs programming included both local and world history courses. The Centre for Continuing Education organized a special series of fourteen lectures during the United Nations Conference on Human Settlements (Habitat) held in Vancouver in June 1976. Over 3,600 people attended the lectures. Thirty years later, UBC Continuing Studies organized Earthblog, a unique community-blogging project and official cultural program of the UN-Habitat World Urban Forum held in Vancouver. More than ten thousand people participated online in Earthblog in 2006.

Throughout the 1970s, the Centre for Continuing Education used educational television broadcasts in its public affairs programming. A half-hour program entitled "UBC Public Affairs" was broadcast on Cablevision Channel 10 between ten and fifteen times each year (see Table 9.1 on p. 177). The episodes in this program dealt with a wide range of local, national, and international current events. In addition to "UBC Public Affairs," the Centre for Continuing Education organized six broadcasts in a series titled "UBC Academics Look at Urban Affairs" in 1972-73, and more than twenty broadcasts per year in a series called "Beyond the Memory of Man" (dealing with classical and medieval history) from 1975 through 1977.

In addition to making public affairs programs available to the general public, the Centre for Continuing Education delivered a multi-year series of workshops and seminars for elected municipal officials. The Centre delivered an annual, two-day "Orientation for Aldermen" as well as seminars targeted to specific regions within British Columbia

*While in the past universities like UBC could follow an agenda that was almost entirely internally stated, society and its institutions now increasingly expect to have a say in our agenda.*

*Walter Uegama*
*Associate Vice President*
*UBC Continuing Studies*
*1998*

Symposium on **Ethics and Aging**

August 16~19, 1984

Seminar on the Charter of Rights and Freedoms:

**Impact on Public Administration**

November 23 and 24, 1984

| YEAR | THEMES |
|------|--------|
| 1971-72 | Foreign ownership in Canada; China; Southern Africa |
| 1972-73 | Drug use; American Elections; Vietnam peace negotiations |
| 1973-74 | Price controls; Indian land claims; Nuclear waste disposal |
| 1974-75 | Alternate energy sources; Canadian immigration policy |
| 1975-76 | New international economic order; Habitat / human settlements |
| 1976-77 | Consumer legislation; Politics of oil in the Middle East |
| 1977-78 | Canadian constitution; Civil liberties issues in British Columbia |
| 1978-79 | Disarmament; Water resources in British Columbia |

**Top left:** Televised public affairs programs in the early 1970s.

**TABLE 9.1:** Selected themes in UBC Public Affairs television, 1970s.

(Vancouver Island and the North Central Municipal Association), and specific issues of importance to municipal officials (capital planning and sewage treatment). The Centre offered programming in local government affairs throughout the 1970s.

In the 1980s, the Centre for Continuing Education offered fewer evening courses and public lectures on current events, in part due to the wider availability of information through the media, and in part because of the decentralization of such activities to faculties and departments across UBC. However, the Centre continued to offer "The International Scene" lecture series and to organize occasional conferences relating to public affairs. For example, in 1981 the Centre co-hosted a conference with the United Nations Association, which attracted over four hundred participants for a discussion of the Brandt Commission report: *North-South: A Program for Survival*. In 1984, the Centre hosted major conferences on "Nuclear War: The Search for Solutions" and "Coalition Building: Social and Economic Justice." In addition to such conferences, through the 1980s the Centre coordinated a series of free public lectures at the Robson Square Media Centre in Vancouver (which later became UBC Robson Square). Many of these lectures were related to current events such as inflation, the Canadian constitution, and scientific developments. In 1985, the Centre held a large public meeting on the new British Columbia *Human Rights Act*, considered by critics to afford less protection

**TABLE 9.2:** Selected themes of public affairs lecture series and forums, 1991-2009.

**Right:** Organizing programs at the Women's Resources Centre during the 1970s.

| YEAR | THEMES |
| --- | --- |
| 1991 | Keeping Canada Together? |
| 1994 | Interpreting the Family in the Nineties: Changes and Challenges |
| 1999 | Creating Jobs: Whose Responsibility? |
| 2004 | An Electoral Ward System for Vancouver? |
| 2009 | Leadership for Change: Making Change Happen |

against discrimination, to air concerns and consider alternatives.[3] In 1990, Robson Square lectures included a series on the theme of "Multiculturalism in Canada: Meeting the Challenge."

Over the past two decades, UBC Continuing Studies has maintained the tradition of organizing public lectures and forums on topics of local, national, and international interest. In most years, UBC Continuing Studies has hosted free, public noon-hour lectures at UBC Robson Square, and organized evening lectures, conferences, and forums at modest cost to participants. Table 9.2 on p. 178 identifies selected themes from these public lectures and forums. In recent years, many of the lectures have been made available as podcasts, reaching thousands of additional participants every year through the UBC channel on iTunesU. UBC Continuing Studies also hosts two annual lectures, the Vancouver Human Rights Lecture and the Milton K. Wong Multiculturalism Lecture, both broadcast on the CBC Radio One program *Ideas* to more than 700,000 listeners across Canada and around the world.

## WOMEN'S RESOURCES CENTRE

In 1970, the Government of Canada released the *Report of the Royal Commission on the Status of Women in Canada*. In January 1971, the Centre for Continuing Education organized a major conference on the report, involving the Commission's chairperson, Florence Bird, and attracting over three hundred representatives of women's organizations, student groups, professional associations, unions, social welfare groups, and the business community. The report and the conference generated substantial discussion and action relating to a wide range of issues influencing the lives of women, including employment outside the home, sharing of childcare responsibilities, access to education, participation in public affairs, and systemic discrimination based on gender. Pat Thom, coordinator of the Daytime Program, had been particularly active in these discussions and planning sessions, and joined with other women to press for a more permanent venue to help provide educational support for women. In 1973, the Centre for Continuing Education established the Women's Resources Centre with the mandate of assisting women "to explore and assess opportunities to re-enter the worlds of education and employment, to develop personal potential, and to find and initiate community projects and involvement." Federal grant funding to the Centre for Continuing Education was crucial to the success of the Daytime Program and the Women's Resources Centre.[4]

In its early years, operating from rented space at the Vancouver Public Library, the Women's Resources Centre organized workshops and lectures similar to those of the Daytime Program, hosted major gatherings such as the "Opportunities for Women" conferences in 1973 and 1975, and established an ambitious, volunteer peer counselling service that would operate for more than thirty years. The counselling service was

*Meeting the Management Challenge – Understanding Power (1980)*

*This workshop will explore current findings and teach you how institutional power systems work to keep women out, how to recognize the traps that keep you powerless, and how to find your own power style. You will learn to read power cues and establish power legitimacy, to use the power impact of costume and body movement, and discover the ways in which your interpersonal style can advance or block your management potential.*

primarily staffed by dozens of volunteer associates who received specialized training and offered personal, career, and educational advice through face-to-face contact and over the telephone. The number of counselling sessions held by the Women's Resources Centre grew dramatically: from 347 in 1974 to 15,887 in 1994.

Clearly, the Women's Resources Centre aided large numbers of women in their personal and career development, both through educational events and individual counselling. Members of staff with the Centre were prominent agents in the engagement of UBC with the broader community – working actively with women's groups, giving presentations at public events, and making women aware of educational resources available through the university.

Over the years, educational programming through the Women's Resources Centre evolved to reflect the key concerns of women in communities and organizations, adjusting emphasis as baby boomers aged and the life situations of many participants changed.[5] Courses in personal and career development continued, and were joined by programs in leadership development and health promotion, as well as events designed to raise awareness of feminist thought and social, political, and cultural issues of importance to women. In 1977, the year that the Women's Resources Centre relocated to a second-floor office on Robson Street, the Centre for Continuing Education established a "Women in Management" program, which offered numerous career development courses throughout British Columbia over the subsequent decade. In the late 1970s and early 1980s, the Women's Resources Centre provided training programs for personnel of "Women's Access Centres" throughout the province. In the latter 1980s, the Centre co-sponsored a major annual seminar: "Woman to Woman: Your Health and Happiness." In the early 1990s, the Centre's training program for its volunteer associates was developed into a "Peer Counselling Certificate Program," a version of which is still offered by UBC Continuing Studies. A few years later, the Centre added a "Certificate in Cross-Cultural Counselling" in response to the increasingly diverse population of British Columbia. In addition to its work with members of the general public, the Women's Resources Centre undertook educational and consulting work with corporate clients, including such major employers as BC Hydro, Canadian Airlines, the Bank of Montreal, the Canadian Red Cross, and the Royal Bank.

In 1998, the mission of the Women's Resources Centre was to promote lifelong learning "in an accessible, non-threatening environment; to serve as a vital link between the community and UBC; to anticipate economic, societal, and cultural trends; and to develop services and programs that will empower our clients." When asked, in 1998, to express the basic philosophy of the Women's Resources Centre, the Centre's director, Ruth Sigal, replied: "I'd say it's a place to teach and empower women, through providing information, counselling and referral, and helping them to set goals for themselves." The Women's Resources Centre moved in 2001 to UBC Robson Square, and was later renamed the

*Many volunteers have stayed with the Women's Resources Centre for 15 to 20 years. There is no other [women's] centre in Canada that uses faculty and students and is situated in the community.*

Ruth Sigal, Director
Women's Resources Centre
2000

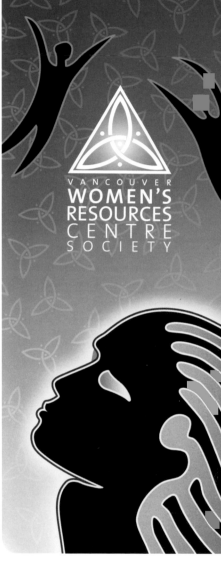

"Life and Career Centre," partly to distinguish it from other social agencies providing complementary services, partly to acknowledge barriers other than gender, and partly to encourage greater participation by men. Although men had been welcome in many of the Women's Resources Centre programs since the 1980s, few had participated.[6]

With a new location and name, the Life and Career Centre continued serving thousands of people each year with courses and counselling services in the areas of personal development and life planning. In 2004, the Centre's counselling service responded to nearly 25,000 inquiries, and the Centre enrolled hundreds of people in courses relating to personal development ("Making Sense of Transition" and "The Path to Self-Esteem"), and skill-building for career and life success ("Effective Communication in the Workplace" and "Creating Healthy Relationships"). The Life and Career Centre continues to provide drop-in counselling and career testing services, as well as to offer lectures and courses dealing with personal and career development. Table 9.3 on p. 182 illustrates some of the courses offered to both men and women over the past thirty years.

The growth of personal and career development courses and services reflected the changing nature of personal identities and careers in British Columbia. Earlier, personal identities were often tied to long-term careers and relatively stable cultural environments. By the end of the century, both men and women in British Columbia were likely to have careers composed of different kinds of jobs, and they were likely to be exposed to multiple and diverse cultural messages via powerful new media. In such circumstances, the provision of courses and consultative services relating to personal and career development helped UBC engage with the fundamental concerns of many British Columbians: who am I, and how am I going to make a living?

**TABLE 9.3:** Courses in personal and career development, 1979–2009.

| YEAR | PERSONAL DEVELOPMENT | CAREER DEVELOPMENT |
|------|----------------------|--------------------|
| 1979 | Coming to Terms with Yourself<br>Bibliotherapy<br>Lessons of Moshe Feldencrais:<br>    Improving Function and Body Awareness<br>Hatha Yoga for More Effective Living<br>T'ai Chi | Considering a Career Change?<br>Do You Know What You Want from Life?<br>How to Run a Meeting<br>So, You Think You'd Like to Work in Sales?<br>Effective Public Speaking |
| 1991 | Balancing Your Life<br>Adult Children of Dysfunctional Families<br>Non-Traditional Breakups<br>Reframing Self-Image<br>Developing Emotional Closeness<br>Exploring the Changes of Adult Life<br>Positive Thinking Revisited<br>Focusing: Overcoming Obstacles<br>    to Personal Change<br>Less Stress | The Positive Interview:<br>    How to Make a Good Impression<br>Career Change: A Jump off the Diving Board<br>Communication Skills<br>Understanding your Personal Style<br>Assertiveness Training<br>Managing Anger<br>Conflict Resolution / Negotiation Skills<br>Public Speaking / Presentation Skills |
| 1999 | Life Planning: A Strategy for Making Decisions<br>Assertiveness Training:<br>    The Art of Positive Communication<br>Positive Thinking Revisited<br>Mastering Anxiety<br>Budget Planning<br>Anger: A Signal Worth Listening To | Take Charge of Your Career<br>Intensive Communication Skills<br>Enhancing People Skills<br>    (The Myers-Briggs Approach)<br>Making Great Presentations |
| 2009 | ACT More, Struggle Less<br>Transforming Stress into Strength<br>Overcoming Perfectionism<br>Assertiveness Training<br>Positive Thinking Revisited<br>The Biology of Empowerment:<br>    Re-Program Your Sub-Conscious for Success | Lead with Your Values<br>The Power of Emotional Intelligence<br>Motivational Interviewing for Healthcare<br>Dealing with Difficult People<br>The Art of Effective Presentations |

## PROGRAMMING FOR SENIORS

In 1977, the Centre for Continuing Education began offering two programs to serve the special interests of older adults: summer courses for retired people, and retirement planning education. Since 1974, UBC had delivered summer programs for seniors under the management of the Summer Session Office whose director had secured a $15,000 grant from the province to cover costs.[7] In the summer of 1977, under the auspices of the Centre for Continuing Education, over 550 retired adults of at least sixty years of age took part in thirty-one courses and a number of social activities hosted on the UBC campus. The number of participants increased to over eight hundred in 1981. Courses varied in content from current events and Canadian literature to genetics and oceanography. To make participation in the courses as convenient and affordable as possible, registration was free of charge, and retired people from outside the Vancouver area were provided with one week of free accommodation in a campus residence. The Centre for Continuing Education offered a Summer Program for Retired People until the early 1990s.

In addition to administering the Summer Program for Retired People, the Centre for Continuing Education promoted the ongoing education of older adults by enabling retired people to participate free of charge in many of its other programs. In 1978, 446 seniors took advantage of that opportunity. Further, beginning in 1978, the Centre collaborated with the West End Senior Learners Group and the West End Community Centre to organize lecture series on topics ranging from "Canada and the Election" to "History of Egyptian Art." By 1980, annual registrations in free courses for seniors through the Centre for Continuing Education had increased to 2,964. In 1985, however, due to financial constraint across UBC, the Centre for Continuing Education began charging tuition fees for the Summer Program for Retired People, and enrolment in the program dropped from over eight hundred participants in the early 1980s to 165 participants in 1987.

*Ageless Pursuits (2010)*

*For close to three decades, UBC Continuing Studies has offered Ageless Pursuits, an intellectually stimulating program that features four individual weeks of lectures, lively discussion, and shared inquiry.*

Third Age Community peer learning group, 1980s.

In 1987, the Centre for Continuing Education established a "Third Age Community of Learners and Scholars" to coordinate educational programming for older adults. President Strangway endorsed the program personally: it would be a good learning experience for participants, and it would have value in connecting UBC with an important segment of the population.[8] Rather than simply provide lectures, the program established peer learning groups who conducted their own research and met to share the results. The program received financial assistance from the Vancouver Foundation and other sources. In 1989-90, membership in the UBC Third Age Community had grown to forty-six retired people, and weekly meetings were held on campus on the themes of "The History of Law," "Pacific Rim Cultures," "19th Century European Literature of Revolution and Social Change," and "20th Century Women Authors and Ethical Issues." By the end of the 1990s, the name for this group had been changed to "Third Age Partners in Learning."

The Third Age Partners in Learning program has employed a pedagogical approach similar to the study group format widely used by the UBC Department of University Extension in the 1930s and 1940s. The Fall 2009 program guide of UBC Continuing Studies described this approach in the following terms:

> In self-directed study groups of approximately 15 members, you meet for two hours each week to explore subjects with others who have similar interests. In addition to the pleasure of studying with like-minded people, the social interaction enhances the experience. At the beginning of each term, an academic specialist gives one preparatory lecture introducing the topic. Each member then selects a related sub-topic to research and reports their findings to the group for discussion. Individual research, life experience, shared perspectives and discussion are all part of the experience. (p. 13)

The Third Age Partners in Learning program has been one means through which UBC Continuing Studies has directly engaged older adults in continuing education. More recently, the Third Age spring lecture series has been renamed "Ageless Pursuits," which attracts, but is certainly not limited to, older adults. Further, UBC Continuing Studies has provided "seniors' discount" pricing on many courses, and a large number of older adults enrol in such courses.

In addition to educational programming tailored specifically for older adults, UBC has delivered retirement planning services for over thirty years. These services included public workshops, a television series ("Tomorrow is Now"), and consulting services to numerous companies, government agencies, and unions. The Centre for Continuing Education offered its first workshops in this field in 1977, and by the 1990s, UBC Continuing Studies provided extensive retirement preparation programs. In 1990, the Centre delivered forty-three retirement planning workshops to clients across British Columbia. Major clients for in-house retirement seminars have included Air Canada, Weyerhaeuser, Labatt's, Chevron, and numerous companies in the forestry industry.

In the 2000s, UBC Continuing Studies focussed its retirement planning education on the provision of in-house workshops for major employers and with the UBC Faculty

Association. In its Fall 2004 program guide, UBC Continuing Studies gave the following rationale for the importance of retirement planning: "Retirement now represents up to a third of a lifetime and is a period of changes, challenges and new beginnings. Preparation is fundamental to a happy and productive retirement" (p. 53). UBC Continuing Studies in-house workshops provided information regarding financial planning, health, housing, lifestyle, and relationship issues. Through such retirement planning workshops, as well as through the Ageless Pursuits program, UBC Continuing Studies responded to another key trend in British Columbia: the tendency for people to live longer and to live a larger proportion of their lives after leaving the labour force.

## PROGRAMMING FOR ABORIGINAL PEOPLE

Since 1970, UBC continuing education units have organized several initiatives designed to engage with the aspirations and educational needs of Aboriginal communities. Although Extension had earlier worked with the province's Aboriginal people, new political currents followed the rejection of the federal government's 1969 white paper which sought to integrate Native people into Prime Minister Trudeau's "just society."

**Top:** First Nations House of Learning in the First Nations Longhouse. **Bottom:** Native Indian Teacher Education Program (NITEP) students, 1974. *UBCA 41.1/142-1*

First Nations leaders saw the white paper as yet another attempt at assimilation and rejected it in favour of self-determination, reinvigoration of Native cultures, control of education, and settlement of land claims. With rising political and public support for Aboriginal claims, the federal government withdrew its white paper, and replaced Indian Agents with Band Councils.

In 1970, with financial support from the federal government, the Centre for Continuing Education and the Faculty of Education established the Indian Education Resources Centre in Brock Hall. In its 1971 annual report, the Centre for Continuing Education wrote that the activities of this new Centre included:

> Distributing books and articles; publishing resource materials; sponsoring courses and programs on Indian culture and education; fostering communications between groups involved in Indian education; promoting involvement of Indian people in educational decision-making; providing facilities for research and projects; working with education committees, and teacher and community groups; and publishing an Indian education newsletter. (p. 41)

The Indian Education Resources Centre was advised by a council of fifteen First Nations teachers, and in the early 1970s it worked in collaboration with the Union of British

**Left:** Graduates of the UBC Certificate in Aboriginal Health and Community Administration. **Right:** Ad featuring House Post by Susan Point (Musqueam). Collection of the UBC Museum of Anthropology, Vancouver, Canada.

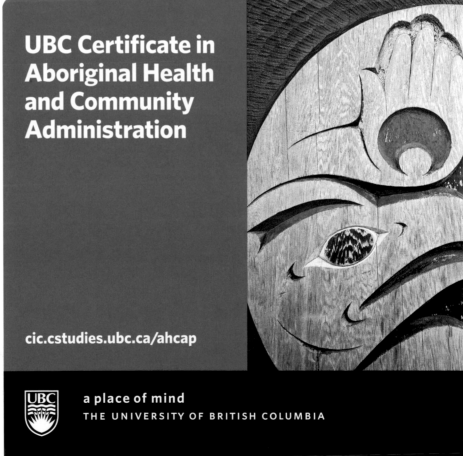

UBC Certificate in Aboriginal Health and Community Administration

cic.cstudies.ubc.ca/ahcap

UBC

a place of mind
THE UNIVERSITY OF BRITISH COLUMBIA

Columbia Indian Chiefs to provide resources for native education in British Columbia. One enduring initiative supported by the Centre was the Native Indian Teacher Education Program (NITEP) launched by the Faculty of Education in 1974, intended to train Aboriginal teachers.[9] As the NITEP program became more established, its resource library absorbed the role of the Indian Education Resources Centre, which closed in 1978.

In 1985, the Community and Regional Planning program of the Centre for Continuing Education developed planning courses specifically for Aboriginal communities. It held an initial workshop in the Northwest Territories, and then delivered a one-week course for chiefs and councillors and a two-week course for band managers, on the UBC campus. The two-week "Introduction to Band Planning" course was offered several times over the next three years, with participants from the three western provinces along with the Yukon and Northwest Territories. In 1987, the Centre also offered a one-week course in "Economic Development Planning" for Aboriginal communities. In 1995, UBC Continuing Studies organized a series of four public lectures on the theme of "Land and Governance" – reflecting a growing public interest in First Nations' land claims proceedings, and encouraged by the provincial government's recognition of Aboriginal title in 1991 and several high profile legal cases.

During the 1990s, as social attitudes toward Canada's First Nations changed and introduced new political relationships, patient but firm leadership from a small number of Aboriginal scholars and Elders was having noticeable results at UBC. Thanks to financial donations, UBC's First Nations House of Learning opened in 1993 to provide a home for Aboriginal faculty and students.[10] Earlier programs designed to facilitate access to degree programs in law and education were joined by others in healthcare and social work.

In 2003, UBC Continuing Studies (through the Centre for Intercultural Communication) collaborated with the First Nations House of Learning, the Institute for Aboriginal Health, the UBC College of Health Disciplines, and the British Columbia Ministry of Health to establish the Certificate in Aboriginal Health Care Administration. Championed by Dr. John Gilbert of the Faculty of Medicine, the certificate program provided basic but comprehensive training in health care administration to those working in First Nations communities and Aboriginal health organizations, following the transfer of health programs and services from the federal government to First Nations and Inuit communities. This ten-month certificate program was composed of five residential workshops at UBC (Communication and Leadership, Fundamentals of Administration, Aboriginal Health Systems, Health Policy, and Information Management) and a practicum. By 2009, this award-winning program had been renamed the UBC Certificate in Aboriginal Health and Community Administration – and continued to be an example of a successful partnership between UBC Continuing Studies (Centre for Intercultural Communication) and the College of Health Disciplines (Institute for Aboriginal Health). The program involves online delivery, facilitating service to remote communities.

*Critical Issues in Aboriginal Life and Thought (2010)*

*Join us at UBC Robson Square for a series of six special dialogues on critical issues in Aboriginal life and thought:*

- *Education: community control*
- *Land: ownership and governance*
- *Resources: control and development*
- *Urban Aboriginals: visibility and representation*
- *Women: law and equality*
- *Art: tradition and expression*

## EDUCATION FOR ENVIRONMENTAL SUSTAINABILITY

Perhaps because of its long history of intensive resource extraction, British Columbia also has a long history of conservation and environmental activism. In the first half of the 20th century, UBC faculty such as botanist John Davidson and agronomist Bert Brink often participated in extension activities where they provided leadership in environmental practices. The environmental movement of the 1960s found fertile ground in British Columbia, both in Vancouver where activists launched Greenpeace in 1971 and at UBC where a young geneticist named David Suzuki began a broadcasting career in 1970 to help people better understand the natural world and the impact of humans upon it. With the "energy crisis" of 1973, interest in energy efficiency and alternative fuels blossomed among UBC engineering faculty and students.

In the 1970s, public affairs programming of the Centre for Continuing Education included courses, lectures, and television broadcasts dealing with environmental issues, including pollution, water resources, waste management, and nuclear power. In 1976-77, the Centre organized two major projects in the increasingly prominent field now called environmental sustainability. The first engaged over five hundred people in a series of three conferences on the theme of "Moving Towards a Conserver Society." The individual conferences were titled "Work as Play," "Doing More with Less" and "Small is Possible," which echoed the title of E.F. Schumacher's 1973 bestseller *Small is Beautiful: Economics as if People Mattered*. The second initiative was a self-help housing program that promoted energy-efficient home construction and culminated in the construction of solar-heated "Acadia House" on the UBC campus by participants in the program. Designed a few years earlier by a UBC student of architecture as a thesis project, Acadia House (located amidst the old army huts of Acadia Camp) cost $15,000, a fraction of the cost of typical solar houses. The following year, the "Conserver Society" program delivered workshops relating to solar energy, and built two additional, energy efficient self-help homes: "Earth House" and "Conservation House." This program educated over 150 participants in the theory and practice of self-help housing and energy conservation. The homes constructed through the program were intended as residences for married students, but in 1982 they were torn down amidst allegations of construction deficiencies.[11]

In the late 1970s and early 1980s, the Centre for Continuing Education maintained its solar energy and self-help housing projects, and organized evening courses on energy management issues. In addition, the Centre periodically organized major conferences relating to environmental sustainability, such as a 1979 event focussed on teaching about energy issues in public schools, and a 1981 event focussed on energy management for municipalities. Field studies and educational travel, as noted earlier, often highlighted environmental issues with trips to areas of ecological significance.

*The people were outstanding. It was a very engaged group; obviously there exists shared interest for sustainability, but there was also a passion that slowly unveiled itself over the course of the week. A group of us still stay in touch and throw ideas at one another about different topics in sustainability.*

*Participant
UBC Continuing Studies
Summer Institute in
Sustainability
2009*

The 1990s saw an increase in concern about issues of sustainability. UBC signed the Talloires Declaration in 1990 that committed the university to sustainable development (a phrase popularized in the report of the World Commission on Environment and Development in 1987), and opened a sustainability office a few years later. Students and faculty at UBC were at the forefront of calls to conserve the planet's threatened eco-system, often joining with environmentalists in the forests of the province to stand up against resource companies.[12] As large environmental protests to protect old growth forests captured world media attention in the early 1990s, UBC Continuing Studies regularly organized lecture series on themes relating to environmental sustainability (see Table 9.4 on p. 190).

UBC Continuing Studies has periodically organized conferences on issues relating to environmental sustainability. Events from the 1990s included a workshop for "Managers of Landfill Operations," a symposium on "Shared Decision Making" in land and resource use, four "International Environmental Summer School" events involving students from Japan, and a conference on "Solid Waste Management."

In addition to organizing public lectures and occasional conferences on environmental issues, UBC Continuing Studies promoted more intensive programs of study in the field

**Top left:** UBC's new Centre for Interactive Research on Sustainability (CIRS), 2011. *Photo: Don Erhardt.* **Top right:** Sustainability courses and programs for personal and professional development, 2011. **Bottom right:** Mike Harcourt, Associate Director of the UBC Continuing Studies Centre for Sustainability.

by establishing the UBC Continuing Studies Centre for Sustainability in 2008, after the success of a week-long UBC Summer Institute in Sustainability. The new Centre expanded the programming beyond environmental sustainability to include social, cultural and economic sustainability. In 2009, the Honourable Mike Harcourt, former premier of British Columbia and former mayor of the City of Vancouver, joined the UBC Continuing Studies Centre for Sustainability on a part-time basis as Associate Director. Bringing his forty years of experience in urban planning, environmental stewardship, and sustainable

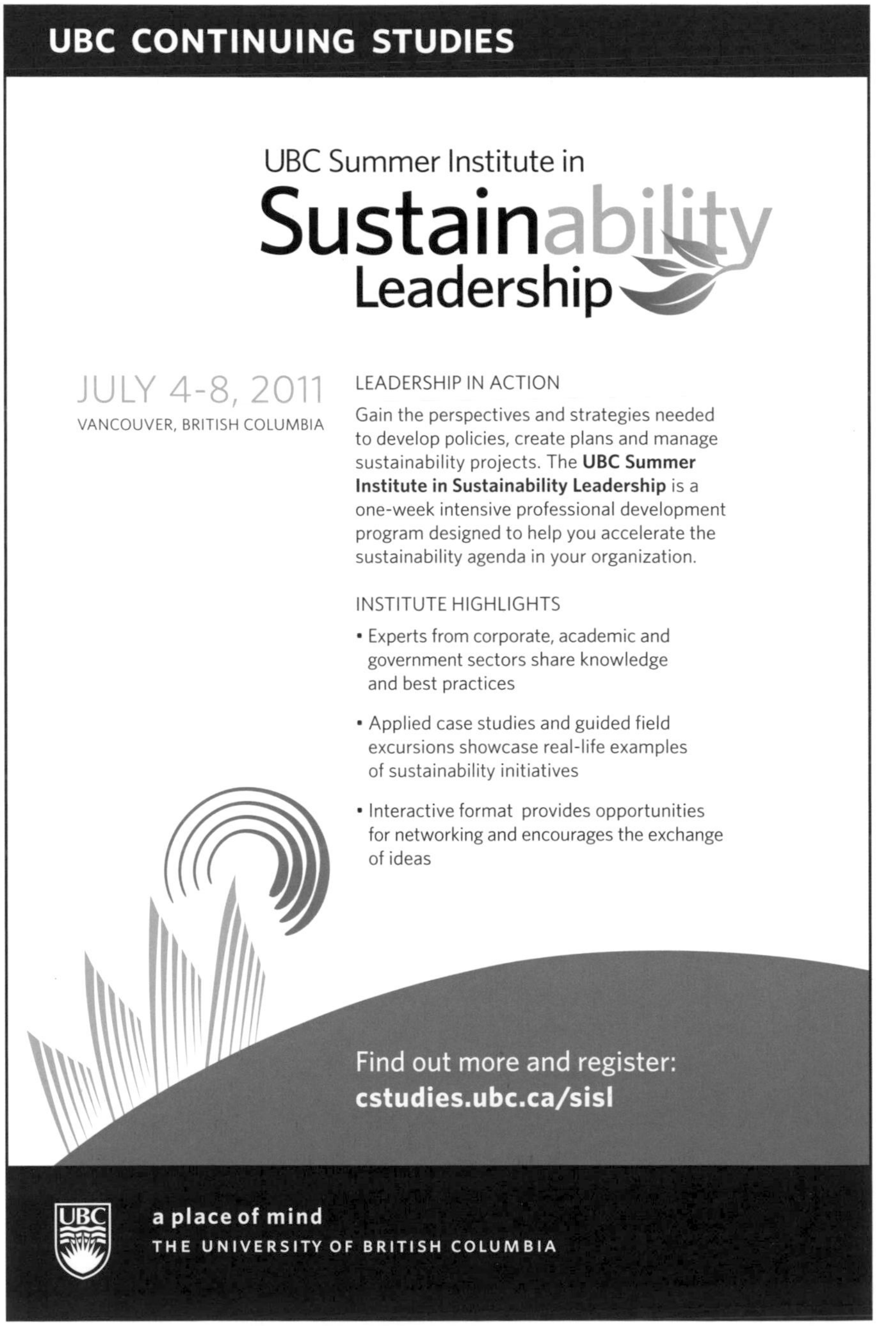

**TABLE 9.4:** Selected lecture series on environmental sustainability, 1991-2008.

| YEAR | THEMES |
|------|--------|
| 1991 | Our Forests: A Citizen's Survey of Current Issues |
| 1994 | Ecological Issues |
| 1999 | The Natural Step to Sustainability |
| 2004 | Biodiversity and Urban Form |
| 2008 | Imagining a Sustainable Future |

**UBC CONTINUING STUDIES**

UBC Summer Institute in
**Sustainability**
Leadership

JULY 4-8, 2011
VANCOUVER, BRITISH COLUMBIA

LEADERSHIP IN ACTION
Gain the perspectives and strategies needed to develop policies, create plans and manage sustainability projects. The **UBC Summer Institute in Sustainability Leadership** is a one-week intensive professional development program designed to help you accelerate the sustainability agenda in your organization.

INSTITUTE HIGHLIGHTS

• Experts from corporate, academic and government sectors share knowledge and best practices

• Applied case studies and guided field excursions showcase real-life examples of sustainability initiatives

• Interactive format provides opportunities for networking and encourages the exchange of ideas

Find out more and register:
**cstudies.ubc.ca/sisl**

UBC
**a place of mind**
THE UNIVERSITY OF BRITISH COLUMBIA

city development, Harcourt helped provide leadership and direction to the new Centre. In 2009, the Centre offered an Award of Achievement in Sustainability Management for students completing one hundred hours of non-degree credit coursework, and a Certificate in Decision Making for Climate Change for students completing four online courses (in collaboration with Northwestern University, the University of California, Irvine, and the University of Washington). As well, week-long Summer Institutes in Sustainability and in Sustainable Urban Design, and public programs such as screening the sci-fi climate change documentary *The Age of Stupid* and hosting Eric Assadourian, director of the Worldwatch Institute in Washington D.C., earned praise for their high quality. The Summer Institute in Sustainability Leadership received an Outstanding Program Award in 2009 from the Western Region of the University Professional and Continuing Education Association, as well as a Program Excellence Award in 2010 from the Canadian Association for University Continuing Education. The establishment of these programs of study reflected both a growing public interest in environmental, social and economic sustainability (the "triple bottom line"), and the emergence of employment opportunities for people with pertinent knowledge and skills.

*chapter summary*

## NURTURING CIVIC ENGAGEMENT

*The continuing education era (1970-present) was influenced by political change, including major movements such as those for Aboriginal rights, feminism, peace, global citizenship, and environmental sustainability.*

*Anticipating and responding to major current events and social issues, the Centre for Continuing Education and UBC Continuing Studies carried on the tradition of their predecessors by offering programs that served to promote a civil and sustainable society.*

*The Daytime Program and the Women's Resources Centre organized courses that addressed the learning needs of women whose roles in society were being redefined. The Indian Education Resources Centre (in collaboration with the Faculty of Education) and the Aboriginal Health and Community Administration program (in collaboration with the Institute for Aboriginal Health) were designed to serve Aboriginal learners and their communities. Innovative lectures, workshops, and conferences on sustainability-related topics can also be traced throughout the decades.*

*In an era when university continuing education units have increasingly operated on a cost-recovery basis, deriving the majority of operating revenues from students and external sponsors, UBC has maintained an impressive balance between programs oriented toward liberal and civic goals and those oriented toward professional goals.*

# The thirty-three years I spent working at UBC Continuing Studies was the best period of my life.

*I always thought that it was a university within a university. Why? UBC Continuing Studies offers programs that expand the mind, improve personal development, broaden social knowledge, take students abroad for new languages and cultural experiences, and provide skills for career advancement. It has always been on the leading edge of lifelong learning for adults in British Columbia. My first Director was Pat Thom – a dynamic woman, full of energy and vision. She initiated the Women's Resources Centre downtown. Marcie Powell, a classy professional, succeeded her as the Director of Daytime Programs. Then there was the late Sol Kort, who was a hero to me. When Sol retired, his successor was Beth Hawkes. Beth and I became lifetime friends instantly. When the Centre was restructured I was transferred to the English Language Institute. There I made connections with Japanese professors with whom I still keep corresponding. My last "boss friend" was Jane Hutton. She is a visionary and Continuing Studies thrived under her leadership. Anyone who has encountered her would never forget Jane! – Linda Fung (2012)*

*Chapter Ten*

# Transformations

This book has shown how the educational programs and services offered by the University Extension Committee, the Department of University Extension, the Centre for Continuing Education, and UBC Continuing Studies have changed dramatically over the decades yet remained committed to consistent purposes. Although dynamic and diverse, changing to meet the demands of contemporary times and the evolution of knowledge and information, the programs and services of these units have maintained a tradition of helping people in British Columbia (and, increasingly, people beyond the province's borders and around the world) to earn a living, understand their world, and participate actively in public affairs and civil society. In this chapter, we assess the balance that has been achieved between professional, liberal, and civic education in extension and continuing education programming at UBC. We argue that the evolution of such programming, in all three spheres, has been driven by major social and institutional changes. Finally, we identify several outcomes of this programming, including the stories of several students who have completed UBC Continuing Studies programs and transformed their personal and professional lives.

## STAYING THE COURSE

Ever since President Klinck presented his "Plan for Adult Education in British Columbia" in 1935, leaders of extension and continuing education at UBC have sought to provide programs that address professional, liberal, and civic goals. The vast range of programs and services identified in this book demonstrates that such goals have indeed characterized the history of the Department of University Extension, the Centre for Continuing Education, and UBC Continuing Studies.

It is important to note that boundaries drawn between professional, liberal, and civic education are conceptual rather than empirical. It is useful to think of extension and continuing education according to these categories, but in reality, programs and services frequently blur the boundaries. Fisheries courses during the 1940s focussed directly on the economic fortunes of those involved, but simultaneously influenced participants' social and political lives. Similarly, since 2008, Summer Institutes in Sustainability addressed an urgent environmental problem while providing participants with new professional identities and new understandings of the world and humanity's place in it. In part, the permeability of these boundaries arises because human activity itself cannot be divided into simple categories. Learners themselves are whole people – not beings neatly sub-divided into occupational, cultural, and citizenship identities. As a consequence, learning derived from a course explicitly dedicated to one area will naturally influence other aspects of a student's life. Although the categorization of educational programs aids both administrative and scholarly work, it can be difficult to designate particular learning experiences as fundamentally professional, liberal, or civic in nature. These *conceptual* categories are useful for making sense of the complex and multifaceted experience of education, but they should not be mistaken as *real* boundaries that somehow limit what people learn through that experience.

What has been the relative balance placed upon these three goals at different periods in the history of UBC? UBC extension and continuing education units fairly consistently placed roughly equal emphasis upon professional education on the one hand, and liberal and civic education on the other. Three indicators help to quantify this conclusion. First, for most years between 1938 and 1965, data exist indicating the number of students enrolled in specific evening courses offered by Extension. For the period as a whole, about one-half of the students enrolled in evening courses were enrolled in courses primarily oriented toward developing their professional capacities. The other half of the student population enrolled in courses dedicated toward personal growth, cultural development, and cultivating an awareness of, and participation in, public affairs. In the 1940s, 1950s and 1960s, there were no long-term changes in the proportion of students enrolled in professional programs; the proportion varied somewhat from year to year, from a low of 28 percent in 1944-45 to a high of 62 percent in 1946-47. However, in all but four years between 1941 and 1965, the proportion of evening course enrolments engaged in professional programs was somewhere between 45 percent and 55 percent.

Second, when we look at more recent decades, we find the same pattern. In the 1970s and 1980s, the Centre for Continuing Education maintained a fairly equal balance between programs oriented primarily toward professional goals, and programs oriented toward liberal and civic goals. For these two decades as a whole, 46 percent of students enrolled in courses having primarily professional or technical objectives. Of course, one must keep in mind that during the 1970s and 1980s the number of degree-credit enrolments, and the number of enrolments in continuing professional education programs delivered by faculties and schools, increased significantly.

Third, in the first decade of the 2000s, UBC Continuing Studies developed numerous programs of study leading to certificates or other credentials. Most of these programs of study have had a professional orientation – they have assisted their graduates to obtain employment or function more effectively in their working lives. However, it is important to note that the substantive fields of study for which UBC Continuing Studies granted credentials were balanced fairly equally between those in business and information technologies, those in languages and culture, and those serving professionals in fields

*It is safe to say that the standing of the University in the community has been very greatly enhanced as a result of its policy of placing its resources at the service of the public through an adult education programme.*

*Gordon Shrum*
*Director of University Extension*
*1942*

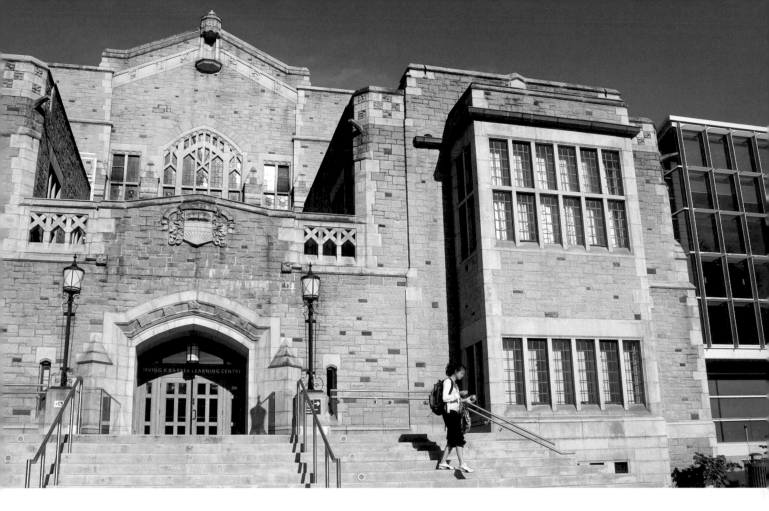

relating to important social issues. Of the twenty-nine certificate programs offered by UBC Continuing Studies in 2009, over half had strong connections to either liberal studies or civic engagement. Clearly, UBC extension and continuing education units have not simply expressed the philosophical virtues of balancing professional, liberal, and civic education – they have actively delivered programs addressing the aspirations of British Columbians with regard to employment, culture, and citizenship.

One other tradition is worth mentioning. Despite various stressors experienced by staff over the years, first-hand accounts of the work climate in UBC Continuing Studies and its predecessors have been overwhelmingly positive; external reviewers over the years have made similar observations. It seems that there was no one "golden age," but an ongoing commitment to congenial working relationships throughout the history of UBC Continuing Studies.

## SOCIAL AND EDUCATIONAL CHANGE

Despite this ongoing balance between professional, liberal, and civic forms of education at UBC, the nature of extension and continuing education programming has been far from static. Course content and delivery have changed profoundly over the years

**Top:** The Heritage Core of the Irving K. Barber Learning Centre at UBC, 2011. **Bottom:** UBC Continuing Studies course calendar celebrating 75 years of lifelong learning at UBC, 2011.

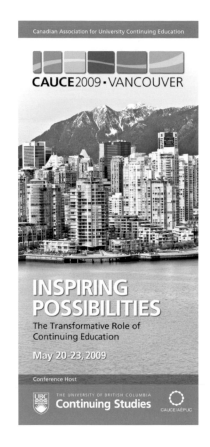

because of changes to the nature of life in British Columbia. Economic and technological changes over the past century have altered the way that people make a living in the province, affecting the nature of professional education. New social realities and insights into the human condition have provided fresh answers to old questions about life's meaning; as people came to understand and express themselves differently, liberal or cultural education has acquired new forms. Finally, with dramatic changes to the British Columbia population, new ways of relating to one another and participating in public affairs, the nature of civic or citizenship education has changed.

Ever since 1935, leaders of extension and continuing education at UBC have argued that social change creates the impetus for lifelong learning, and that the university has both opportunity and responsibility to provide relevant educational programs. The establishment of agricultural extension, home economics, and fisheries education programs at UBC fit the historical project of constructing a provincial economy based on the production and sale of primary commodities. As employment in the provincial economy shifted toward the provision of services rather than the production of these staple commodities, and as British Columbians increasingly lived in cities rather than the countryside, the nature of continuing professional education at UBC changed.

The rise of continuing education programs in business and management reflected the increasing complexity of organizational forms, labour relations, and profit-seeking strategies among companies in the evolution of industrial and post-industrial production

## CAUCE2009·VANCOUVER

### INSPIRING POSSIBILITIES: THE TRANSFORMATIVE ROLE OF CONTINUING EDUCATION

*Hosted by UBC Continuing Studies in Vancouver: May 20-23, 2009*

Over 200 national and international delegates attended the 56th Annual Conference of the Canadian Association for University Continuing Education (CAUCE) that was planned and hosted by UBC Continuing Studies at the Westin Bayshore in Vancouver.

This national conference of adult education professionals focused on the transformative role of university continuing education – both on campus and in the community.

Conference themes explored the ways in which our programs and practices inspire positive changes in the individuals, universities, organizations and communities we serve. Transformative changes in our units, our institutions and our field were also examined. Three conference tracks included: The Teaching and Learning Continuum; Operating Models and Strategies; and Forces of Change.

#### Keynote Speakers

The program included two keynote speakers. **Mike Harcourt**, former BC premier and Vancouver mayor, expressed his views on the role of university continuing education in the transformation of cities (introduced by Vice President Academic and Provost, David Farrar). **Carla Qualtrough**, human rights lawyer and former Paralympic athlete, shared her experiences advocating for the values of fairness, diversity and inclusion (introduced by Vice President External, Legal and Community Relations, Stephen Owen).

in British Columbia. The emergence of continuing professional education programs in fields such as education, health care, engineering, and social work reflected the professionalization of these fields, the increasing numbers of people working in them, the rise of a middle class, and the intensification of competition for professional status, what historian Harold Perkin has called "the rise of professional society."[1] The growth of degree-credit educational programs for part-time learners, and the emergence and proliferation of certificate programs, reflected the increasing levels of formal educational attainment among British Columbians and the growing necessity for people to possess post-secondary credentials in order to obtain jobs in an economy characterized for periods of time by significant levels of unemployment and underemployment. As more and more goods and services in the economy depended upon new information technologies for their production, distribution, and sale, continuing education programs in computer science and information technology became increasingly prominent.

Just as economic and technological changes guided the evolution of professional programming at UBC, so too did cultural change guide the evolution of continuing education in the liberal arts. The emergence of the mass media of radio, television, and commercial cinema meant that the major liberal arts programs of the 1930s and 1940s – extension lectures, film showings, and library services – declined in their attractiveness. At the same time, dominant sensibilities and tastes in the province shifted from British to Anglo-Canadian, and more recently to multicultural. The transition from modern to postmodern forms of cultural life, including increased scepticism regarding authoritative accounts of the world, increased fragmentation of experience over the course of the lifespan, and decreased certainty regarding knowledge and identity, has led to a shift in liberal arts programming away from teaching the foundations of Western culture, and toward facilitating reflection upon diverse life experiences, and helping people construct and express meaningful identities. The globalization of economic and cultural life, in its many and sometimes conflicting aspects, has fuelled the popularity of international and language programs. While it may be easier to understand the connections between changing employment patterns and shifts in the provision of professional programs, the changing patterns of cultural experience and personal identities have helped structure the evolution of continuing education.

Social change has also transformed the nature of citizenship education and civic engagement in British Columbia over the past seventy-five years. At the most obvious level, current events programs have shifted as the nature of those events changed. At a more subtle level, there have been important challenges to the very nature of how citizenship and public affairs have been conceptualized. Notions of citizenship in the early 1900s were influenced by frontier capitalism mixed with British imperial sensibilities, in the post Second World War era by a new and independent Canadian and British Columbian political identity conjoined with "welfare state" policies, and in the later 20th century by

*The UBC continuing education story is one of encouraging curiosity and reflection, developing ingenuity and critical thinking, stimulating dialogue and learning new skills for thousands of learners throughout our many communities, local to global.*

*Jane Hutton*
*Associate Vice President*
*Continuing Studies*
*2005*

a "neo-liberal" political agenda that endorsed both economic free markets and individual rights. In the new millennium, notions of "global citizenship" gained currency. Universal claims to things such as "the national interest" and "the rights and duties of citizens" have been, in recent decades, shown to obscure and in some cases oppress the particular interests of many individuals and groups. In part as a result, there has been a shift away from general citizenship education and toward the provision of educational programs that engage with the specific experiences and aspirations of particular populations. At UBC, this has been demonstrated in the growth of continuing education programming for women, older adults, and Aboriginal people, and in the provision of programs concerning specific issues such as environmental sustainability and health and wellness.

The increasing participation of women in the labour market is likely the social change which has had the most profound influence on university continuing education over the past fifty years. In professional education, the aspirations of women to develop their knowledge and skills and to obtain credentials to compete in the labour market, have helped drive an enormous expansion of continuing professional education programs. In liberal studies and public affairs, the women's movement has had a fundamental role in reshaping continuing education programs. Women now constitute the majority of students at UBC Continuing Studies and at all major university continuing education units across Canada. Women's changing roles in economic, cultural, and political life have shaped, to a great extent, the evolution of continuing education in recent decades.

One of the key claims of feminism – that the personal is political – is integral to understanding the connections between social change and the evolution of continuing education programming for professional, liberal, and civic goals. With the rise of a post-industrial economy and of women's participation in the wage labour market, patterns of labour relations and employment have also changed: rather than experiencing long periods of stable employment with one employer or within one field, many British Columbians increasingly change jobs, employers, and even fields of activity, several times over the course of their working lives. This has obvious and well-known implications for the provision of continuing education for professional purposes. However, it is also central to continuing education programs designed to help people understand themselves and others, and to participate actively in public affairs.

The discontinuous nature of employment is part of a larger fragmentation of cultural experience in the contemporary world. As people's productive activities change more frequently, and as globalization and new information technologies bring an increasing number of diverse cultural messages into people's lives, the project of constructing a coherent and stable personal identity becomes more difficult. Within such a postmodern context, liberal studies becomes less about helping individuals understand "their culture" and more about helping people construct an individual sense of self as they interact with others in a culturally diverse landscape. At the same time, civic education becomes less about helping citizens participate in public affairs, and more about constructing patterns

*Universities help us discover who we are and they open the doors to all we might be. They do this not only by imparting knowledge, but also by fostering growth.*

*Stephen Toope*
*UBC President*
*2011*

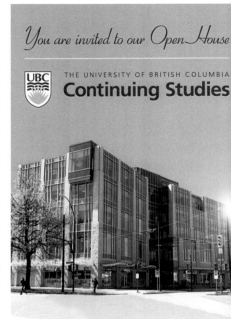

You are an invited to our *Open House*

**Left:** View of Carr Hall, site of the Centre for Continuing Education. **Right:** Invitation to the opening of the UBC Continuing Studies site at the David Strangway Building, 2005.

of citizenship that make sense for different people at different times in their lives. In short, politics is increasingly integrated with economics and culture. In some ways, the key political issues today are rooted in age-old cultural and economic questions: who am I, what is important to me, and how am I going to make a living and contribute to my society?

## TRANSFORMING LIVES

Clearly, social change and the evolution of extension and continuing education programming at UBC have been closely related for the past seventy-five years, and have been marked at several times by organizational transitions such as the creation of the Department of University Extension and the Centre for Continuing Education. Social, institutional, and programmatic transformations have been integral to the history of extension and continuing education work at UBC, and are likely to continue in the future.

Another type of transformation has been central to the story that we have told – one that has been "between the lines" of our account of the programs and services that constituted the most visible part of the work of extension and continuing education at UBC. We are referring here to the transformations experienced by those who participated in these programs and services, some of which may have been visible to others (for example, gaining skills and credentials that led participants to greater career success) and

TRANSFORMATIONS    199

some of which may have stayed largely inside the participants themselves (for example, coming to understand the world more fully, or coming to have more confidence in one's ability to act in that world).

The programs and services provided by UBC extension and continuing education units over the past seventy-five years consistently have benefitted adult learners. Hundreds of thousands of people have participated in a diverse range of programs over the years. Many of these people have become more effective in their work, obtained new jobs or promotions, gained access to opportunities for further education, or built more profitable businesses. Many have come to understand and express themselves in their world at a more mature and sophisticated level. Many have considered, discussed, and even acted on key local, national, and international issues. Although these benefits are difficult to quantify, there are thousands of stories of people whose professional, personal, and civic lives have been enriched and transformed through participating in UBC extension and continuing education programs.

In short, the Department of University Extension, the Centre for Continuing Education, and UBC Continuing Studies have helped hundreds of thousands of people develop the full range of their human potential: their knowledge, their skills, their self-awareness, their understanding of others, and their commitment to act in the world. Indeed, participating in extension and continuing education programs has often been a transformative experience for both local and international students – helping them to change their lives for the better. The benefits from such change have reached beyond the individuals involved. As people have participated in extension and continuing education programs, they have become better able to contribute to the families, organizations, and communities in which they live and work. In this way, UBC has strengthened the economic, cultural, and social fabric of the communities it serves.

It is important to note that one of the communities most strengthened by continuing education programming has been UBC itself. Numerous members of faculty and staff have participated in UBC Continuing Studies courses and programs over the years, in areas ranging from intercultural communication and the liberal arts, to information technology and career development. UBC has provided tuition fee support to facilitate the participation of staff in continuing education programs, and such participation has contributed to the personal and professional development of many members of the UBC community. Through the work of staff in places such as the Writing Centre and the English Language Institute, UBC Continuing Studies has fostered the academic success of many students following undergraduate programs of study at UBC.

Of course, the transformations that have taken place in the lives of adult learners, and the impact that those learners have had on their families, workplaces, and communities, are difficult to summarize here. Many of the learners who participated in the programs and services of the Department of University Extension are now deceased, and we must

*To live a life abundantly requires more than a high school education or a university degree. It implies lifelong learning.*

*John Friesen*
*Director of University*
*Extension*
*1961*

leave to future researchers any attempt to explore systematically the transformative impact of UBC Continuing Studies experiences on those who are still alive. However, some indication of the transformative nature of extension and continuing education can be seen in the stories of students who have graduated from contemporary programs.

To conclude our story of transformations, we are including brief stories of a some recent students. These narratives touch upon four contemporary programming streams: life-long learning and community engagement; technology and the professions; skills and viewpoints for a global community; and academic success for UBC undergraduates. We believe that the following profiles help illustrate the transformative impact of extension and continuing education work over the past eight decades.

Just as social, institutional, and programmatic transformations have been common themes in the past seventy-five years at UBC, so too have significant personal changes often been part of the experience of adult learners whose lives have been touched by those who work with the Department of University Extension, the Centre for Continuing Education, and UBC Continuing Studies.

*UBC Continuing Studies inspires positive and often transformational changes in the individuals, organizations, and communities we serve.*

*UBC Continuing Studies Highlights Review 2010/11*

*Transforming Lives Throug*

"Don't fear the technology," **Bonnie Bishop** advises students considering the Certificate in Multimedia Studies offered by UBC Continuing Studies. With a strong background in graphic arts, Bonnie began the program to expand her knowledge and skills in digital technology. She learned many technical and business skills, but she also acquired a great deal of self-reliance and the confidence to branch into web design. Shortly after she graduated, she was hired as a web designer for an agency that offers educational materials for interior designers, architects, and government agencies. Bonnie plans to continue to explore web design and interactivity, as well as design for mobile devices.

Photo: Martin Dee

**James Milligan** decided he wanted to do work that had a positive impact on the world. Inspired by campaigns like Make Poverty History and Live 8, he started to wonder how he could be involved in something that would give back. In addition to completing a leadership program through the Sauder School of Business Executive Education, James worked to obtain the UBC Continuing Studies Award of Achievement in Sustainability Management and the UBC Certificate in Project Management at UBC Robson Square. Before long, he started his own company, Social Conscience, which sells fair trade soccer balls, volleyballs and basketballs. "I wanted to get more involved in the community," Milligan says, "and this was a perfect fit. There's so much work I want to do, and I love what I'm doing. This business has the potential to make a difference."

A series of unforeseen circumstances led **Jas Cheema** to enroll in the UBC Continuing Studies Certificate in Intercultural Studies in 2004. Her work with immigrants and community organizations made her an ideal student for the program, which provided her with an opportunity both to formalize her earlier knowledge and to consider the theoretical underpinnings of her work. After completing the certificate program, Jas went on to earn a Master's degree from Royal Roads University and begin her own diversity consulting business. Currently, as Leader, Diversity Services for Fraser Health Authority, Jas is laying the foundations for more equitable and culturally competent healthcare services in the largest health region in British Columbia.

**Rena Dhir** found her time studying for the Certificate in Immigration: Laws, Policies, and Procedures to be busy and rewarding, not surprising for someone also working as a CGA and raising a young family. With the certificate completed, Rena passed the licensing exam and began consulting. However, a new and even more challenging opportunity arose when she applied for a vacant position with the Immigration and Refugee Board of Canada, to which she was subsequently appointed in 2009, and reappointed in 2011. Despite the challenges, Rena enjoys the rewards of her new career direction, for which she thanks her immigration studies at UBC Continuing Studies.

Born in Toronto but raised in Japan, **Daniel Budgell** grew up with a foot in two cultures. He came to the UBC Continuing Studies English Language Institute in 2001 to improve his English so he could pursue a UBC degree in biology. After six months, he had learned not only how to write a better essay, but also to appreciate our shared humanity despite diverse backgrounds. Daniel completed his studies and then a biology degree, but remained with the ELI as a Cultural Assistant. His intercultural appreciation and compassion were engaged during a visit to Tanzania, when he learned that the street children who approached him for money really wanted an education and the opportunity to create a future. He was soon caring for and educating three hundred homeless and displaced children, prompting him to register a charity. Daniel considers himself lucky to have found such great purpose and meaning for his life.

*The UBC Continuing Studies website (cstudies.ubc.ca) regularly features stories about a wide range of students who have completed lifelong learning programs at UBC.*

# Endnotes

**Note:** Archival fonds and collections are contained in the UBC Archives unless otherwise noted. References to specific events, courses, and programs are typically made without citing archival locations. In general, information regarding specific events, courses, and programs is derived from reports, promotional materials, and calendars found either at UBC Archives or in a collection of historical documents held by UBC Continuing Studies.

## INTRODUCTION

[1] *UBC Annual*, 1916, "Invocation" by President Wesbrook, p. iii.

[2] Report of the UBC President, 1947-48, p. 25.

[3] *University of British Columbia 2001-2002 Annual Report*, p. 2.

[4] Blythe Eagles fonds, Box 15-65, Leonard Klinck, "A Plan for Adult Education in British Columbia" (transcript), 16 November 1935.

[5] Note that UBC annual reports typically cover a period spanning two calendar years, from September 1 in the first year to August 31 in the second year. For ease of reading, the dates of annual reports are presented in the text by naming the second of the two years covered in the report. In this example, Friesen's 1965 report actually covered the period from September 1, 1964 through August 31, 1965. In some cases, activities reported as taking place in one year actually commenced in the previous year.

[6] Report of the UBC President, 1969-70, p. 28.

[7] UBC, *Annual Report of the Centre for Continuing Education*, 1969-70, p. 7.

[8] UBC, *Annual Report of the Centre for Continuing Education*, 1977-78, p. 1.

[9] UBC, *Annual Report of UBC Continuing Studies*, 1993-94, p. iii.

[10] Provincial statistics cited for the period from 1911 through 1971 are based upon census data found in the following publications: Canada, Census and Statistics Office (1911) *Fifth Census of Canada, 1911* (Ottawa, King's Printer); Canada, Census and Statistics Office (1921) *Sixth Census of Canada, 1921* (Ottawa, King's Printer); Canada, Dominion Bureau of Statistics (1931) *Seventh Census of Canada, 1931* (Ottawa, King's Printer); Canada, Dominion Bureau of Statistics (1941) *Eighth Census of Canada, 1941* (Ottawa, King's Printer); Canada, Dominion Bureau of Statistics (1951) *Ninth Census of Canada, 1951* (Ottawa, King's Printer); Canada, Dominion Bureau of Statistics (1961) *1961 Census of Canada* (Ottawa, Ministry of Trade and Commerce); Statistics Canada (1971) *1971 Census of Canada* (Ottawa, Statistics Canada).

[11] Provincial statistics cited for the period from 1981 through 2001 are based upon census data compiled by Statistics Canada and presented in the form of a digital database: Statistics Canada (2005) *PCensus, 1981-2001* (Ottawa, Statistics Canada).

[12] Statistics Canada, *Historical Statistics of Canada*, 2nd ed. (Ottawa: Statistics Canada, 1983), Table W504-512.

[13] Statistics Canada, "University degrees, diplomas and certificates granted, by program level and instructional program (Bachelor's and other undergraduate degrees)," last modified April 3, 2012, http://www.statcan.gc.ca/tables-tableaux/sum-som/l01/cst01/educ52a-eng.htm

[14] W. Clark, "100 years of education," *Education Quarterly Review* 7, 3 (2001): 18-23.

[15] Association of Universities and Colleges of Canada, *Trends in Higher Education: Volume 1 – Enrolment* (Ottawa: AUCC, 2007).

[16] http://www.library.ubc.ca/archives/enrolmnt.html

## CHAPTER ONE

[1] Much of the background information on UBC can be found in Eric Damer and Herbert Rosengarten, *UBC: The First 100 Years* (Vancouver: The University of British Columbia, 2009). Jean Barman, *The West Beyond the West* (Toronto: University of Toronto Press, 1991), table 5 "British Columbia Population by Ethnic Origin, 1871-1981."

[2] Scott McLean, "University Extension and Social Change: Positioning a 'University of the People' in Saskatchewan," *Adult Education Quarterly* 58, 1 (2007): 3-21.

[3] Eric Damer, "The Vancouver Institute and the Highjacking of Mutual Enlightenment," *The Canadian Journal for the Study of Adult Education* 13, 1 (May 1999): 61-79.

[4] Theodore Shannon and Clay Shoenfeld, *University Extension* (New York: The Center for Applied Research in Education, 1965), 14-15.

[5] Scott McLean, "University Extension and Social Change"; Scott McLean, "'A Work Second to None': Positioning Extension at the University of Alberta, 1912-1975," *Studies in the Education of*

*Adults* 39, 1 (2007): 77-91; Scott McLean, *Reaching out into the World: A History of Extension at the University of Saskatchewan, 1910-2007* (Saskatoon: University Extension Press, 2007).

6 Cited in the *Annual Report of the Department of Extension*, University of Alberta, 1963, p. 3.

7 UBC Department of University Extension Fonds (hereafter "Extension Fonds"), Box 2-7, brochure, 1917, "Short Course in Horticulture."

8 Extension Fonds, Box 5-1, Blythe Eagles, "Agricultural Extension at U.B.C. – Past and Present," paper presented at a seminar on *Agricultural Extension in British Columbia* on May 18, 1961, pp. 11-12.

9 Eric Damer, *Discovery by Design* (Vancouver: Ronsdale Press, 2002), 30-31.

10 Gordon Selman, "A History of the Extension and Adult Education Services at the University of British Columbia 1915-1955" (MA thesis, The University of British Columbia, 1963), 34.

11 UBC Archives, Scrapbooks, *passim*; Selman, "A History," 36; David C. Jones, "The Strategy of Rural Enlightenment: Consolidation in Chilliwack, BC," in *Shaping the Schools of the Canadian West*, eds. David C. Jones, Nancy M. Sheehan, and Robert M. Stamp, (Calgary: Detselig, 1979), 139.

12 "May Abandon Agricultural Faculty: Course is Too Costly," *Daily World*, 20 March 1922, p. 1. Issues of the *UBC Calendar* retained the description of the extension courses, but added "not offered" each year after 1923.

13 Selman, "A History," 37.

14 Extension Fonds, Box 2-7, brochure, 1931, "Ninth Annual Series of Short Courses."

15 Damer and Rosengarten, *UBC: The First 100 Years*, 7, 23; UBC Board of Governors (BoG) Minutes, 28 February 1916.

16 UBC Senate Minutes, 13 December 1916; BoG Minutes, 13 March 1917. Appointments made in Applied Science and Chemistry included E.T. Hodge, J.M. Turnbull, and R.W. Brock, who also served on the Chamber of Mines executive (honorary or active). UBC faculty were regular speakers at Chamber events; see also clippings in the UBC Scrapbooks.

17 UBC Archives, Academy of Science Collection, Box 2-28, 1924, brochure, British Columbia Chamber of Mines. The brochure emphasizes Vancouver's need for investment capital.

18 BoG Minutes, 1 December 1916; Senate Minutes, 19 February 1930.

19 David Brownstein, "Sunday Walks and Seed Traps: The Many Natural Histories of British Columbia Forest Conservation, 1890-1925" (PhD diss., The University of British Columbia, 2006).

20 Selman, "A History," 40.

21 Extension Fonds, Box 1-3, Report of June 1919, The University Extension Committee, p. 1.

22 Ibid.

23 Attendance data reported in the annual reports of the University Extension Committee, Extension Fonds, Box 1-3, 7, 15.

24 Attendance data reported in the annual reports of the University Extension Committee, held in the Continuing Studies Collection.

25 Extension Fonds, Box 1-5 through 1-29 and Box 2-1 through 2-4. Page numbers to reports included in the text for this section also refer to reports included in these files.

26 Damer and Rosengarten, *UBC: The First 100 Years*, 49.

27 UBC Scrapbooks; Robert A.J. McDonald, *Making Vancouver* (Vancouver: UBC Press, 1996). The labour press at times regarded UBC as an elite institution. *B.C. Federationist*, 19 November 1915 (clipping in UBC Scrapbooks); Selman, "A History," 44.

28 Eric Damer, "The Vancouver Institute and the Highjacking of Mutual Enlightenment," *The Canadian Journal for Studies in Adult Education* 13, 1 (May 1999): 61-79.

29 UBC Senate Minutes, 14 May 1919.

30 F. Henry Johnson, *A History of Public Education in British Columbia* (Vancouver: University of British Columbia, 1964), 86; also see issues of the *UBC Calendar* during the 1920s. At first, only teachers with senior matriculation (grade thirteen, or first-year university) could earn Summer Session credit, but in 1924 Senate ruled to permit junior matriculants the opportunity: UBC Senate Minutes, 15 October 1924.

31 Selman, "A History," 140-145; UBC *Calendar*, 1935-36.

32 Glennis Zilm and Ethel Warbinek, *Legacy: A History of Nursing Education at the University of British Columbia 1919-1994* (Vancouver: UBC School of Nursing, 1994), 35, 56; Calendars, *UBC Summer Session*, 1923-1931; Personal communication, 2011.

33 Damer and Rosengarten, *UBC: The First 100 Years*, 83.

34 Damer and Rosengarten, *UBC: The First 100 Years*, chap. 5; Scott McLean, "Discovering Adult Education at McGill and UBC," *Canadian Journal for the Study of Adult Education* 22, 1 (2009): 1-20.

35 University Extension Collection, Graham A. Drew (collector), Box 1-2, Alden Barss, "A Proposal..." TMS, January 1934.

36 See Barss Fonds, Box 13-2, 11 January 1934, "Carnegie Corporation Grant Suggested Projects."

37 Selman, "A History," 57-64.

38 Alden Barrs, "A Proposal..."

39 Klinck, "A Plan for Adult Education in British Columbia."

## CHAPTER TWO

1 Robert England, *Living, Learning, Remembering* (Vancouver: Centre for Continuing Education, UBC, 1980), 73-85.

2 Harry T. Logan, *Tuum Est: A History of the University of British Columbia* (Vancouver: The University of British Columbia, 1958), 121.

3 Cole Harris, "The Struggle with Distance," chap. in *The Resettlement of British Columbia* (Vancouver: UBC Press, 1997), 161-193; Barman, *The West*, 260-261.

4 Gordon Shrum, *Gordon Shrum: An Autobiography* (Vancouver: The University of British Columbia Press, 1986).

5 Peter Waite, *Lord of Point Grey: Larry MacKenzie of U.B.C* (Vancouver: The University of British Columbia Press, 1987);

for the shared values, a moderate "Christian socialism," see Eric Damer, "The Study of Adult Education at UBC, 1957-1985" (PhD diss., The University of British Columbia, 2000).

[6] Kathryn Anne Kennedy, "John K. Friesen: Adult Educator, Mentor and Humanitarian" (MA thesis, The University of British Columbia, 1992), 111; Damer, "The Study of Adult Education," 5.

[7] UBC *Calendar*, 1950-51 and 1957-58.

[8] Barman, *The West*, Tables 5 and 7.

[9] Gordon Selman, *A Decade of Transition: The Extension Department of The University of British Columbia 1960 to 1970*, Occasional Papers in Continuing Education no. 10 (Vancouver: The Centre for Continuing Education, The University of British Columbia, 1975), 20; Kulich, *Former UBC Extension Directors Reminisce, 1936-1976* (Vancouver: Centre for Continuing Education, UBC, 1976), 29. The *Calendar* in 1963-64 listed twenty-four full-time staff in the Department, while the 1966-67 *Calendar* listed only seventeen, four of whom had continuing professional education responsibilities. Numbers were back to twenty-three in 1967, seven of whom were directly responsible for continuing professional education.

[10] Kennedy, "John K. Friesen," 195-212, 219.

[11] Kennedy, "John K. Friesen," 174-178.

## CHAPTER THREE

[1] Continuing Studies Collection, 18 September 1937, "Report on the Projects Initiated and Conducted by the Extension Department of the University of British Columbia from October 1st, 1936 to August 31st, 1937, and Paid for out of Funds Provided by the Carnegie Corporation of New York," p. 4; Report of the UBC President, 1938, p. 25.

[2] "Need Adult Education," *The Daily Province*, 1 December 1934 (clipping in Barss Fonds, Box 13-2).

[3] Vancouver City Archives, Major Matthews Collection, Add. MSS 54, 503-C-3, newspaper clippings p. 149, 152, 156, 170 and 503-C-4 p. 5, 7, 9, 10, 13, 14, 18 and photos of North Vancouver produce, 1933; Selman, "A History," 129.

[4] Cole Harris (with David Demeritt), "Farming and Rural Life," chap. in *The Resettlement of British Columbia* (Vancouver: UBC Press, 1997), 219-249; John Douglas Belshaw and David J. Mitchell, "The Economy Since the Great War," in *The Pacific Province: A History of British Columbia*, ed. Hugh M. Johnston (Vancouver: Douglas and McIntyre, 1996), 324-325.

[5] UBC, *Annual Report of the Department of University Extension*, 1945-1946, p. 10.

[6] UBC Senate Minutes, 4 April 1946 and 27 August 1952.

[7] Kulich, *Former UBC Extension Directors Reminisce*, 23-24.

[8] Quoted in Selman, "A History," 97.

[9] Alvin Finkel and Margaret Conrad, *History of the Canadian Peoples vol. 2*, 2nd edition (Toronto: Copp Clark, 1998), 271; Carol Dennison, "'Housekeepers of the Community': The British Columbia Women's Institutes, 1909-1946," in *Knowledge for the People: The Struggle for Adult Learning in English-Speaking Canada 1828-1973*, ed. Michael R. Welton (Toronto: OISE Press, 1987), 52-72.

[10] Lee Stewart, "The Proper and Logical Study for Womankind: Home Economics at UBC," chap. in *"It's Up to You": Women at UBC in the Early Years* (Vancouver: UBC Press, 1990), 43-65.

[11] Selman, "A History," 114.

[12] Dennison, "Housekeepers of the Community," 60.

[13] Denise Charleston, Phyl Babichuk-Mowatt, and Alison Lane, "Character Education in Junior and Senior High Schools," The Homeroom, April 2001, http://www.viu.ca/homeroom/content/topics/programs/2001/CHARED/index.htm

[14] Kulich, *Former UBC Extension Directors Reminisce*, 24.

[15] University Extension Fonds, Box 5-37, "Home Economics Services."

[16] Census of Canada, 1961.

[17] UBC, *Annual Report of the Department of University Extension*, 1936-37; Kulich, *Former UBC Extension Directors Reminisce*, 20; Ian McPherson, *Co-operation, Conflict, and Consensus: B.C. Central and the Credit Union Movement to 1994* (Vancouver: BC Central Credit Union, 1995), 25-27, 29, 32.

[18] UBC, *Annual Report of the Department of University Extension*, 1939-40, p. 15.

[19] Selman, "A History," 104-105.

[20] Selman, "A History," 109, 114.

[21] Belshaw and Mitchell, "The Economy Since the Great War," 324.

[22] *UBC Graduate Chronicle* (May 1937): 5, 7.

[23] Allan Irving, "The Development of a Provincial Welfare State: British Columbia 1900-1939," in *The Benevolent State*, eds. Allan Moscovitch and Jim Albert (Toronto: Garamond Press, 1987), 155-174.

[24] Selman, "A History," 137.

[25] Penney Clark, Mona Gleason, and Stephen Petrina, "Preschools for Science? The Child Study Centre at the University of British Columbia, 1960-1997," TMS; Doug Owram, *Born at the Right Time: A History of the Baby Boom Generation* (Toronto: University of Toronto Press, 1997), chap. 2.

[26] UBC Calendar, 1940-41, p. 174. The course textbook, Fowler D. Brooks' *Child Psychology*, had a large section on mental hygiene.

[27] Owram, *Born at the Right Time*, 34-45; Gillian Weiss, "An Essential Year for the Child: The Kindergarten in British Columbia," in *Schooling and Society in 20th Century British Columbia*, eds. J. Donald Wilson and David C. Jones (Calgary: Detselig, 1980), 139-161.

[28] Weiss, "An Essential Year for the Child," 154-155.

[29] Damer, "The Study of Adult Education at UBC," 11-12.

[30] UBC, *Annual Report of the Department of University Extension*, 1959-60.

[31] Selman, "A History," 140-45; 149-50.

[32] UBC Senate Minutes, 10 May 1949, 26 August 1949.

[33] UBC, *Annual Report of the Department of University Extension*, 1948-49.

[34] Report of the UBC President, 1956-57, p. 27.

# CHAPTER FOUR

[1] "Alumni Hear Learning Plea," UBC Scrapbook 23, p. 89.

[2] *UBC Alumni Chronicle* (Summer 1961): 28 and (Winter 1961): 35.

[3] UBC, *Annual Report of the Department of University Extension*, 1953-54, p. 28.

[4] Report of the UBC President, 1936-37, p. 5.

[5] *The Encyclopedia of British Columbia*, 2000 ed., s.v. "Halpern, Ida"; William Bruneau and David Gordon Duke, *Jean Coulthard: A Life in Music* (Vancouver: Ronsdale Press, 2005), 71; Barman, *The West*, 245.

[6] Bruneau and Duke, *Jean Coulthard*, 72.

[7] Bruneau and Duke, *Jean Coulthard*, 58, 72.

[8] Selman, "A History," 188.

[9] Bente Roed Cochran, *Printmaking in Alberta 1945-1985* (Edmonton: The University of Alberta Press), 119.

[10] Rachelle Chinnery, "Significant Material: Ceramics of British Columbia 1945-1960," in *A Modern Life: Art and Design in British Columbia 1945-1960*, eds. Ian Thom and Alan Elder (Vancouver: Arsenal Pulp Press, 2004), 87-88.

[11] Debra Sloan, "Origins of a Ceramic Culture: The First Fifty Years of the BC Potters Guild 1955 – 2005," TMS., http://www.debrasloan.com/articles/Origins_of_%20a_Ceramic_Culture.doc

[12] Kulich, *Former UBC Extension Directors Reminisce*, 22.

[13] Canadian Theatre Encyclopedia, "Sydney Risk," 18 January 2006, http://www.canadiantheatre.com/dict.pl?term=Risk%2C%20Sydney; Canadian Theatre Encyclopedia, "Joy Coghill," 25 January 2010, http://www.canadiantheatre.com/dict.pl?term=Joy%20Coghill

[14] "A Holiday with a Difference," *UBC Alumni Chronicle* (Summer 1952): 7-8.

[15] Jean Falardeau, "The University Summer Session: A Visitor Looks at UBC," *UBC Alumni Chronicle* (Autumn 1957): 20-21; Selman, "A History," 191.

[16] "Couple's Legacy Takes Flight at UBC Science," *Synergy: Journal of UBC Science*, 2 (2009): 4.

[17] Damer and Rosengarten, *UBC: The First 100 Years*, 32; Damer, *Discovery by Design*, 56.

[18] Damer and Rosengarten, *UBC: The First 100 Years*, 128.

[19] UBC, Report of the University Librarian to the Senate, 39th Year, 1954, p. 24; UBC, Report of the University Librarian to the Senate, 40th Year, 1955, p. 24.

[20] Juliet Pollard, "Propaganda for Democracy: John Grierson and Adult Education During the Second World War," in *Knowledge for the People: The Struggle for Adult Learning in English-Speaking Canada 1828-1973*, ed. Michael R. Welton (Toronto: OISE Press, 1987), 129-150. For a slightly different view of Grierson's social and educational vision, see Brian Low, "'Lessons in Living': Film Propaganda and Progressive Education in Rural British Columbia, 1944," in *Children, Teachers, and Schools in the History of British Columbia 2nd edition*, eds. Jean Barman and Mona Gleason (Calgary: Detselig, 2003), 343-361.

[21] UBC, Thirteenth Report of the Library Committee to the Senate, 1942, p. 10.

# CHAPTER FIVE

[1] UBC, *Annual Report of the Department of University Extension*, 1941-42, p. 9.

[2] Selman, "A History," 90.

[3] Extension Fonds, Box 7-11, Memorandum from J.R. Kidd, 26 June 1950.

[4] Joseph H. Kett, *The Pursuit of Knowledge Under Difficulties* (Stanford: Stanford University Press, 1994), 424-425.

[5] UBC Continuing Studies Collection, unpublished report: *Study-Discussion...The First Three Years*, 1957–1960, p. 5.

[6] Ross Lambertson, "The Black, Brown, White and Red Blues: The Beating of Clarence Clemons," *The Canadian Historical Review* 85, 4 (December 2004): 755-776.

[7] Damer and Rosengarten, *UBC: The First 100 Years*, 65; E. Paulson, G. Zilm and E. Warbinek, "Profile of a Leader: Pioneer Government Advisor: Laura Holland, RN, RRC, CBE, LLD (1883-1956)," *Nursing Leadership* 13, 3 (September, 2000): 36-39.

[8] Kulich, *Former UBC Extension Directors Reminisce*, 25.

[9] Extension Fonds, Box 7-1, 17 December 1946, Shrum to British Council.

[10] George S. Tomkins, *A Common Countenance: Stability and Change in the Canadian Curriculum* (Scarborough: Prentice-Hall, 1986), 280, 362.

[11] See Damer, "The Study of Adult Education at UBC, 1957-1985," and Kennedy, "John K. Friesen."

# CHAPTER SIX

[1] Scott McLean, "Extending Resources, Fostering Progress, or Meeting Needs? University Extension and Continuing Education in Western Canada," *British Journal of Sociology of Education* 29, 1 (2008): 91-103. Scott McLean, "About Us: Expressing the Purpose of University Continuing Education in Canada," *Canadian Journal of University Continuing Education* 33, 2 (2007): 65-86.

[2] UBC, *Annual Report of the Centre for Continuing Education*, 1969-70, p. 7.

[3] Gordon Selman, *Felt Along the Heart, A Life in Adult Education*, Monographs on Comparative and Area Studies in Adult Education (Vancouver: UBC Centre for Continuing Education, 1994), 71-72; Report of the UBC President, 1971, p. 32.

[4] UBC Senate Minutes, 10 June 1970; Report of the UBC President, 1970, p. 28; Selman, "A Decade of Transition," 31, 32.

[5] Selman, *Felt Along the Heart*, 62-83; Kulich, *Former UBC Extension Directors Reminisce*, 46.

[6] Damer and Rosengarten, *UBC: The First 100 Years*, 206; Faculty Association fonds, Box 12-35, 6 June 1979, Brockett to Slaymaker.

[7] Centre for Continuing Education Fonds (hereafter "CCE Fonds"), Box 1-2, "Goals and Directions," 1977; Damer and Rosengarten, *UBC: The First 100 Years*, 215, 223. Chase, *Post-Secondary Enrolments in the '80s* (Burnaby: SFU Office of Analytic Studies, 1979); see especially reports and correspondence in CCE, Box 5-1.

[8] CCE Fonds, Box 5-1, 27 May 1977, Edwards to Shaw.

[9] CCE Fonds, Box 8-6, Minutes of meetings held autumn, 1974.

[10] Anne Ironside, Pat Thom, Ruth Sigal, and Susan Griffin, *UBC Women's Resources Centre: The First 25 Years* (Vancouver: The University of British Columbia, 1998), 42.

[11] CCE Fonds, Box 3-27, 12 November 1975, Minutes.

[12] Interview, July 2010.

[13] Interview, July 2010.

[14] CCE Fonds, Box 3-27, 15 December 1975, Minutes.

[15] Jindra Kulich, "Lifelong Education and the University of British Columbia," in *Looking Beyond* (The University of British Columbia, 1981), 9.

[16] Report of the UBC President, 1976, p. 10.

[17] Interview, July 2010.

[18] CCE Fonds, Box 1-2, "Goals and Directions: Language Institute-Present and Future," 1977; Interviews, July 2010.

[19] Report of the UBC President, 1974, p. 59.

[20] The Robson Street office was used by the Women's Resources Centre.

[21] CCE Fonds, Box 1-12, 8 February 1984, Memo.

[22] Mike Sasges, "Fighting the Battle of the Budget," *UBC Alumni Chronicle* (Summer 1984): 14-15.

[23] CCE Fonds, Box 1-12, 16 November 1983 and 7 December 1983, Minutes.

[24] CCE Fonds, Box 1-12 19 February 1985, Kulich to Russell; 6 March 1985, Minutes.

[25] Damer and Rosengarten, *UBC: The First 100 Years*, 236.

[26] CCE Fonds, Box 1-12, 3 April 1985, Minutes; 1 May 1985, Agenda; 5 June 1985, Minutes; Box 1-13, 11 September 1985, Minutes.

[27] CCE Fonds, Box 1-12, 3 April 1985, Minutes; 5 June 1985, Minutes; CCE Fonds, Box 1-13, 11 September 1985, Minutes; CCE Fonds, Box 1-12, 6 March 1985, Minutes.

[28] Chris Petty, "Mission: Impossible?" *UBC Alumni Chronicle* (Fall 1988): 12-15; Damer and Rosengarten, 240-247.

[29] CCE Fonds, Box 1-13, 8 January 1986, Minutes.

[30] CCE Fonds, Box 1-13, [n.d.], Continuing Education [response to draft mission statement questions].

[31] CCE Fonds, Box 1-13, 5 February 1986, Minutes.

[32] CCE Fonds, Box 9-1&2, Report of the Task Force on Continuing Education, p. 12.

[33] CCE Fonds, Box 11-6, Appendix 5, "A Response to the Report of the Task Force."

[34] CCE Fonds, Box 9-3, various letters December 1989, January and February 1990.

[35] This memo was not found, but the contents can be inferred by the response given by the Community Advisory Committee. CCE Fonds, Box 9-3, 19 April 1990, Moore to Strangway.

[36] Damer and Rosengarten, *UBC: The First 100 Years*, 240.

[37] Senate Minutes, 23 May 1990; CCE Fonds, Box 9-3, 18 May 1990, Strangway to Members of Community Advisory Committee; 22 May 1990, Moore to DWS (phone message); 4 June 1990, Friesen to Strangway.

[38] CCE Fonds, Box 11-7, "Five Year Plan: Introduction and Context."

[39] Interview, July 2010.

[40] CCE Fonds, 11-6, part 5, "International Division."

[41] Note that while we use the term "ESL – English as a Second Language" in this book, the term "EAL – English as an Additional Language" has become more commonly used at UBC Continuing Studies and elsewhere, to reflect the fact that many students of English already speak more than one other language.

[42] Barman, *The West,* 348.

[43] CCE Fonds, Box 11-7, Appendix 12, Five Year Plan.

[44] "Continuing Education," *UBC Alumni Chronicle* (Fall 1995): 21.

[45] CCE Fonds, Box 11-1, April 1997, "The University of British Columbia Review of Continuing Studies Review Team Report"; "The Matrix Then and Now," 1992 and 1998, clearly show a great loss of "general public programs" (especially fine arts, science, culture, and travel) and a great increase in pre-academic language, high-tech, and vocational certificate programs.

[46] Damer and Rosengarten, *UBC: The First 100 Years*, 294.

[47] See budgets listed at http://www2.finance.ubc.ca/budgets/documents/BudgetSummaryBook2005-06_000.pdf

[48] Review of Continuing Studies/Report of the Review Committee, January 2007.

## CHAPTER SEVEN

[1] *The Encyclopaedia of British Columbia*, 2000 ed., s.v. "Agriculture."

[2] Philip Moir, "A Brief Review of a Decade of Education-Extension Services" and "General Systems Theory Applied to Program Development in Education-Extension," TMS.

[3] Senate Minutes, 12 September 1979; 12 October 1983.

[4] Interview, July 2010. The Vancouver Police Museum exists today.

[5] Damer and Rosengarten, *UBC: The First 100 Years*, 257.

[6] Wesley Pue, *Law School: The Story of Legal Education in British Columbia* (Vancouver: University of British Columbia Faculty of Law, 1995), 277-278.

[7] UBC Senate Minutes, 12 September 1979; 11 September 1985.

[8] UBC Centre for Continuing Education, 1984 Winter-Spring non-credit courses catalogue.

[9] CCE Fonds, Box 1-2, 29 December 1976, Duff to Vince.

[10] CCE Fonds, Box 1-2, Local Government Programs – 1977 Objectives and Preliminary Timetable.

[11] Interviews, July 2010.

[12] Paul D. Lehrman, "Digicon 83," *Creative Computing* 10, 4 (April 1984): 164, http://www.atarimagazines.com/creative/v10n4/164_Digicon_83.php; interview, August 2010.

[13] Mark Wilson, "Science/Technology," in *The Greater Vancouver Book: An Urban Encyclopaedia* ed. Chuck Davis (Vancouver: The Linkman Press, 1997), 514-515; Linda Richards, "Computing in Greater Vancouver," in *The Greater Vancouver Book*, 518-519.

[14] Interview, July 2010.

[15] External Review of UBC Continuing Studies, November 29-December 1, 2006, p. 55.

[16] External Review of UBC Continuing Studies, November 29-December 1, 2006, p. 57.

[17] Damer and Rosengarten, *UBC: The First 100 Years*, 223.

[18] Interview, July 2010.

[19] CCE Fonds, Box 11-1, "A Report to the UBC Board of Governors," June 1998.

[20] Senate Minutes, 17 February 1988.

[21] UBC Calendar, 1992-93, p. 21.

[22] "UBC Powerful Draw for International Students," *UBC Reports*, 20 March 1997, p. 1.

[23] Personal Collection, Continuing Education - Review of Continuing Education April 1, 1996, to March 31, 1997, p. 5. Note that the provincial NDP froze tuition in 1996, a year after federal transfers for post-secondary education were slashed.

[24] Damer and Rosengarten, *UBC: The First 100 Years*, 259.


## CHAPTER EIGHT

[1] CCE Fonds, Box 1-2, 25 January 1977, Sol to Vince; Interview, July 2010.

[2] Interview, July 2010.

[3] CCE Fonds, Box 11-14, 28 August 1992, Strangway to Uegama.

[4] Interview, July 2010.

[5] Interview, August 2010.

[6] CCE Fonds, Box 1-13, 5 March 1986, Minutes.

[7] CCE Fonds, Box 11-7, 20 December 1995, Vertesi to Uegama; Appendix 10; CCE Fonds Box 9-5, Kulich to Birch, 23 October 1987, "Proposed Development for the English Language Institute"; 29 January 1990, McLean to Strangway; 16 February 1990, McLean to Birch; 4 December 1990, Barb to Vera.

[8] CCE Fonds, Box 11-7, Appendix 12, 2 December 1996, Five Year Plan.

[9] CCE Fonds, Box 11-1, "A Report to the UBC Board of Governors," June 1998; Interview, August 2010.

[10] Interview, July 2010.

[11] Interview, July 2010.


## CHAPTER NINE

[1] Anne Ironside, Pat Thom, Ruth Sigal, and Susan Griffin, *UBC Women's Resources Centre: The First 25 Years* (Vancouver: The University of British Columbia, 1998), 8.

[2] Damer and Rosengarten, *UBC: The First 100 Years*, 209.

[3] Abstract of W.W. Black, "Human Rights in British Columbia: Equality Postponed," 1984-1985 *Canadian Human Rights Yearbook*, p. 219, http://heinonline.org/HOL/LandingPage?collection=journals&handle=hein.journals/canhry1984&div=14&id=&page=

[4] Ironside and Thom, *UBC Women's Resources Centre*, 11.

[5] Interview, July 2010.

[6] Interview, July 2010.

[7] Don Wells, "Pair o' Norm(al) Activity," *Alumni Chronicle* (Summer 1999): 12-13.

[8] CCE Fonds, Box 9-18, 11 August 1987, Strangway to Kulich.

[9] Damer and Rosengarten, *UBC: The First 100 Years*, 208.

[10] Damer and Rosengarten, *UBC: The First 100 Years*, 255.

[11] "UBC hikes rent on solar home," *The Ubyssey*, 23 September 1977, p. 3; "Future clouding for solar housing," *The Ubyssey*, 11 March 1980, p. 3; "Houses destroyed despite use," *The Ubyssey*, 7 January 1982, p. 1.

[12] Damer and Rosengarten, *UBC: The First 100 Years*, 252.


## CHAPTER TEN

[1] Harold Perkin, *The Rise of Professional Society: England Since 1880* (London: Routledge, 1990).

# Lifelong Learning at UBC

## UBC CONTINUING STUDIES: PROGRAM OVERVIEW AND LEADERSHIP

The following outline provides an overview of UBC Continuing Studies programs as of 2012, as well as a partial list of program directors and professional staff who provide leadership for these programs.

### Executive Director's Office

Judith Plessis, Executive Director
Mary Holmes, Associate Executive Director (Communications and Strategic Initiatives)
Peter Moroney, Associate Executive Director (Professional Programs and Services)

### Centre for Intercultural Communication

Karen Rolston, Director
Jamie Donaldson, Pat Marshall, Joenita Paulrajan: Program Managers; Emily Wu: Program Coordinator

- Customized Programs for Organizations
- International Professional Exchange Programs
- Pre-Departure/Re-Entry Intercultural Workshops for Clients Working Internationally
- Programs for International Teaching Assistants
- Training the Intercultural and Diversity Trainer
- Certificate Programs:
    Aboriginal Health and Community Administration
    Immigration: Laws, Policies and Procedures
    Intercultural Studies
    International Development

### Centre for Sustainability

William Koty, Director
Mike Harcourt, Associate Director
Diana McKenzie: Program Leader

- Sustainability Lectures
- Sustainability Management
- Summer Institute in Sustainability Leadership
- Green Building and LEED® Credentials
- Certificate Program with Other Institutions:
    Decision Making for Climate Change (with Northwestern University, University of California Irvine, and University of Washington)

### Community Programs and Centre for Cultural Planning and Development (CCPD)

Don Black, Director
Burke Taylor, Community Director, CCPD
Dianne Olsen, Assistant Program Leader, CCPD

- Arts, Humanities and Public Affairs
- Cultural Planning and Development
- Public Lectures and Podcasts
- Programs for Seniors
- Certificate Programs:
    Garden Design
    Liberal Studies

### English Language Institute

Mike Weiss, Director
Andrew Scales, Academic Director
Jas Gill, Senior Academic Programmer
Gwen Semenoff, Administrative Director
Sarah ter Keurs, Program Manager
Susan Curtis, Head Teacher IEP and Assessment
Craig Huish, Head Teacher IEP and Assessment
Sylvia Ozbalt, Head Teacher Short Programs
Ali Pahlavanlu, Head Teacher Student/Instructor Advising
Denise Tonner, Head Teacher Computer Assisted Language Learning

- English and University Culture
- English for Business Communication
- English for the Global Citizen
- English for English Teachers
- Intensive English Program (IEP)
- Certificate Programs:
    Advanced English Language Teaching
    English Language

### International Preparatory Programs

Allan English, General Manager
Lily Gu, Mark Wisniewski: Program Coordinators

- International Undergraduate Study Preparation Program
- International Graduate Study Preparation Program

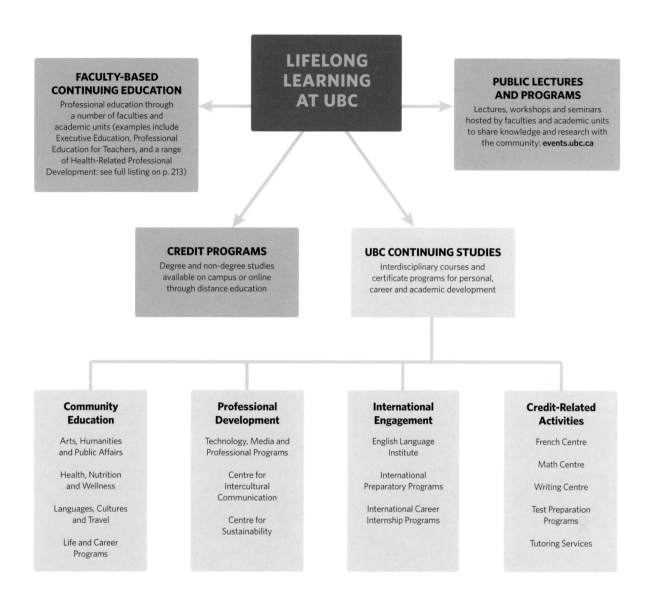

**LIFELONG LEARNING AT UBC**

**FACULTY-BASED CONTINUING EDUCATION**

Professional education through a number of faculties and academic units (examples include Executive Education, Professional Education for Teachers, and a range of Health-Related Professional Development: see full listing on p. 213)

**PUBLIC LECTURES AND PROGRAMS**

Lectures, workshops and seminars hosted by faculties and academic units to share knowledge and research with the community: **events.ubc.ca**

**CREDIT PROGRAMS**

Degree and non-degree studies available on campus or online through distance education

**UBC CONTINUING STUDIES**

Interdisciplinary courses and certificate programs for personal, career and academic development

**Community Education**

Arts, Humanities and Public Affairs

Health, Nutrition and Wellness

Languages, Cultures and Travel

Life and Career Programs

**Professional Development**

Technology, Media and Professional Programs

Centre for Intercultural Communication

Centre for Sustainability

**International Engagement**

English Language Institute

International Preparatory Programs

International Career Internship Programs

**Credit-Related Activities**

French Centre

Math Centre

Writing Centre

Test Preparation Programs

Tutoring Services

## International Career Internship Programs

Jennifer Mielguj, Senior Program Leader
Allan Dias, Dana Schindel, Marg Toronchuk:
Program and Internship Coordinators

- Global Academics:
    Global Academics Internship Program
    Global Career Development with Internship
    Global Career Foundations
    Global Relations
    GlobalTech

## French Centre and Math Centre

Francis Andrew, Director
Tea Inkinen, Administrative Manager

- French Centre:
    Explore (Summer Language Bursary Program)
    for University Students
    Institut de Français, UBC à Québec for BC Teachers
    Spring English or French with Canadians
    Centre de la Francophonie de UBC
    (with Faculties of Arts and Education)
- Math Centre:
    Pre-Calculus Courses

## Languages, Cultures and Travel Programs

Lang Sun, Director
Hyoshin Kim, Nina Parr: Program Leaders
Tea Inkinen, Administrative Manager

- Asia-Pacific Language Initiative
- Conversational Language Programs
- Culinary Arts and Culture
- Languages for Business Purposes
- Travel Programs
- Understanding Wine Program
- Certificate Programs:
    French Language and Culture
    French Regional Cuisine
    Practical and Business Spanish
    Translation and Interpretation for Business
    (Chinese/English, Korean/English)

## Life and Career Programs

Deena Boeck, Program Director
Sally Halliday, Managing Director, Counselling and
Program Development
Jacquie Digeso, Manager of Assessment Services
Dan Fortier, Administrative Manager

- Peer Counselling Services (Free Drop-In)
- Career Assessment, Consultation and Development
- Counselling and Human Resource Professions
- Interpersonal Skills for the Workplace
- Personal Growth and Change
- Health and Wellness
- Workplace Wellness
- Programs for Health Care and Human Service Professions
- Retirement Planning
- Test Preparation Programs
- Certificate Program:
    Peer Counselling

## Technology, Media and Professional Programs

Peter Moroney, Director
Raquel Collins, Associate Director
Vince Wong, Managing Director
Fiona McAuley, Jennifer Mielguj: Senior Program Leaders
Eileen Chow, Manpreet Dhillon, Lynn Fujino, Stephanie
Jackson, Jasmin Lee, Diana McKenzie, Phil Stenfors-Hayes:
Program Leaders
Faid Saffou, Labs Manager
Su Yon Sohn, Natalie Tung: Online Learning Systems
Doug Gehl, Administrative Manager

- Business and Technology Management
- Applied Technology and IT
- Digital Media and Communications

- Certificate Program:
    Multimedia and Web Development
- Certificate Programs with Sauder School of Business:
    Business Analysis
    Integrated Marketing Strategy
    Program Management (also in collaboration
    with Faculty of Applied Science)
    Project Management (also in collaboration
    with Faculty of Applied Science)
- Certificate Programs with Other Institutions:
    Web Intelligence (with University of California Irvine)
    Network Administration and Security Professional
    (with BCIT)
    Technology Support Professional (with BCIT)
- Awards of Achievement
    Project Management Using Microsoft Project
    Social Media
    Web Analytics

## Writing Centre

Ramona Montagnes, Director
Tea Inkinen, Administrative Manager
Vera Lowe, Supervisor, Tutor Programs

- Academic Writing
- Personal and Creative Writing
- Professional Writing
- Tutoring Services

## Strategic Initiatives

Mary Holmes, Director
Monica Killeen, Strategic Projects Manager

- Enhancements in Services for Adult Learners
- Strategic Alliances with Campus and Community Partners
- Summer Institute and Destination UBC Initiatives
- Advancement of Continuing Education through Professional
  Associations and Strategic Working Groups

## Program Support Services

**Finance and Accounting**
Mike Weiss, Director
Lisa Chau, Manager

**Information Technology**
Vince Wong, Director
Jonathan Gilmore, Manager, Technical Services and
IT Project Development
Rade Ljustina, Manager, Infrastructure and Networking
Winnie Low, Manager, Information Systems and
Business Solutions

**Marketing Services**
Mary Holmes, Director
Tanya Reid, Manager

## FACULTY-BASED CONTINUING PROFESSIONAL EDUCATION

UBC Continuing Studies is the largest continuing education unit at UBC and reports to the Provost and Vice President Academic. Other faculty-based continuing professional education units serve specialized disciplines and report to their respective deans. In addition to these units, some colleges, schools and academic departments offer a variety of educational events that serve professionals working in associated fields and, in some cases, members of the general public. The following listing outlines continuing professional education activities as of 2012.

### Applied Science

UBC's Faculty of Applied Science hosts lectures in specific fields such as architecture and landscape architecture, community and regional planning, engineering, and nursing, and provides a certificate program in Mining Studies.

### Arts

The UBC Faculty of Arts offers professional development through an advanced certificate program in Library, Archival and Information Studies, and diploma programs in Music Performance and in Piano Studies. (Public programs are also offered through UBC cultural attractions and concert halls.)

### Business

The Sauder School of Business at UBC provides a broad range of courses and programs through the following continuing professional education units:

- Executive Education (open enrolment and customized corporate programs, international executive programs)
- Real Estate Division (online professional development and licensing programs)

A CGA program, as well as diploma programs in Accounting and in Sales and Marketing Management are also available. The Business Families Centre hosts professional development seminars, and the Centre for CEO Leadership facilitates peer-to-peer learning.

### Education

The UBC Faculty of Education provides a wide range of continuing professional education courses, institutes, certificates, diplomas, and master's degrees in diverse content areas. Offerings are often in collaboration with K-12 education partners, but also serve educators in early childhood, post-secondary and adult vocational settings.

### Forestry

The UBC Faculty of Forestry offers professional development for wood products manufacturers through the Centre for Advanced Wood Processing.

### Health Sciences

UBC's health sciences faculties deliver a wide variety of courses, programs, online learning and conferences through the following continuing professional education units:

- UBC Faculty of Dentistry (Continuing Dental Education)
- UBC Faculty of Medicine (Continuing Professional Development in Medicine; School of Population and Public Health)
- UBC Faculty of Pharmaceutical Sciences (Continuing Pharmacy Professional Development)

Interdisciplinary professional education is also offered by:

- Interprofessional Continuing Education at UBC
- College of Health Disciplines

### Land and Food Systems

UBC's Faculty of Land and Food Systems hosts lectures in specialized fields related to maintaining a sustainable food supply and responsible use of resources. (Public programs are also offered through the UBC Farm.)

### Law

The UBC Faculty of Law provides lectures and National Centre for Business Law educational events accredited for continuing professional development by the Law Society of British Columbia.

### Science

The UBC Faculty of Science offers professional workshops to the scientific community. (Public programs are also offered through UBC science attractions and venues.)

## DISTANCE LEARNING AND FACULTY DEVELOPMENT

UBC's Centre for Teaching, Learning and Technology (CTLT) supports faculties that offer distance learning courses and programs to students who prefer technology-enabled learning modes, seek scheduling flexibility and/or are unable to come to campus. All courses offered by CTLT carry full credit toward degree programs. CTLT also delivers an ongoing development program to support faculty members in their teaching and learning endeavours, and to provide information on current research on teaching and learning theories and methods.

## ALUMNI ENGAGEMENT

Surveys of UBC alumni report strong interest in lifelong learning. Faculty-based continuing professional education units serve alumni by providing ongoing professional development related to their disciplines. UBC Continuing Studies courses, programs and summer institutes also serve alumni seeking personal or career development. UBC Alumni Affairs hosts educational travel programs, and delivers a UBC Dialogues lecture series in various communities in the Lower Mainland, as well as other cities in Canada and internationally.

3% of 18–24 year old Canadians attended university

1931
UNIVERSITY SHORT COURSE on HORTICULTURE
January 19th to January 24th

Second World War shaped extension programming

First English as a second language courses offered by UBC in 1961

British Columbia population less than 400,000 people

Great Depression crippled UBC

PHONOGRAPH RECORD LOAN LIBRARY

Summer School of the Arts thrived from 1946 through 1965

| 1915 | 1925 | 1935 | 1945 | 1955 |

| 1910 | 1920 | 1930 | 1940 | 1950 | 1960 |

First extension work at UBC: short courses and public lectures in agriculture and mining

UBC extension lectures are offered throughout the province

Carnegie Corporation grant sparked a broad program of extension work

Educational Programme for British Columbia Fishermen operated from 1940 through the 1960s

Living Room Learning expanded across British Columbia from 1957 to 1964

LIVING ROOM LEARNING

Information technology programming expanded rapidly

One-quarter of British Columbia population of 4 million speak a first language other than English

Federal Government released the Report of the Royal Commission on the Status of Women in Canada

UBC Continuing Studies Writing Centre established in 1992

First cohort of Conditional Admission students began in Summer 2011

**1965**　　**1975**　　**1985**　　**1995**　　**2005**　　**2015**

**1970**　　**1980**　　**1990**　　**2000**　　**2010**

First UBC certificate programs (Adult Education; Administration for Engineers; Criminology) begin in latter 1960s

Women's Resources Centre provided counselling services to over 10,000 people per year

Internet-based communication spawned widespread economic and educational change

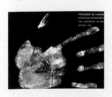

First televised degree-credit course at UBC launched in 1976

20% of 18-24 year old Canadians attended university

Globalization influences work, leisure, and educational programming

# Index

Notes